# New People

# New People

## MISCEGENATION and MULATTOES in the UNITED STATES

### Joel Williamson

LOUISIANA STATE UNIVERSITY PRESS

Baton Rouge and London

Published by arrangement with the author
Originally published by The Free Press
All rights reserved
Manufactured in the United States of America
Library of Congress Catalog Card Number: 80-65201

Louisiana Paperback Edition, 1995
04 03 02 01 00 99 98 97 96 95   5 4 3 2 1


ISBN 0-8071-2035-9 (pbk.)

Library of Congress Cataloging in Publication Data

Williamson, Joel.
    New people.

    Includes index.
        1. Mulattoes—United States.  2. Miscegenation—
United States.  3.  United States—Race relations.  I.
Title.
E185.62.W54        305.8'00973        80-65201

The paper in this book meets the guidelines for permanence and
durability of the Committee on Production guidelines for Book
Longevity of the Council on Library Resources. ∞

*For my mother*
*Carrie Mae*
*and my father*
*James Henry*

"You must take us for ourselves alone—we are new people."

John Warwick, in *The House behind the Cedars,*
by Charles W. Chesnutt

# Contents

# Preface

$F$OR some three years now, desultorily at first and very intensively during seven months in 1977–1978, I have been attempting to write what might be called an "outline" history of miscegenation and mulattoes in the United States. I use the word "outline" because, given the state of the art, I feel that such an approximation is as well as I can do. References to these twin subjects abound, and there are excellent articles and dissertations on specific aspects of each. But there has been published no single study that attempts to cover the whole ground, or even most of it, in the historical vein. Indeed, the only wholly relevant book was published in 1918 by the sociologist Edward B. Reuter.[1]

In this outline history I offer a theme. The theme is encapsulated in the short title *New People*. I take the term "new people" from a phrase used by Charles W. Chesnutt, a turn-of-the-century Negro writer. In his novel *The House behind the Cedars* Chesnutt introduced a mulatto character, John Warwick, who, along with his sister, had "passed" for white and made his way well up into the planter aristocracy of South Carolina. At one point in the story Warwick explained to a white friend that "you must take us for ourselves alone— we are new people." [2] The term seems beautifully fitting. Mulattoes in America are a new people, new not just in the surface way of a new physical type, but new in the vital way of constituting a new culture that is both African and European, each transformed in America and married to one another. Precisely as John Warwick said of himself and his sister, the mix in America must be taken for themselves alone and understood as a new people.

Because the great majority of American Negroes are in fact of mixed ancestry, and because mulattoes and pure blacks came ultimately to fuse their cultural heritages, what begins in the colonial period as mulatto history and culture ends in the twentieth century as Negro history and culture. Thus, understanding the history of the mulatto becomes one way of understanding something of the experience of the Negro, the Afro-American, in this new land.

It seems useful at the outset to make clear what I mean by certain frequently used terms. "Miscegenation" is meant to include a broad range of intimacy, from the most ephemeral interracial sexual contacts to marriage and children. It includes the mixing of blacks and mulattoes as well as the mixing of whites with either blacks or mulattoes. I hope the reader will indulge me in my use of the terms "white," "black," "mulatto," and "Negro." Admittedly, they are very loose and laden with powerful emotional charges. But most who read this book will know their weaknesses and recognize their strengths as necessary symbols in talking about these subjects. For Caucasians "white" will be used. For people of African heritage unmixed with Caucasians on this side of the Atlantic I shall use the term "black." "Mulatto" in the United States has generally been understood to refer to people in whom the mixture of black and white is visible. Such, for instance, was the use made of the word in the United States Census from 1850 to 1920. I shall use the term, however, to refer to people with any mixture at all of black and white ancestry. For groups of people that include both mulattoes and blacks I shall use the term "Negro."

Strictly speaking, a "mulatto" was a person who was half black and half white. A "quadroon" was one-quarter black. An "octoroon" was one-eighth black. Although Anglo-Americans did not ordinarily make such distinctions, Americans of Latin backgrounds had words for persons one-sixteenth or one-sixty-fourth black and for mixtures between mulattoes and blacks. In Latin cultures, as in Louisiana, a person three-quarters black was called a "griffe" or a "sambo," and a person seven-eighths black was called a "sacatra" or a "mango." Of course, as people of a certain mixture mated with people of another mixture, the array of fractions became vast and the possibilities infinite. Ultimately titles were approximations, so that if someone was referred to as a quadroon, it meant that he was closer to a quadroon than to either a mulatto or an octoroon. Lastly, there was also miscegenation between American Indians and Negroes. Offspring of such unions were usually called "mustees," a term derived from the

Latin American word "mestizo," often used to indicate a person of European and Indian ancestry.

Viewed in the world context and over the centuries, the mixing of peoples of different colors and features that occurred in America was, of course, but a continuation of a process that is practically as old as the history of humankind. Whites and blacks had been mixing in Africa, Europe, and Asia for eons before Columbus sailed the western ocean, and they mixed in Latin America for a century before either white Englishmen or black Africans came to the Virginia shore. Consequently, the blacks who first came to America were, as a group, in some degree already mixed with whites—and vice versa. Further, some of the first Negroes who came to British North America came from the West Indies, where a more immediate mixing had occurred. Therefore, when we speak of the mixing of black and white in America, we are in actuality speaking relatively. In the broad sweep of recorded history, black was never totally black, and white was never entirely white.

In writing this book, it has seemed useful to preserve the flavor of the thinking of past times by occasionally using the terms the people themselves used in the ways they used them. For example, in the past people often thought that character and culture were carried, quite literally, in the blood. Thus they would sometimes characterize persons of mixed ancestry as having "mixed blood," meaning to suggest a cultural as well as a physical mixture. There has also existed a folk concept of race. Scientific scholars generally agree that there is actually no such thing as race, that mixing has been universal and perpetual and that human traits so overlap that it is impossible to describe the characteristics of one "race" to the exclusion of all others. These scholars prefer to think in terms of a "gene pool" that produces certain traits among an inbred people more frequently than among others. What seem to be races, one might say, are actually clusters of traits. But even though blood did not itself carry character and culture, and, scientifically, races did not really exist, I will sometimes speak as if they did.

Finally, in discussing the white South, I will use the terms "upper class," "planters," and "slaveholders" almost interchangeably. While it is still debated whether or not the slaveholding planters controlled the society of the South, it is not much debated. Rather clearly they were the elite, they set the tone of the culture, and people who were not, strictly speaking, slaveholders and planters seemed generally to share their values and do their bidding. Moreover, many people who at first glance might seem to be only ministers, lawyers, or city businessmen will, upon investigation, be found to own plantations and slaves. Planters might be distinguished from small slaveholders by the fact that they did not work in the fields with their own hands; rather they devoted their energies totally to the management of other people's labor. In 1860 there were perhaps 100,000 people belonging to the planter families of the South and constituting a white elite.

Just as there was a white leadership, there was a Negro leadership. The Negro leadership included blacks and mulattoes. In the North, Negro leadership generally included people of both elements. However, before the twentieth century the Negro population in the North was not large, and it did not amount to more than 10 percent of the total number of Negroes in America. In the South before emancipation in 1865, only one class of Negroes seems to have had considerable power. These were the free mulattoes. Their power was always limited, of course, by the imperatives of the slave society in which they lived; but insofar as there was an elite of Negroes in the Old South, it was they. The free mulatto elite existed virtually everywhere in the South, but its presence was most striking in the two places in which free mulattoes lived close together in considerable numbers—in the Charleston District in South Carolina, and in some parishes in lower Louisiana and in New Orleans. These two mulatto communities in the lower South produced elites composed of self-conscious conservators and leading promoters of the values of their groups, and these elites seemed to set the tone for the antebellum Negro South. All of this is not to deny the existence of a significant black world, a black leadership, a black elite, or sometimes a merging of black and mulatto worlds, leaders, and elites. It is, rather, only to focus upon the subjects of our study and to search out—almost to vivisect from the living whole—the role of the mulatto elite in American history. Over several decades after emancipation the distinctive mulatto elite disappeared, but it is virtually impossible to relate the history of Afro-America without appreciating the special role of these special people.

In this work I have tried very hard to hack through the semantic jungle of race relations with full care for the feelings of all. It is impossible to do the task without irritating someone, and doubtless my choice of words will sometimes offend. I regret that. I can only say that I feel compelled to offer my findings thus, and that I myself attach no invidious distinctions to color in the skin of humanity—or to the lack of it.

Joel Williamson, *Center for
Advanced Studies in the Behavioral
Sciences*, Stanford, California

# Acknowledgments

THE writing of this book has been for me often an exciting and sometimes an ecstatic experience—feelings that arose both from my enthusiasm for the subject and from the circumstances in which I worked. I wrote nearly all of the manuscript during my stay at the Center for Advanced Study in the Behavioral Sciences in Stanford, California, during the academic year 1977–1978. This book is infused with the spirit of the community of half a hundred scholars among whom I lived happily day by day. Professional scholars at the Center were tremendously supportive, and so too was the staff, rich as it is in the warm blood of human sympathy and common-sense intellectuality, and from whom logistical aid flowed easily and gladly. Great credit for the maintenance of such a rare ambience is due to the Board of Trustees of the Center, to Director Gardner Lindzey, and to Associate Director Preston Cutler.

Much in this book came from work that I have been doing over the last fifteen years in race relations in the South since emancipation. The results of that work should appear in print in 1981 or soon thereafter, but it seems appropriate that I recognize here the Guggenheim Foundation, the American Council of Learned Societies, and the Department of History and the Faculty Research Council of the University of North Carolina for fellowships, grants, and leaves all generously given in support of the larger work. I wish also to say with gratitude that my stay at the Center for Advanced Study was funded in part by the National Endowment for the Humanities (FC-26278-76-1030).

I owe deeply personal thanks to a number of friends who helped me in specific ways. Agnes Page of the Center nursed the first typescript through infancy with great care and vast faith. She went not one but literally many extra miles between her office and my study in the pursuit of perfection. Agnes was totally encouraging and, at that stage of the writing, worth a platoon of critics. In that same vein I happily name Libby Sajo and Baylor Hicks, my fond and steady companions of the year, who bore me through the first writing with the terrific intelligence and sensitivity that is both the individual gift of each and their mutual wealth, and Sherry Wilson, my thoughtful and highly perceptive instructor in the art of humanistic description and appreciation. I wish also to thank Rosalie I. Radcliffe of the Department of History of the University of North Carolina in Chapel Hill for her generous encouragement and for shaping, with her usual keen eye and expert hand, the manuscript into final form for the publisher.

I am indebted to Professor Kenneth M. Stampp of the University of California in Berkeley for giving me excellent advice on the manuscript in the original version, especially that portion dealing with the antebellum period. I want also to acknowledge the assistance of Professor Robert Toplin of the University of North Carolina at Wilmington for aid in the same area. Finally, I owe great thanks to Professors George B. Tindall of the University of North Carolina at Chapel Hill, Carl Degler of Stanford University, Nell Painter of the University of Pennsylvania, and George Fredrickson of Northwestern University for giving me the benefit of their special knowledge in the areas of miscegenation and mulattoes in conversations over the years. With each of these I have not always been a good student but I have never been an ungrateful one.

# New People

# Introduction

IN the 1920s, in the age of the flapper and the Broadway extravaganza, there was a popular novel and Broadway musical by Edna Ferber called *Showboat*. The showboat was a floating theater that in the 1870s moved up and down the Mississippi. In the company was Julie, the best actress, a thin, darkling young woman. Her devoted lover was Steve, a blond Adonis and a boy at heart, who was usually cast, incongruously, as the villain in showboat productions. Julie, it was discovered, was a Negro passing for white, and a Mississippi sheriff came aboard to arrest the couple for violating the state's anti-miscegenation law. As the sheriff approached, Steve used his knife to prick Julie's finger. Bending his head over the wound, he sucked and swallowed some of her blood. Just as the sheriff was about to take the couple away, Steve looked him in the eye and demanded, "You wouldn't call a man a white man that's got Negro blood in him, would you?" "No, I wouldn't; not in Mississippi," the sheriff stoutly replied. "One drop of nigger blood makes you a nigger in these parts." [1]

Julie and Steve went free because, in those parts, in the eyes of the dominant whites the merest hint of Negro blood automatically made a person all Negro. Indeed the fact was that in the 1920s the Mississippi sheriff was speaking for the whole of America. By that time the racial code of the South pervaded the nation, and Negroes as well as whites had come to accept as universal what came to be called "the one-drop rule."

The one-drop rule was also readily adopted by students of society in the 1920s. The young Negro sociologist Horace Mann Bond, himself more white than black, caught beautifully the irony of making black people out of white in a scholarly article published at the end of the decade. There had been no "ripple of amusement" in a recent meeting, he observed, when a seemingly "blue-eyed Anglo-Saxon" speaker asserted "the necessity that all of us black men in America and the world stand together!" There was a time, Bond said, when light-skinned Negroes held themselves aloof from their darker brothers. But that time had faded because those who most desired to be white had passed and slipped quietly into the white world, and the remainder had turned their energies "upon the immediate task of racial survival." The happy result was that "there is here no widespread wasting of energies or efforts on the creation and maintenance of an intermediate group." [2]

In America we still live with the paradox that white is black. Occasionally people who are visibly white declare themselves black, and millions of Americans who are more European than African in their heritage insist, sometimes defiantly, upon their blackness. Our paradox is unique. In other societies where two races have met and mixed, the progeny have usually formed a third element allied more or less with the dominant race. Where black and white have met, the pattern has been that mixed bloods formed the usual intermediate group, distinct even as it was tied in some way to the group at each end. In Dutch South Africa such a distinction was made, and in various forms it has been made in Latin America. Why is it that the pattern was broken in the United States? Why is it that American mulattoes of all shades have been brusquely relegated to a single Negro caste along with blacks and, further, have come eagerly to embrace that identity?

The answer begins with the fact that indeed it was not always so, and not everywhere so. Before 1850 in South Carolina and in the lower South generally the master class was at the same time especially harsh upon the black slave mass and especially lenient toward the relatively few free mulattoes. In short, mulattoness did count, real distinctions were made, and the one-drop rule did not always prevail. Before 1850 race relations in the lower South partook of the character of race relations among its Latin American and especially its West Indian neighbors, where the harshest slavery somehow bred the greatest freedom for free mulattoes and mulattoes used their freedom to pursue and achieve white culture. The upper South and the rest of America, on the other hand, constructed their race relations out of whole— if rather thin—cloth. After a hundred years of experimentation, in which the lower classes seemed to be rather slow learners, these areas arrived at the one-drop rule early in the eighteenth century.

After 1850, a long-running intolerance of miscegenation and mulattoes among whites in the upper South joined with the rising and crystallizing intolerance among whites in the lower South to exert tremendous pressures upon both whites and mulattoes. Whites who mixed found themselves abused and ostracized. Under heavy fire from a seemingly universal racism, the previous ambivalence of mulattoes toward both whites and blacks turned during the Civil War toward a steadily growing affinity with blacks. In Reconstruction the engagement of mulattoes and blacks was firmly cemented, though obvious vestiges of a preference for lightness lingered for two or three generations. By the 1920s the great mass of mulattoes saw their destiny as properly united only with that of their darker brothers and sisters. They saw themselves as fusing with blacks and together forming a whole people in embryo.

Negroes in America in the 1920s were indeed a new people. First, they were a new people physically. Social scientists soon developed some thirty specific traits (varying from "sitting height" to thirty-three shades of skin coloring, each with an identifying number) that they laboriously measured and elaborately described to prove the existence of a new physical type. Second and much more important, Negroes were a new people culturally. Negro language and literature, Negro music and dance, and Negro achievement in the visual and performing arts were all rising to undeniable beauty in the 1920s. In each case the art was like that of white America, but different. Elements of Negro culture merged and found signal expression in what came to be called the Harlem Renaissance. Along with cultural awareness inevitably came self-awareness. Awareness included a sense of being different both from other contemporary Americans and from preceding Negro generations. The Negro elite encapsulated the mood in the phrase "the new Negro." The phrase carried the idea that the Negro was neither African nor European, but both—and something more. Chromatically he was neither black nor white, but rather brown. The term "brown America" gained currency in the 1930s and 1940s, and it was applied culturally as well as physically. In those years it seemed apt.

In the 1960s brown America disappeared, to be replaced by black America and the emergence of the nearly perfect paradox in which white could be unblinkingly black. The drive for a biracial society had reached its culmination, finally not by white dictation, but rather by the eager embracement of "blackness" by American Negroes.

Describing the paradox is not so important, of course, as understanding what it means in human terms; and to explain its meaning is to study the history of miscegenation and mulattoes in America. Who were the mixers, and what happened to their children and their children's children down through the generations? Where were they, and when? How did mulattoes perceive themselves, and how did they perceive whites and blacks? How did whites and blacks perceive mulattoes? And how did each respond, and in the responses change the perceptions? To struggle with these questions is to struggle with that fascinating and defiant tangle, the infinitely interwoven "seamless web" of human interrelations, a web that covers broad space and many people, and moves through time at ever unevenly changing rates. It is also to impress upon ourselves that there are individuals in history as well as aggregates, and that there is human time as well as solar time. It is to remind ourselves that in the lives of individuals and groups of individuals time is elastic, and pulse beats often measure time better than clocks.

# CHAPTER I

# Genesis

ONE great fact about race relations in the South from the beginning and into the twentieth century is that there have been two Souths, one reaching down from Pennsylvania into North Carolina, and the other continuing southward to the Gulf of Mexico. In the first section (p. 6) of the six into which this chapter is divided we look at the beginnings of mulatto America in the upper South, a story that commences with the settlement of Jamestown in 1607. In the second section (p. 14) we focus upon miscegenation in the lower South, a very different story that begins with the settlement of Charles Town in 1670. In the third section (p. 24) we bring these two stories together by way of the census of 1850, the first national census that attempted to count mulattoes separately from blacks. That census was flawed, of course, as the census is always flawed. In this case it was marred by an undercount, for the special reason that census takers were not always able to distinguish between mulattoes and people of purely African ancestry, and for the usual reason that the census takers simply did not get to every place where there were mulattoes. Still, we are working here only with large numbers, usually numbers for whole states, and those numbers display patterns that relate to patterns derived from other sources, statistical and individual. The third section lays out patterns exhibited in the census, and those patterns reinforce and elaborate the history recounted in our first and second sections. Furthermore, and rather surprisingly, a close look at the broad census carries us strikingly beyond what we have previously perceived in working along the racial fault line lying between the upper South and the lower.

The fourth section (p. 33) is an attempt to build a model to explain how and, more importantly, why we came to this certain picture evident in the census of 1850. The model builds upon the census of 1850, strongly buttressed by a large number of state and colonial censuses taken before that time. This is a conscious experiment by a historian to construct a model that will help him probe a phenomenon in the past and explicate the results of his study much as do his colleagues in social science, usually in dealing with contemporary matters. First it attempts to define the conditions that would produce relatively many or relatively few people of mixed ancestry. Then it explores those conditions in the Caribbean, the lower South, the upper South, and the North. Incidentally, it offers concise and often revealing comparisons between the South and the Caribbean on one side and the South and the North on the other.[1]

The fifth section (p. 42) on "mavericks" describes and explores continuing miscegenation between whites and Negroes after the first great wave of mixing had passed early in the eighteenth century. Some of the children of this later mixing were supremely important in the mulatto world that followed the first great wave. They and their progeny became a part of an elite in the mulatto world that led, ultimately, in a cultural fusion with the darker mass. These people provided a disproportionately large share of the leadership for Negro people at large during the Civil War and Reconstruction, and up into the Harlem Renaissance. They begin in the eighteenth century, they swell tremendously in importance in the nineteenth, and they reach up into the most vital happenings in Afro-American history in the twentieth. They are a tie that binds the beginnings with what we see about us today.

The sixth and final section (p. 56) recapitulates the first five sections. It says again where mulattoness came from and where it went up to 1850, working in some attention to mixing and mulattoes in the westward migration into the Southern interior. It also begins the marrying of black and mulatto, physically and culturally, that is to be the central theme of the remainder of the book.

Mulattoness is a quality almost as old—if not, indeed, fully as old—as blackness in British North America. The first significant mixing of blacks and whites came in the seventeenth and early eighteenth centuries, by far the most of it in the Chesapeake world of Virginia and Maryland. Most of these first mulattoes were probably the offspring not of white planters and their black slave women, as were many of the later issue, but rather of white "servants" and blacks. These whites were indentured servants—English, Scotch, Irish—most of whom had obligated themselves to serve a master for a term of years to pay their passage across the Atlantic. Servants not slaves were the numerous class among the "unfree" in Virginia and Maryland in the seventeenth century. In Virginia in 1648, for example, there were only 300 Negroes amid 15,000 English, while in 1665 it was estimated that there were some 10,000 servant men in the colony. Of 40,000 people in Virginia in 1671, 2,000 were slaves while 6,000 were servants.[2] The remainder included many people then free who had come as servants. In addition to servants who volunteered to migrate to America under indenture, British courts during the first century of settlement sentenced some 4,400 criminals, paupers, and other undesirables to servitude in the Chesapeake colonies. It seems highly probable that these white servants, voluntary and involuntary, contributed much to the foundation of a large mulatto population in the American colonies. The work of these people was menial, and they lived and labored closely with blacks both slave and free.[3] Probably they simply took their lovers from the class most readily available, black or white, and without great regard for color. They did so in defiance of a color code of goodness and badness in the English tradition, a code that was sometimes applied invidiously to black Africans. These laboring people themselves had in a sense been aliens at home, they were aliens in America, and they were not so deeply steeped in the color code as were their betters. They were more likely to respond to the body than to the mind, and the result was the first wave of mulatto offspring in the new land.

The authorities in the Chesapeake world early set a stern face against miscegenation, whether in the form of interracial sex or interracial marriage. Repeatedly during the seventeenth century, the rulers of Virginia and Maryland acted against miscegenation and its mulatto children. One of the oldest colonial records extant concerns a man named Hugh Davis who, in Virginia in 1630, was sentenced "to be soundly whipped, before an assembly of Negroes and others for abusing himself to the dishonor of God and shame of Christians, by defiling his body in lying with a Negro, which fault he is to acknowledge next Sabbath day." In 1640 a similar case brought a somewhat different punishment from the Virginia court. "Whereas Robert Sweat hath begotten with child a negro woman belonging unto Lieutenant

Sheppard," Sweat was to do public penance at James City Church during service on the following Sabbath and the woman was to be "whipt at the whipping post."[4] Four years later the court first inserted the term "mulatto" in its formal record when it ruled that "A Mulatto named Manuel" was to be a slave.[5]

The first mulattoes were of uncertain status. In Virginia the ruling whites required a half century of legislative experimentation before they were able to translate their attitudes toward mulattoes into a relatively complete body of law. In 1662 the assembly passed the first of a series of acts designed to discourage miscegenation and to relegate mulattoes to an inferior position. In that year it flatly declared that mulatto children of slave mothers would be slaves. In so deciding, the assembly wrenched itself away from the English rule that the child followed the status of its father, but it settled the issue of status for a large proportion (perhaps more than half) of the mulattoes in Virginia in a few words. The same act imposed double penalties upon "any christian" that "shall committ ffornication with a negro man or woman."[6] If the punishment fit the crime, sexual intercourse by a Christian with a black person was twice as evil as sexual intercourse with a white person.

Mulatto children of white mothers posed a more difficult problem. They were to be free, but their freedom soon proved unwelcome to the whites. In 1691 the assembly denounced such children as "that abominable mixture and spurious issue" and attacked the problem vigorously. It declared that any English woman who gave birth to "a bastard child by any negro or mulatto" was to suffer a very heavy fine or five years of servitude, and the child was to be sold as a servant until it attained the age of thirty. While the assembly did not prohibit interracial marriage outright, it ordered the white party involved in such a union banished from the colony within three months of the ceremony.[7] In 1705 the legislature stiffened the sentence against white persons who married Negroes or mulattoes to six months in jail. Further, it repeated the sentence for English women having mulatto children and extended the time of service of such children to thirty-one years.[8]

Court records suggest that Virginia officials were not slow in enforcing the laws against miscegenation. For instance, provisions of the law of 1691 were levied against a poor white woman in Elizabeth City County in the 1690s, as the manuscript record indicates:

> Whereas by the law it is provided that in case any English woman
> being free shall have a mulatto bastard child borne of her body, she

shall pay fifteen pounds sterling or be sold for five years and such bastard to be sold as servants until they attain the age of thirty years and for as much as Ann Wall of this county a free English woman being convicted of having two mulattoe bastards by a negro begotten and borne of her body contrary to ye law. It is therefore ordered that ye said Ann Wall doe serve Mr. Peter Hobson or his assigns (of Norfolk County) the term of five years from ye date hereof and her said two mulatto bastards to serve ye said Hobson in like manner until they attain each of them unto ye age of thirty years as ye said law directs ye same being consideration of ye sum of one thousand pounds of legal tobacco and cask and payment of costs and sheriffs due ye said Ann Wall, and it is further ordered that in case ye said Ann Wall after she is free from her said master doe at any time presume to come into this county shall be banished to ye Island of Barbadoes.[9]

Elizabeth City County was not alone in having to cope with white mothers of mulatto children. Between 1690 and 1698 fourteen white women in Westmoreland County were convicted of having given birth to nineteen bastards, of whom four were mulattoes. At the same time thirteen women were punished in Norfolk County for bearing the same number of illegitimates, of whom three were mulattoes. In Lancaster from 1702 to 1712 twenty-six white women bore thirty-two bastards, of whom nine were mulatto, and suffered the usual punishment.[10] The vestry book of Bristol Parish recorded eight mulatto children bound out in the space of six years beginning in 1724.[11]

While the legislature and the law acted thus to deter future miscegenation and to hold in either slavery or prolonged servitude such mulatto children as were born, the definition of the official status of free persons of mixed ancestry already within the population posed a problem more difficult still and one that Virginia was not able to solve with relative satisfaction until the twentieth century. In the early colonial period a few mulattoes prospered and even owned slaves themselves, but many others were not so fortunate. Indeed, free mulattoes were often poor, and enough were vagabonds and rogues to excite the disfavor of the governing elite. In legislation free mulattoes were frequently listed in sequences with servants, Negroes, slaves, mustees, and Indians. It was as if in the minds of the lawmakers free mulattoes were considered a separate category to be ranked with those other subordinate and often troublesome elements. In 1691, in the same act in which it attacked white mothers of mulatto children, the Virginia Assembly moved both to discourage further manumissions by compelling masters to send their freedmen out of the colony and to encourage officials to break up bands of "negroes, mulattoes, and other slaves [perhaps Indians]" who had fled to "lie hid and lurk in obscure places." The implication was strong that freed mulattoes established themselves in remote areas where they welcomed runaways and preyed upon the property of local citizens.[12] In 1705 the Virginia legislature prohibited Negroes, Indians, or mulattoes from holding office in the colony and defined a mulatto as "the child of an Indian and the child, grand child, or great grand child of a negro." It also refused to allow mulattoes and others to be witnesses in cases at law.[13] By 1723 Virginia was ready to deny the equal citizenship of free mulattoes in a wide range of categories. In that year the assembly provided that they should no longer vote and allowed them to possess firearms only under special, highly restrictive circumstances. In addition, it moved to make private emancipation by owners even more difficult and to tax free mulatto women discriminatorily.[14]

Maryland, first settled in 1634, was not far behind its southern neighbor. The authorities in that colony quickly decided that mulatto children of slave mothers would be slaves. Like the Virginians, they had more difficulty deciding what to do with mulatto children of white mothers. In 1664 the legislature fumbled at the problem by enacting a law to discourage the marriage to "Negro Slaues" of "divers freeborne English women forgetfull of their free Condicon and to the disgrace of our Nation." The law, even more stringent than that in Virginia, provided that such women must serve the masters of their husbands during the lifetime of the husband, and that the "Issue of such freeborne woemmen soe marryed shall be Slaues as their fathers were."[15] Some masters apparently took advantage of the law by pushing their white women servants into marriages with their Negro slaves for the purpose of obtaining their labor for extended periods and enslaving their children. Consequently, in 1681 the legislature modified its stand to exempt from the penalty women thus forced and, further, to declare their mulatto children free. Tradition has it that the legislature in this act responded to the specific case of "Irish Nell" Butler, a servant of the proprietor of the colony, Lord Baltimore, who had married a black man. However, at the same time that it moved to relieve women servants pressed into marriage with black men, the all-male legislature also took occasion to make a scathing denunciation of the willing marriage of white women to Negroes. It was, they declared with either great presumption or fantastic insight into feminine motivation, "always to the Satisfaction of their Lascivious & Lustfull desires," and concluded that such behavior was "to the disgrace not only of the English butt allso of many other Christian

Nations."[16] In 1715 the Maryland Assembly forbade ministers and magistrates to marry whites to "any Negro whatsoever, or Mulatto Slave." In subsequent years it moved further to prohibit the marriage of mulattoes to blacks and to punish severely all parties to illegal marriages—white, black, and mulatto.[17] By the law of 1715 whites and free mulattoes could still marry legally. Moreover, throughout the period of slavery Maryland made a distinction between the mulatto offspring of white women and mulattoes generally. Not only could the former marry whites and testify in court, they also were punished as if white when convicted of crimes. Possibly, the legislature in 1715 chose to allow whites and free mulattoes to marry in part to benefit this class. After the mid-colonial period, however, the number of mulatto children born of white mothers became negligible.

In the two decades between 1705 and 1725 authorities in each of the colonies from New Hampshire to South Carolina were coming to legal conclusions not unlike those of Virginia and Maryland. Pennsylvania in particular went through much the same sequence as those two colonies in attempting to curb first the mixing and then the marriage of white servants, both men and women, with black slaves. Especially in the vicinity of Philadelphia were the numbers of mulattoes high. One community known as "Mulatto Hall" became entirely mulatto and was abandoned and isolated by the whites. Finally, in 1725–1726 Pennsylvania enacted a general law prohibiting interracial unions of all kinds, punishing white parents of mulatto children, and remanding the children of white women to servitude for thirty-one years.[18]

What was happening in the colonies in relation to miscegenation and mulattoes in that first century of settlement was possibly a part of a larger British story in which the ruling class was struggling to regain control of the lower orders. In seventeenth-century England there was a "better sort" and a "meaner sort." As a result of the "enclosure movement" begun in the early modern period, peasants had been squeezed out of their homes, and the lands they had once farmed given over by the landlords to the raising of sheep for wool. Often the dispossessed took to the roads to become perpetual vagrants and rogues. In the sixteenth century Queen Elizabeth attempted to tie them down in the so-called "poor laws." By the time America was settled, these people were a nuisance in the mother country, and there were a great many of them. America was an obvious place to dump these surplus persons, and they came by the thousands, primarily to the upper South and the middle Atlantic states. In America they proved no more easily manageable than in Britain. To make a society with large numbers of these displaced people was indeed a great challenge for colonial leadership.

The problem of building a British society in the Chesapeake world was complicated by the fact that its settlers were not as a whole representative of the residents of Great Britain. Its parts included many kinds of persons present in the mother country—aristocrats, bourgeoisie, artisans, laborers, priests, farmers, men, women, and children—but in proportions varying widely from those at home. To recast English society in the New World was rather like attempting to make a familiar cake in an unfamiliar kitchen with a haphazard cupboard. Many of the ingredients were there, but there was too much vinegar and not enough sugar. The result was that the "better sort" in Virginia and Maryland had first to inventory their human materials—white, black, red, mustee, and mulatto—and then decide what they would make of them. Certainly, they could not simply construct another England. In terms of miscegenation and mulattoes, it took about half a century (ending with the first legislation in 1662) to begin to decide what they wanted and another half century to realize, more or less effectively, their intentions. In the effort, laws were passed and repassed, extravagant declarations were made, and heavy punishments meted out.

The task of organizing a British society in the Chesapeake area was made even more difficult by the importation of wave after wave of newcomers—not always English or even British—flooding into the underclass and perpetuating indiscipline. During the first century of settlement great waves of the "meaner sort" were brought over, used up, worn out, and cast aside. Remnants of them were socialized and survived. In the second quarter of the eighteenth century the influx of these people into the Chesapeake Bay area slowed, and the American elite at last managed to press their people into prescribed molds and form a relatively unified society out of what had been a chance conglomeration of individuals. Increasingly the higher orders were able to impose their will concerning miscegenation and mulattoes, as well as other things, upon the lower orders.

Initially it was probably simply the idea of miscegenation and mulattoes rather than the quantity of interracial sex, marriage, and offspring that so outraged authorities in the Chesapeake region. On the eve of the American Revolution the number of mulattoes in the area probably did not exceed 3 percent of the total population. Moreover, these few were spread evenly over the countryside of the first settled areas east of the Blue Ridge Mountains, either as slaves, laborers, or small farmers, and they seemed, in numbers and power, largely unthreatening. Mulattoes in Maryland appear fairly representative of mulattoes in the upper South generally, and, fortunately for future students, a count of mulattoes was made in that colony in 1755, the only broad count of these people made in America before 1850. Living among 108,000 whites and 45,000 blacks were some 3,600 mulattoes, or 2.4 percent of the total population, of whom about 1,500 were free. Possibly most of the free mulattoes owed their freedom to white maternity in the seventeenth century. The 2,100 mulatto slaves were probably mostly the descendants of white fathers who shared at least some of the verve of Hugh Davis, that lusty and original Virginian.[19] If it followed the Maryland ratios, Virginia counted about 9,600 mulattoes at that time, 4,000 of whom were free. Delaware, a third colony with a relatively high proportion of mulattoes, probably had very small fractions of these numbers.

By the middle of the eighteenth century the ruling elite in the Chesapeake world seems to have lost much of its earlier anxiety about mulattoes. The legal status of mixed bloods was still only loosely defined, though in the white mind they were firmly classed as Negroes and in effect lumped on that side of the race bar. With them was a rather disparate collage of people of Indian and black ancestry, known as mustees, and offspring of Indian and white parents. For the most part, these people grew out of relations with the several hundred Indian slaves taken in each colony in the first few decades of settlement and cast indiscriminately with black slaves and white servants.

During the Revolutionary era, however, ideology and economics combined to cause masters in the upper South to emancipate numbers of slaves, black as well as mulatto. The free Negro population, which had been about 20 percent black, rapidly darkened to 60 percent black. The authorities again took alarm. Legislatures acted to draw a clear and hard line between the increased and ample privileges of white citizens, now free of the English monarchy, and the restricted privileges of free Negroes. Inevitably they were forced to define legally what was a Negro. States in the upper South generally followed the lead of Virginia, which in 1785 defined a Negro as a person with a black parent or grandparent.[20]

The legal definition as white of free people with anything less than one-fourth of black blood soon became a sore upon the social body of Virginia and remained such for half a century. This rather generous fraction classed as white some free people who were clearly Negro. Thus in Virginia there were some people who were significantly black, visibly black, and known to be black, but by the law of the land and the rulings of the courts had the privileges of whites. The possession of those prerogatives was valuable, as, for example, when one was about to be lashed by the police for some petty offense. In Virginia, and especially in Richmond, shady characters rushed to claim the privileges of whiteness and to pursue dissolute and scandalous lives under their shelter. As sectional tensions mounted, public opinion grew more and more intolerant of this anomalous people, people who were legally white and socially black. External pressures demanded internal order and there could be no anomalies; everything at all black must be unfree and white must be privileged. Mulattoes must be made black, and the unfreedom of blacks must be defined and made universal.[21]

In the history of the mulatto there are two Souths. In the upper South (taken as North Carolina and northward and westward), mulattoes appeared very early in the colonial period and in relatively large numbers. Probably most of the first mulattoes were born of white parents, male or female, of the underclass. Compared with mulattoes in the lower South, they came to be very numerous and improved their numbers over the generations, in large measure by effecting unions among themselves. Many mulattoes in the upper South were free. These tended to be rural folk either poor or of modest means, and they were spread fairly evenly across the first set-tled areas. In the upper South mulattoes in the mass, having sprung from elements of the lower orders, were generally treated by the white elite much as if they were black. Among the elite in the upper South, the one-drop rule was the rule in all but the legal sense well before the American Revolution.

In the lower South, in contrast, mulattoes appeared later and built their numbers slowly but continuously in the eighteenth and nine-teenth centuries. An important number were born of well-to-do white fathers, and many of these were recognized and sponsored by their fathers, sometimes as slaves, sometimes as free. Mulattoes in the lower South before the Civil War never became so numerous as those in the upper South, and not nearly so many of them were free. Yet when they were free, they tended to dominate the free Negro com-munity both in numbers and influence until emancipation became general. The topmost few, the lightest and the brightest, quite literally the crème de la crème, lived very well—nearly on a par with their white neighbors, to whom they were tied by bonds of kinship and culture. It was the elite of the free mulattoes who touched most intimately the skin of white society. In the upper South, whites came to regard the lightest of free mulattoes as often dissolute and difficult people. In the lower South before the 1850s, the white elite seemed to value them in important ways. Especially in South Carolina around Charleston and in lower Louisiana—the places where free mulattoes were most numerous, most affluent, and most cultivated—were they appreciated. In the 1850s that relatively tolerant order would rapidly deteriorate. But until then free mulattoes in these enclaves enjoyed a status markedly elevated above that of the black mass, slave and free.

Free mulattoes of the more affluent sort in the lower South were treated by influential whites as a third class, an acceptable and sometimes valuable intermediate element between black and white, slave and free. In the lower South mulatto relations had a distinct West Indian flavor. That flavor grew out of the direct immigration of people and institutions from the West Indies into eastern Carolina and lower Louisiana during the first years of colonization and continuing contact between the islands and the continent. Unlike early settlement in the Chesapeake world, first settlement in the lower South was characterized by great plantations employing large numbers of Negro slaves. The great number of slaves gave abundant sexual opportunity to white masters and overseers. Those liaisons produced children, but not so many as in the upper South because the number of whites involved was limited to a relatively small number of white men. Some of these children the masters cared for and made free. Some they established in trades or businesses in the cities. Many remained slaves and filled the ranks of domestic servants. Over time free mulatto clans emerged, especially in Charleston and New Orleans, interlocking rings of families almost as prosperous, nearly as cultured, and fully as exclusive as those of their planter kin. Just as the planter class dominated white culture, the elite free people of color dominated free Negro culture.

In the lower South in the Revolutionary era there were few sentiments and no economics to breed emancipation. Lower South rebels felt no conflict between freedom for themselves and slavery for their slaves. The result was that a relatively small free Negro community remained small and heavily mulatto, about 75 percent so.[22] Native-born free mulattoes and free Negroes generally were not yet seen as a threat in the lower South. They not only were tolerated, they were in some ways valued, and with good reason. In the lower South the ratio of blacks to whites ran high in the areas where the plantations were concentrated, the black belts. Fearful whites prudently imposed stringent controls upon their black slaves, and they looked to their mulatto kin for help. Ironically, in the lower South as in the West Indies, the blackest and harshest slavery bred the greatest freedom and the highest status for free mulattoes.

The West Indian influence in South Carolina was direct, and it was large. Indeed, South Carolina virtually began its life as an extension of the British West Indian colony of Barbados. On Barbados, and the other British islands of the West Indies, slavery and a pattern of race relations that placed mulattoes above blacks were already well established in 1670 when the first permanent settlement was made in South Carolina. During the first ten years of its existence more than half of the settlers whose origins are known came from the islands. Moreover, the richest and the most influential came directly out of the 175 families that dominated the economic, political, and social life of Barbados. Between 1670 and 1730 six Barbadians became governors of the Carolina colony, and four of these were members of the richest planter families on that island. Also, more than a score of persons who secured large grants of land around Charleston were from the eminent Barbadian families. The Barbadians brought with them to the mainland not only gangs of slaves previously seasoned to the plantation regime but also a pattern of race relations and a social fabric into which that pattern was already tightly knit.[23]

Among the British mainland colonies Carolina was uniquely black. It became so rapidly after the introduction of rice culture in the 1690s. Accustomed in the islands to a plantation slavery that imported vast numbers of Africans, Carolina rice planters had little difficulty finding labor to support their newfound prosperity. As early as 1708 South Carolina probably had a black majority.[24] On the eve of the Revolution the ratio in the low country ran about three blacks to every one white—a ratio not far from that of Barbados. As in some Latin American cultures, South Carolina combined a harsh and massive slavery with a curious toleration of miscegenation between white men and black women. Early white colonists without wives apparently mixed rather freely with slaves, and especially with slaves already light in color.

South Carolina was unique among the British American mainland colonies not only in its blackness and easy mixing but also in that some whites positively and publicly defended interracial sex. In 1732, for instance, the *South Carolina Gazette* drew arguments from both sides when it published a clever poem entitled "The Cameleon Lover" that suggested that miscegenationists would "imbibe the *Blackness* of their *Charmer's* Skin." In the next issue "Albus," fabricating a pseu-

donym that claimed the essence of both white and English, charged
that miscegenation was a malignancy approaching epidemic proportions in the colony. "Sable," on the other side, responded sym-
pathetically to the lover whose taste ran to "the *dark* Beauties of the
*Sable* Race." [25] A few years later another attack upon white men having relations with black women was boldly met by an anonymous
poet who ended his verse with the taunt, "Kiss black or white, why
need it trouble you?" [26]

South Carolina shared much with the British West Indies, yet there
were differences between the two cultures. A primal difference was
that life on the continent was much more livable than in those over-
crowded, underfed, sometimes dry and disease-ridden tropical islands.
On the mainland life was simply more salubrious. Whatever was
planted seemed soon to grow, not only crops, but numbers of people
as well—whether black, white, or brown. Contrary to the practice in
the West Indies, English colonists commonly brought their wives
and children to Carolina, where in time they flourished and increased.
As white sex and white families grew, the pressure for interracial sex
and mulatto families diminished. Interracial sex outside of marriage
came under attack, not only in the press but also in the legislature. In
1717 an act of the assembly provided that "any white woman,
whether free or a servant, that shall suffer herself to be got with child
by a negro or other slave or free negro, . . . shall become a servant
for . . . seven years." The children of such unions were to be bound
for twenty-one years if male and eighteen years if female. Further,
white men who impregnated Negro women were to suffer the same
punishment.[27] In 1721 the legislature moved against free Negroes, including free mulattoes, by providing explicitly that only "free White
men" should vote, thus ending some voting by free Negroes. In the
next year the legislature required the outmigration of emancipated
slaves, and in 1740 it in effect required a special act of the legislature
for each emancipation.[28] All of this took place before a backdrop of a
rapidly swelling black slave population, threats from the Spanish out-
posts in Florida, and a rising sense of insecurity among white Carolinians.

Even though pressures changed and there was some shifting in the
attitudes and behavior of the white community, until the 1850s South
Carolinians maintained a striking tolerance of free mulattoes and an
amazing resistance to the outright outlawing of interracial marriage.
Indeed, throughout the era of slavery racial intermarriage was *never*
prohibited in South Carolina, nor was it punished by law. The
Palmetto State also refused to relegate free mulattoes to the status of

blacks, slave or free. Even the discovery of the alleged Vesey insur-
rectionary plot of 1822, while it left white Carolinians chary about
the great number of blacks in their midst and about free Negroes
from outside, did not turn them against members of the resident free
mulatto elite, whom they continued to regard as allies in the struggle
to control the slave mass.[29]

A legislative commission appointed to investigate the Vesey plot
and the general state of race relations reported its opinion that free
mulattoes were "a barrier between our own color and that of the
black—and, in cases of insurrection, are more likely to enlist themselves under the banners of the whites." There were good reasons, the
commission felt, to rely upon the mulatto elite in a racial conflict.
"Most of them are industrious, sober, hardworking mechanics, who
have large families and considerable property; and so far as we are
acquainted with their temper, and disposition of their feelings, abhor
the idea of association with the blacks in any enterprise that may
have for its object the revolution of their condition. It must be recol-
lected also, that the greater part of them own slaves, and are, therefore so far interested in this species of property as to keep them on the
watch, and induce them to disclose any plans that may be injurious to
our peace—experience justifies this conclusion." Recognizing "the
value of the services they have performed," the commission thought
that the free mulatto elite should be sustained in the state. At the same
time, however, it thought it wise to "regulate their *degree* [exact position in society] when placed in opposition to our own." In brief,
the commission opted for the retention and clarification of the three-
tier society that had evolved.[30]

The authorities of South Carolina, unlike those of Virginia, steadfastly refused to attempt a fractional definition of blackness for
mulattoes. Perfectly revealing in this connection was the thinking of
Judge William Harper. In 1835 he refused to rule on the whiteness or
blackness of a free person of color involved in a case simply according to the proportion of white blood in his veins. "We cannot say
what admixture of negro blood will make a colored person," he declared. "The condition of the individual is not to be determined solely
by distinct and visible mixture of negro blood, but by reputation, by
his reception into society, and his having commonly exercised the
privileges of a white man. . . . it may be well and proper, that a man
of worth, honesty, industry, and respectability, should have the rank
of a white man, while a vagabond of the same degree of blood should
be confined to the inferior caste. It is hardly necessary to say that a
slave cannot be a white man." [31] Above the realm of slavery where the

slave could not, of course, be white, one could hardly imagine a more perfect rejection of the one-drop rule.

In one case Judge Harper left to the jury the decision as to whether two witnesses, who happened to be brothers, were white or not because, as he said, "it belongs for them to settle questions of common usage and the meaning of popular terms. . . ." In the evidence supplied to the jury, the court offered a highly interesting genealogy. "It appeared that the father of the witnesses was a white man and the mother, a descendant in the third generation of a half-breed who had a white wife; their mother's father was the issue of this marriage, and he also married a white woman; so that the witness[es] had one-sixteenth part of African blood." The black heritage of these witnesses was almost certainly invisible, but the acceptance of their darker progenitors into the white world was no less than astounding. "The maternal grandfather of the witness[es], although of dark complexion, had been recognized as a white man, received into society, and exercised political privilege as such; their mother was uniformly treated as a white woman; and their relations of the same admixture have married into respectable families, and one of them has been a candidate for the state legislature. The witnesses were ordinarily fair and exhibited none of the distinctive mark of the African race; they are respectable, have always been received into society, and recognized as white men—one of them a militia officer, and their caste had never been questioned until now." [32]

Thus the door to whiteness for free people of some color was kept firmly and judiciously open in South Carolina. Known and visible mulattoes could by behavior and reputation be "white," and people of mixed blood could and did marry into white families. In contrast with the upper South, where the animus against free mulattoes of any sort began early and continued strong and where people of slightly mixed blood did not marry into white families of elevated status, South Carolina was strikingly "soft" on free mulattoes of the upper echelons through the 1840s. In this respect it shared a characteristic of race relations common among its Caribbean and Latin neighbors to the south.

In 1850 some 4,400 free mulattoes lived in South Carolina. Of these, more than half, 2,554, lived in Charleston, where they formed a quarter of the total Negro population. As in the cities of Latin America where black slaves were numerous and whites were relatively few, free mulattoes filled many of the trades as bootmakers, carpenters, tailors, etc., and reached up into business and the professions. Some Charleston mulattoes, such as the Kinlochs, Noisettes, and McKinlays, were almost as wealthy and as cultured as their well-to-do white neighbors. And they were nearly as white.[33] The toleration of free mulattoes that was general in Charleston also existed in the Carolina countryside. O. Vernon Burton has uncovered evidences of such feelings in a very close study of Edgefield District, where in 1850 some 250 free Negroes, of whom about three-quarters were mulattoes, lived easily among 20,000 whites. Indeed, he concluded, "The barriers in Edgefield District between whites and free blacks were not so formidable as historians have thought." So loose were the bonds imposed upon these people, he suggested, that they intermarried with whites, and some perhaps passed easily over into the white world.[34] Possibly this condition existed precisely because some 24,000 slaves, vastly black, were held in severe bondage in the same county.

The Carolina preference for mulattoes extended down into slavery. In 1850 there were 12,000 mulatto slaves in the state. These occupied more than their share of places as domestics and artisans at the summit of the slave world. In the Palmetto State mulattoness was, in a sense, a continuum that tied rather smoothly into freedom and whiteness at one end, stretched through the free and the dark, and disappeared at the other end into bondage through mulattoes who were slaves.

Just as South Carolina was largely an evolution of British culture by way of Barbados, lower Louisiana was largely an evolution of French culture through the island of Santo Domingo and directly from the continent. During its colonial era, until acquired by the United States in 1803, Louisiana was possessed by both France and Spain. These nations simply expanded onto the mainland the racial systems they had generated in the islands of the Caribbean. The connection was reinforced in the 1790s when the French, driven out of Haiti by mulatto revolutionaries, transplanted island culture to lower Louisiana. Within a few years they perfected the cultivation of sugar for the region, and a small but rich and flourishing society emerged. In this sugar country black slaves were numerous and mulatto slaves not lacking. There also rose a free mulatto population of some size and, at the top, of impressive wealth. Many of those who became wealthy did so as slave-owning planters in the parishes west of the Crescent City. In 1830 eight of the eleven Negroes in America who owned more than fifty slaves were Louisianans.[35] The census of 1850 counted 242 free persons of color in Louisiana as planters, some of whom were very rich. These were especially strong in St. Landry, Iberville, Plaquemines, and Natchitoches parishes, and they were committed to a social and economic order that promoted their security as slaveholders.[36] Nowhere in America did mulattoes rise so high as in lower Louisiana. There they included large planters and slaveholders who were wealthy, who were Catholic, whose children were sometimes educated in France, and who joined their white counterparts in the promotion of one of the most elegant Creole cultures in the New World.

Gary B. Mills has studied closely a community of these *gens de couleur libre* that emerged along the Cane River in Natchitoches Parish in the late eighteenth century. The founding spirit of the colony was Marie Thérèze Coincoin, a woman of purely African ancestry. Marie Thérèze was born in 1742 of newly imported slaves whose loyalty to their African heritage was such that they gave at least three of their children African names. Family tradition relates that Marie Thérèze herself spoke an African language fluently and was trained by her parents in the medicinal uses of roots and herbs. In time she became the mistress of Claude Thomas Pierre Metoyer, a young man of means who came from France to settle in the colony in 1767. In 1778 when she had borne him seven children, Pierre purchased Marie Thérèze and freed her. Thereafter he arranged for the freedom of all of their children and the settlement upon them of one-third of his very large estate. In the 1790s Marie Thérèze began to build the considerable fortune, including land and slaves, that she would leave to her children to add to the legacy of their father. Her eldest son, Augustin Metoyer, became the patriarch of this family and of the allied families in the community, a clan that came to include some 400 people by 1860.[37]

The wealth of the Metoyers, derived primarily from the planting of cotton, was impressive. In 1830 they owned 287 slaves, more than any other free mulatto family in the South. Augustin and his brother Louis each possessed fifty-four slaves; this, along with their large land holdings, placed them well up in the ranks of slaveholding planters. Augustin's son, François, owned 1,000 acres of improved land in 1850 when only five other planters in the parish, all white, owned as many. When Augustin died, his estate was valued at $141,000. All of these things Marie Thérèze and her children achieved by the favor of influential whites, including Pierre Metoyer, the father of the children, by the generous policy of the Spanish government in giving away large grants of land, and by hard work and business acumen.[38]

The early Metoyers were half European and half African, but they soon established themselves as a third element. "They successfully rejected identification with any established racial order," as Gary Mills asserted, "and achieved recognition as a distinct racial ethnic group." That was a slow and careful process in which they divorced themselves from the blacks but did not allow themselves to melt into the white world—as, for instance, the Gibsons in South Carolina had done. In the beginning, the Metoyers used a part of their wealth to buy their mulatto relatives out of slavery, including husbands and wives, present and prospective. Some of the Metoyer women also became the lovers of white men of substance and produced children who later married into the clan. By the time Augustin had become the patriarch, however, marriages were carefully arranged so as to preserve the clan's intermediate position. Blacks were scorned as mates, but so too were whites refused. Some spouses were brought in from the mulatto community in New Orleans, but primarily the Metoyers married one another intensively and shared the inbred character common to mulatto communities of eminence in the South.[39]

The wealth of the Cane River Creoles of color gave them the means to maintain themselves with poise and dignity in a white-dominated world. Lending and selling, borrowing and buying across the race line at a great rate, "the men of the colony were accepted, economically, in the highest levels of Natchitoches society." They paid white lawyers to defend their rights in the courts, and they used their money and their white relatives in politics to promote their interests. With these certain lines of communication open, the men of the colony maintained a "degree of social parity" with the well-to-do whites. Augustin Metoyer built a church for the community, an inspiration he had conceived as a youth while traveling in Europe with his father. It was the only Catholic church in the area, and Augustin invited his white neighbors to attend, setting aside eight pews for them immediately behind his own. They came, and for two generations the planter elites, white and mulatto, worshipped together. The wealth of the Cane River people also gave them a quality of life and a culture that commanded respect from their white neighbors. "Large and stately homes, furnished with taste and style, graced many of their plantations," wrote Gary Mills. "Musical training developed in their youth an appreciation of the arts. Education, even including university study in Europe in some cases, equipped their offspring for a role as southern planters of distinction." During the first half of the nineteenth century, Cane River's Creoles of color enjoyed a golden age, building and preserving for themselves a middle space between black and white.[40]

Mulatto planters in Louisiana were an impressive group, but it was in New Orleans that the continuing interchange between blacks and whites, sexual and otherwise, reached the highest and most fascinating level. In his study of the city, John Blassingame found that "the pervasiveness of miscegenation" became "the most unique feature of race relations in antebellum New Orleans." As in Latin America, there was a steady surplus of whites males and mulatto females in the city. So common was mixing among the elites of both races that it came to be institutionalized in "quadroon balls." These were regular and public affairs at which wealthy and cultured white men formally courted prospective mulatto mistresses. When the man had made his choice, he met the woman and her parents to offer an arrangement, a "placage," in which he agreed to maintain the woman in a certain style and provide for any children who might be born of the union. If his offer was accepted, the woman was established in a household of her own, less than a wife and a bit more than a concubine. Sometimes the arrangement evolved into a permanent one; more often it endured a matter of months or years. Liaisons also occurred between white women and mulatto men, but, true to the Latin pattern, these were notably less frequent. Blassingame concluded not only that interracial sex was common in New Orleans but that there were "also a number of black-white marriages in spite of the antebellum law prohibiting them." As in South Carolina, many very light mulattoes ultimately passed over the color line into whiteness. In New Orleans as elsewhere there was an official and a professed social intention of discriminating against people of color, but Blassingame found that the mulatto community breached the color bar often enough to maintain for itself a "relatively rich" social life.[41]

Both sentiment and practicality contributed to the reluctance of the upper class in the lower South to press free mulattoes into an undifferentiated blackness. Wealthy Southern white men were not always willing to alienate forever their darker children from the finer things of life. Thus there was a seeming softness at the top edge of mulatto existence in the lower South. Deep South Southerners possessed a "remarkable ability," as one close scholar found, "to resist the Upper South tendency to jumble all Negroes together."[42] On the practical side, authorities in the lower South had long faced a relatively large and hostile black slave population. If the report of the South Carolina legislative commission appointed to study the Vesey plot is an accurate indication, those authorities had learned to think of the free Negro community as a useful ally in controlling that sometimes alien mass. Free mulattoes were the beginning of a connection, however tenuous, that reached down into the menacing black majority and back again to insure whites against unpleasant surprises.

Far from jumbling all blacks together, lower South Southerners and particularly deep South Southerners, like their Latin American neighbors, were able to make minute distinctions among mulattoes by degree of mixture, running the scale out both ways from the half-and-half center to join the darkest with the lightest and giving names to each slight variation. For instance, a Louisiana Creole might call a person one-sixteenth black a "meamelouc" and a person one-sixty-fourth black a "sang-mele," and in some places a person three-quarters black would be called a "sambo" and a person seven-eighths black would be a "mango"—distinctions that were totally foreign to the upper South.[43] "Mulatto" itself was an Iberian word, and it was the gentlemen of the deep South who virtually made a class out of "quadroons" (a word of Spanish and French origins) and went on sometimes to misappropriate "mustee" from "mestizo," meaning a mixture of European and Indian, and apply it to persons one-eighth black. Until the 1850s mulattoness in the social order of the lower South had a quality different from its quality in the upper South, and that difference was to have a curious impact upon race relations in the whole of the South from emancipation into the twentieth century.[44]

The census of 1850 supports the conclusion that there was a significant division between the histories of the mulattoes of the upper South and the lower. It also supports the idea that the lower South shared certain West Indian characteristics in its treatment of miscegenation and mulattoes while the upper South did not. Finally, its figures, taken with others, suggest further generalizations concerning the origins and evolution of the mulatto population.

In 1850 the census takers counted mulattoes for the first time, relying simply upon the eye of the beholder to recognize a person of mixed ancestry. In that year in the whole of the United States, the census listed 406,000 people visibly mulatto out of a Negro population of 3,639,000. Thus mulattoes constituted 11.2 percent of the Negro population and 1.8 percent of the national total. Free mulattoes numbered 159,000, slave mulattoes 247,000. Mulattoes outside of the South, all of whom were free, were heavily concentrated in the area from New York to Indiana. Of the 57,000 mulattoes in the North and West, more than half, 30,000, lived in the two states of Pennsylvania and Ohio. Three-quarters, 43,000, lived in those two states plus New York and Indiana. The remaining 14,000 were spread fairly evenly through the population from Maine to California.[45]

Some 350,000 mulattoes lived south of Mason's and Dixon's line, that is, south of Pennsylvania, where they formed 3.6 percent of the total population.[46] It is striking that Virginia alone supported 80,000, or nearly a quarter of these. It is even more striking that Virginia and her child state Kentucky counted a third of all the mulattoes in the South. Add Missouri and Virginia's "sisters" to the east—Maryland, Delaware, and the District of Columbia—and in this narrow band of America one counts 154,000, or roughly half (44 percent) of all the mulattoes in the South. Moving southward to include North Carolina and Tennessee, one counts 212,000, or more than half of those in the entire nation and nearly two-thirds of the total number in the South.[47] The upper South, clearly, was the heartland of mulattoness in America, just as the deep South was the heartland of blackness. It seems fully as appropriate to speak of the upper South in 1850 as the "mulatto belt" as it is to refer to the lower South as the "black belt."

In 1850 slightly more than a third, 137,000 or 39 percent, of the mulattoes in the South lived in the lower South. They were spread from South Carolina into northern Florida and across to Texas. The largest concentrations were in lower Louisiana and eastern South Carolina. Interestingly, in both areas free mulattoes outnumbered slave mulattoes two to one. Free mulattoes in the lower South were not only free, but unusually prosperous in terms of occupation, wealth, and land and slave holdings. Moreover, they constituted a great majority of the free Negro population, about 75 percent in the lower South as against 35 percent in the upper South. Evidently free blacks in the upper South came to be most numerous only during the era of the American Revolution, when a rising number of private emancipations in that area produced more black freedmen than mulatto because most slaves were black[48] The Maryland census of 1755, significantly, had counted 1,460 free mulattoes, 80.4 percent of the total number of free Negroes, as opposed to 357 free blacks. In 1850 the state counted 14,000 free mulattoes, 18.7 percent of the total number of free Negroes, as opposed to 61,000 free blacks.[49] The lower South did not share that Revolutionary enthusiasm, with the result that its free Negro population remained about three-quarters mulatto, a ratio that prevailed until the Civil War.

The salient statistical fact about mulattoes in the lower South in 1850 was that the great mass of them were slaves. Free mulattoes numbered only 24,000, or 17.3 percent of the total mulatto population, as against 79,000, or 37.1 percent, for the upper South. Outside of the first-settled areas they were especially sparse. If one subtracts the free mulattoes of South Carolina, 5,000, and Louisiana, 14,000, only 5,000 remain in the other six states of the lower South. The specific figures for each state are significant: Alabama 1,700, Georgia 1,500, Florida 700, Mississippi 600, Arkansas 400, and Texas 300. Apparently, the newer the settlement, the fewer were the free mulattoes. Looking at the overall statistics on mulattoes in these six states, one is impressed not by their freedom, but by their slavery. Out of 86,000 mulattoes, 81,000, or 93.9 percent, were slaves. In Mississippi not one mulatto in twenty was free, a ratio generally shared by Georgia, Alabama, Arkansas, Florida, and Texas.[50] Color the lower South dark . . . and color it very slave.

In addition to suggesting significant differences in numbers and freedom between mulattoes in the upper South and those in the lower South, the census of 1850 offers another revealing line of division—one between what might be called the "old slave South," consisting of those areas settled early in the colonial period, and the "new slave South," consisting of those areas settled subsequently. By far the greater proportions of free to slave mulattoes appeared in those states that had been settled before the 1730s. Thus in the upper South in the old slave states of Delaware, Maryland (including the District of Columbia), Virginia, and North Carolina fully half, 50.5 percent, of the mulattoes were free, while in the new slave states of Kentucky, Tennessee, and Missouri only 10.4 percent were free. Carried south, the pattern held. South Carolina and Louisiana were the oldest colonies in the lower South. In these two states 36.3 percent of the mulattoes were free, while in the new slave states of Georgia, Mississippi, Alabama, Arkansas, Florida, and Texas only 6.1 percent were free.[51]

Thus in both the upper South and the lower, free mulattoes were very much the creatures of early settlement. In the old slave South free mulattoes ranked high both in raw numbers and in proportion to slave mulattoes. It is an arresting fact that in 1850, 90,000 free mulattoes, or 87.7 percent of all free mulattoes in the South, lived in the old slave South, while only 13,000 were counted in those areas later settled. Of these 90,000 free mulattoes, 71,200 lived in the upper South, while 18,500 lived in the lower. Almost half, 46.7 percent, of the mulattoes in the old slave South were free, while only 8.0 percent in the new slave South were so. This great divergence occurred even

though the total number of mulattoes in the old slave South was not
vastly greater than their number in the new slave South, some 192,000
to 157,000.[52]

Mulatto slaves were sufficiently plentiful in the first-settled areas
so that it could not be said that they were very much the creatures of
later settlement. Still, mulattoness and slavery went together to an as-
toundingly high degree in those nine Southern states that were last
colonized. In that whole broad geography from Missouri to Florida
between the first British settlements in the Chesapeake and Carolina
areas and the first French settlements in Louisiana, 92 percent of the
mulattoes were slaves, and there were some 144,000 of them. In making slaves of mulattoes, Kentucky, Tennessee, and Missouri were
much closer to Georgia, Mississippi, Alabama, Arkansas, Florida, and
Texas than they were to their mother states to the east.

Interestingly, the new slave South included the state of Georgia,
and, statistically speaking, ought to be extended to include the later-
settled portions of South Carolina and Louisiana. Even though Georgia was first permanently settled in the 1730s and became a slave
colony in the 1750s, in the census of 1850 it fits squarely into the
profile of the new slave South, with 93.7 percent of its mulattoes
being slaves. Georgia appears to have been, in a sense, the first planta-
tion-slave frontier. The sudden opening in 1749 of southeastern Georgia by the trustees of the colony to settlement by slaveholders brought
a veritable flood of slaves into the area. By 1773 there were about
33,000 people in that portion of the colony, of whom 15,000 were
slaves.[53] Perhaps it was the sudden influx of slaves, largely blacks from
South Carolina, plus the proximity of the Spanish in Florida that led
the legislature in 1765 to pass a rather remarkable law inviting free
mulattoes and mestizos to settle in the colony. It offered them the
status of white men, except the privileges of voting for and sitting as
members of the assembly. Thus in Georgia free mulattoes were distinctly separated from free blacks and specially favored, a generosity
that may have sprung from the perceived needs of the frontier
colony.[54]

The geography of the new slave South included large portions of
South Carolina and Louisiana, where the later-settled areas shared the
profile of the new slave South while the remainder more closely approximated that of the old slave South. In South Carolina, 66.2 percent of the mulattoes in the Charleston District were free while only
14 percent of those in the remainder were. In Louisiana, 61.3 percent
of the mulattoes in the New Orleans Parish were free while 30 percent

of those outside the parish were. Further, if one reaches out from New Orleans to include three country parishes of the Creole core, he counts 11,000 of the 14,000 free mulattoes in the Pelican State.[55]

Whatever it was that brought about a high rate of freedom for mulattoes was associated with the first-settled places. In the lower South Louisiana might be unique because of its relatively late settlement, but the cases of Georgia and back-country South Carolina strongly suggest that the conditions that would have created a relatively large free mulatto population in those areas had already passed away in the 1750s, and perhaps even in the 1730s when up-country South Carolina began to be settled. In the upper South the timing of the closing out of freedom for mulattoes is more difficult to establish. Certainly the age had passed when Kentucky was settled in the 1770s, 1780s, and 1790s. Probably it had passed well before that, and perhaps it was already rapidly passing in the 1720s.

The basic reasons for the existence of a large proportion of free mulattoes in the old slave South probably differed between the upper South and the lower. In the upper South there was a seventeenth-century free mulatto tradition upon which to build. Then in the period from about 1690 to about 1720 the black population in Virginia and the rest of the upper South increased rapidly even as the underclass of indentured servants and ex-indentured servants was dissolving. At the same time, free white women were approaching numerical parity with free white men. White women were no longer at a high premium, and white women in or moving out of the servant class may well have taken as mates black or mulatto slaves; or they may have taken black or mulatto freemen, some of whom possessed property and skills promising security. It could be that the meeting of considerable numbers of black men and white women of the lower orders under these circumstances bred the first great wave of free mulattoes. These mulatto children began to flow into the rather loose molds established by the relatively few mulattoes in the seventeenth century, overran them, and flooded the countryside, much to the consternation of the ruling powers.

As the free mulatto population swelled, authorities, as we have seen, took action to impede its growth and diminish its freedom. Meanwhile the influx of a mass of cheap black slave labor tended to squeeze white servants out of the cruder tasks and upward. Higher types of labor bred higher status for servants, ex-servants, immigrants, and the underclass of whites generally. Higher types of labor and higher status probably bred, too, an increasing tendency on the part of members of the underclass to hold themselves aloof from blacks and mulattoes and to identify their future in America with the pure whiteness their betters had long encouraged. Probably in that "lost generation" at the beginning of the eighteenth century, racism in America took a new and not so faltering step forward.

In Virginia racism gained definition, ironically, to become a part of a world that was even then crystallizing into the society that produced the Washingtons, Jeffersons, Madisons, Randolphs, and Lees of the Revolutionary generation and a new high sense of personal liberty. This is an irony that Edmund S. Morgan caught succinctly in the title of his study *American Slavery, American Freedom.* In that work he depicted in seventeenth-century Virginia a virulent prejudice among whites against Indians, a vague and nebulous prejudice against Africans, and a bitter conflict between the authorities and whites of the underclass. Early sentiments against Africans living in Virginia seemed to be based as much upon their not being Christian and English as upon their not being white. By the end of the first quarter of the eighteenth century, however, the authorities were moving rapidly to draw a race line and to ally themselves with the white masses to control all of the colored elements—blacks, mulattoes, Indians, and mustees, slave and free.[56] New mixing between blacks and whites would be greatly impeded in the new order, but mulattoes would persist. A reservoir of free mulattoes had already been created. They were fruitful, and they did replenish the earth. After the Revolution, with a layer of newly emancipated mulattoes added to their ranks, the reservoir was large enough and sufficiently vital to survive the hostilities that white people heaped upon mulattoes . . . and to grow.

In South Carolina, as in Louisiana, a later start and the Latin influence produced a much smaller number of free mulattoes than in the upper South, but many of those were children of the master class that saw fit to free them.[57] Aided specially by their kinship with upperclass whites, these increased over time, not only in numbers but, often, in wealth and culture as well. Some married light or white and over generations entered the top realm of the system as planters; others became merchants and tradesmen in the cities. And some free mulatto families of substance were openly allowed to melt into the white world. South Carolina did have tremors of nervousness about mixing and mulattoes, and these sometimes surfaced in legislation. But before the 1850s it did not move to damage severely the freedom of mulattoes already free, or to tax them specially, or even to deny them weapons, as did Virginia. All during the slave period there was no law in South Carolina prohibiting or punishing interracial marriage. Further, the state would almost attain the twentieth century before it first attempted to define legally what separated black from white—even as all agreed, upper South and lower, that a slave could not be white. It may have been that in the beginning colonial South Carolina thought it needed its mulatto community, caught as it was between a recurrently bloody Indian frontier, the menacing Spanish in Florida, and a sudden vast swell of Africans at home. It expressed its need with a measure of tolerance, and the tolerance gathered a momentum and institutions of its own and persisted after the reasons for its origins had disappeared.[58]

The story of the Gideon Gibson family illustrates well the difference between the lot of free mulattoes in the upper South and the lower in the early years of the eighteenth century. Gibson was originally a Virginian. He was a free person of color, a carpenter, and the owner of seven slaves. He led his clan to settle in the Santee River country on the South Carolina frontier about 1731. There were several white women in the clan, perhaps out of the ranks of the servant class in Virginia. Gideon's own wife was white. His father had been a free mulatto, probably heir to the grudging freedom that seventeenth-century Virginia had allowed free mulattoes. Possibly the Gibsons felt the effect of rising discrimination against their class so evident in Virginia in the preceding decades and were thus spurred to make the move to South Carolina. Hailed before the governor to explain their presence, however, Gideon Gibson simply said it was for the "better support of his Family." The governor allowed Gibson and his people to stay, as he reported to an inquiring assembly, "in Consideration of his Wifes being a white woman and Several White women Capable of working and being Serviceable in the Country." Possibly the governor also welcomed their being firmly settled out in the wilds of Santee between the recently very troublesome Indians and the highly profitable rice plantations along the coast. The Gibson case suggests that the prejudice against interracial unions could be eased readily enough in colonial Carolina if the parties were not vagabonds and had the kind of status that light color, generations of good behavior as freemen, and a trade, land, and slaves could give them.

The subsequent history of the Gibsons indicates a striking tolerance by white Carolinians of free mulattoes of substance in their communities. Moreover, it indicates that whites of status and wealth were willing to intermarry with light mulattoes of status and wealth. In the 1730s the Gibsons acquired land on the Carolina frontier and raised a numerous and influential clan. One of Gideon's daughters first married an English settler and planter named George Saunders. When he was killed in an accident, she improved her position by marrying one of the richest men in the area. Her brother, named Gideon like his father, became the leader of the family clan. He acquired a 550-acre tract from the colony in 1736 near Sandy Bluff on the Santee and established a family seat called Hickory Grove. He was very active in community affairs and in 1766 won note as a leader in the Regulator movement, a spontaneous rising of vigilante groups organized to suppress frontier banditti. For a time this brought him the unfavorable attention of the authorities. Especially did it earn him the enmity of a militia colonel sent to punish the Regulators for taking the law into their own hands. All of the colonel's men defected to Gibson's side, and the vengeful colonel, as a member of the South Carolina legislature, attacked Gibson on the floor of the House of Representatives on the ground of his color. Henry Laurens, a leading Charleston merchant and one of the few Carolinians in the Revolutionary era to attack slavery openly, challenged Gibson's critics to compare the red and white, associated with Englishness, of Gibson's face with that of the average member of the assembly of French Huguenot ancestry. There the debate concerning Gibson's color abruptly ended. The justice of the Regulator cause was soon recognized, and Gibson became a hero of the movement. During the Revolutionary War, Gideon Gibson was shot dead by a local guerrilla chief whom he had just hosted at breakfast and upbraided for brutally whipping an elderly Tory. On the frontier, it would seem that ambivalence was not confined to matters racial.

The Gibson family continued to flourish and to spread. One of Gideon's sons, Jordan, went west with Daniel Boone in 1774. Another, Stephen, grew wealthy and moved off to Georgia in 1800. There his daughter reputedly married a prominent man named Thomas Butler King. Some left and others stayed, but all married into local elites with seeming ease. When the historian of the area published his account in 1867, he gave the Gibsons full play among the eminent families, but he did not mention their African ancestry. That ancestry was clearly visible in the colonial records, and it was probably common knowledge in the neighborhood. There was one drop and more of black blood in the Gibson family, but no one made an issue of it after the Regulator incident, and clearly it did not prevent these wealthy people from marrying comfortably into the white world. The whites who mixed with the Gibsons in the most vital areas of their lives were distinctly saying in the personal and social realm what Judge Harper said in the judicial realm in 1835—that one could not prescribe the number of drops of African blood that made one black rather than white, and character counted against color. Such acceptance of people of mixed blood into the higher social realm of the white world was unheard of in the upper South. Yet it was a phenomenon that Vernon Burton saw still happening in Edgefield District and Marina Wikramanayake observed generally in the state of South Carolina in the years before the Civil War.[59]

The Gibson family illustrates an important variant in the mulatto experience in America. Unlike the Metoyer and other families who chose to maintain themselves distinctly as a third element in the society, marrying neither white nor black, the Gibsons and others opted to dissolve their African ancestry in seas of whiteness. As generation after generation married into the white world, the African connection became more and more tenuous. No African names for their children, no practicing of African herbal medicine, no continuations of African culture for the Gibsons. Indeed, soon one would have to search hard for any distinctions of color or feature that would link them to their African past. By the early twentieth century the black blood of the Gibsons had spread so thin as to become absolutely invisible and its presence more suspected than known, even to many of those who carried it.

The old slave South was remarkable for its high proportion of free mulattoes; the new slave South was equally remarkable for its dearth of free mulattoes. The few free mulattoes in the new slave South were scattered in handfuls across the states, and lesser numbers were directly and closely related to recentness of settlement.[60] Of the seven Southern states admitted to the Union after 1796, only two, Louisiana and Alabama, both of which still carried signs of their Latin origins, had more than 1,000 free mulattoes in 1850. The two frontier slave states of Texas (257) and Arkansas (407) could not muster 1,000 between them. Even with Florida (703) and Mississippi (635) added, they barely counted 2,000. Further, the two new slave states with the most free mulattoes, Tennessee and Kentucky, had been admitted to the Union in the eighteenth century. Evidently the numbers of free mulattoes in the new slave South grew exceedingly slowly, and only in part because of laws prohibiting emancipation. Indeed, not every state prohibited emancipation by individual masters. Missouri never did so, Arkansas only in 1858, and Kentucky only in 1850.[61] The dearth was due in part to the fact that few free mulattoes migrated into the new slave South. Free mulattoes were not very mobile in the South, and when they moved, they did not often move into the new slave states. Perhaps most of the free mulattoes in these states in 1850 owed their freedom to slaveholding fathers or grandfathers or great-grandfathers who wanted their children free. These parents do not appear to have been numerous. Freedom, seemingly, was a thing achieved either early in the colonial period or one by one later, and free mulatto communities in areas newly settled grew with terrific slowness.

In sum, the figures in the census of 1850 suggest that the free mulatto population generated its numerical base very early in the colonial period, and that later accretions from new mixtures of whites and Negroes were, in terms of numbers, inconsequential. Freedom for mulattoes existed in enclaves along the coast line of the South, and especially in the upper South. The figures also suggest that mulatto slavery was strong and rising in 1850. Slavery was a special feature of mulattoness in the lower South, but, dividing the South in another way, it was a more striking feature in those states settled after the 1720s. The large numbers of mulatto slaves on the slave frontiers suggest that mulatto slavery leaped eagerly onto ground newly opened and swelled rapidly as the area matured. Taken altogether, the census of 1850 illustrates not mulatto freedom, but a virulent mulatto slavery.

How did it happen that the upper South in 1850 had become a "mulatto belt" supporting some two-thirds of the mulattoes in the South and maintaining a pattern of relations distinctly different from that in the lower South? The organization of a detailed answer might be centered around a demographic model. It seems safe to assume that miscegenation and the appearance of a mulatto population required three elements: opportunity, inclination, and time. Opportunity involved, first, bringing Negroes and whites into the same general area; second, the existence of both men and women among those brought together; and, third, bringing the potential miscegenationists together under circumstances in which sexual relations could occur. Inclination assumes a basic sex drive in each individual, more or less inhibited in the Freudian sense in its exercise across race lines by the demands of the society in which the individual lives. Finally, the number of mulattoes ultimately relates directly to the operation of opportunity and inclination over time.

The fundamental requirement for producing a large number of mulatto children is a large number of women of childbearing capacity of one race and relatively few men of the other race. Under ordinary circumstances it appears that a woman between the ages of fifteen and forty-five could bear a child every two years. Possibly a man could father several children a day over a long span of years. If the production of children were the primary objective of a society, an Amazonian model featuring many women and few men would be very close to the ideal arrangement. Obviously, however, European, African, and American societies have not organized themselves for this end. On the contrary, they have invested heavily in fostering one-to-one long-running relationships between men and women. The result is that tremendous pressures have traditionally been brought upon individuals to have one mate at a time and to prolong the relationship. These pressures seemed to have been highly effective in America among blacks, whites, and mulattoes, and to have influenced the history of miscegenation.

The first ingredient in opportunity was simply getting white people and black people together in the same general areas. The numbers and the ratio in which they came together were very important in determining the numbers of mulatto offspring. Other things being equal, a large initial mulatto population occurred when a large number of whites and a large number of blacks were brought together. Where there were many whites and few blacks, as in New England, few mulattoes were born. Where there were few whites and many blacks—as in Barbados, where the ratio in 1713 ran three to one black over white, or Jamaica, where the ratio was eight to one—also few mulattoes were born.

In the lower South, in colonial South Carolina and Louisiana, where great numbers of slaves were introduced over a short period of time and Negroes came to outnumber whites by a large majority, few mulattoes were born. The white population of Carolina was never very large in the colonial period. In the first thirty years after Charleston was settled in 1670, the Negro population also remained small. In the 1690s rice cultivation was introduced and began to flourish. The Negro population swelled rather suddenly from several hundred to an estimated 4,100 in 1708, in which year it probably surpassed the white. In the next dozen years, with importations and a natural increase, the number of Negroes tripled to 11,700 as opposed to a white population of only 6,580. Beginning in 1726, the importation of slaves accelerated to a still higher rate with the result that by 1740 the slave population had grown to 40,000. On the eve of the Revolution, Charleston itself was half white and half Negro, counting some 14,000 people. In the rural areas of rice-country South Carolina there were 72,000 Negroes and some 25,000 whites. Thus Carolina rapidly passed from a small colony in which whites outnumbered blacks to a rapidly growing one in which blacks comprised 51.1 percent of the population in 1708, 64.0 percent in 1721, and 70.6 percent on the eve of the Revolution. With relatively few whites present in the black belt and the races evenly matched only briefly, one could expect few mulattoes to appear in colonial South Carolina.[62]

In terms of racial ratios, the upper South, on the other hand, at one time supported conditions nearly ideal for the proliferation of a large mulatto population. Most especially was this true in Virginia. Whereas the Negro population in that colony had numbered only 300 out of 15,000 in 1648, 2,000 out of 40,000 in 1670, and 3,000 out of 70,000 to 80,000 in 1681, the figure grew rapidly to 23,000 by 1715, while the white population remained relatively static at about 72,500. In 1756, one estimate had it that 120,000 Negroes existed in the colony with 173,000 whites. In Virginia in 1790, by the first federal census, there were 306,000 Negroes, slave and free, with some 452,000 whites. To recapitulate, whites in seventeenth-century Virginia overwhelmed Negroes in numbers much as they did in New England. Between 1670 and 1681 Negroes were actually losing relative strength, as their percentage of the total population dropped from 5 percent to 4 percent. In 1708 the trend was shifting due to large importations of slaves. By 1715 some 24.1 percent of the population was Negro. By 1756, when Maryland was about 30 percent Negro, Virginia was 41 percent—ratios that held fairly firm for a century.[63] No other colony had such large numbers of both blacks and whites as Virginia, nor such a near and long-running balance between the two.

The rate of miscegenation and the number of mulattoes in the total population were also influenced by sex ratios. If only British women had come to America and imported only African men, all of the new Americans obviously would soon have been mulattoes. Lamentably, our information about sex ratios among both whites and blacks in the early settlements is partial and scattered. What we do know, however, tends to indicate that sex ratios among Britishers in the New World had a common pattern. The first migrants were mostly males, who were followed by women in considerable numbers. There was always more or less a "starving time" in which the population became seasoned to the environment. Subsequently the female population gained parity with the male. In the last stage parity was often promoted by men moving off to new frontiers. This pattern prevailed in New England. It also prevailed in the West Indies, where it is often erroneously assumed that white men lived perpetually without white mates. It is true that in the early years in the islands white men did vastly outnumber white women. In Barbados and St. Christopher some 94 percent of the first settlers were males. In Jamaica in 1661, 85 percent of the white population was male. By 1720, however, the population of both Barbados and the Leeward Islands had passed through parity to become slightly more female than male.[64] These events were hastened by white men going off to pioneer new territories, especially in Jamaica. On the large island of Jamaica, where there remained lands available for exploitation, the ratio rested during the mid-eighteenth century at three to two.[65]

Blacks, like whites, exhibited a remarkable capacity for achieving a balance between the sexes. A count of some 60,000 slaves brought into the West Indies by the Royal African Company between 1673 and 1711 indicates that they were 60 percent male. However, the male preponderance evaporated with great rapidity. Even during these years of large-scale importations, the slave gangs in the islands were slightly more female than male. It appears that everywhere in British America, from Maine to Barbados, both white and Negro women simply survived at a greater rate than did men. That near balance was upset in the West Indies only later in the eighteenth century as planters turned to massive importations of slave men to meet their needs for labor and thus overturned the natural balance.[66]

The settlement of the Chesapeake world was begun by men. The first large group of immigrant white women arrived at Jamestown in 1619, the very same year in which the first significant group of Negroes arrived. The women numbered over a hundred while the Negroes numbered a few more than a score. By about 1700 the ratio of white men to white women in Virginia was three to two. This sexual imbalance existed at a time when relatively large numbers of African slaves were flooding into the colony. There was also a sexual imbalance among black people in favor of men, but blacks were African slaves, the most alien and the least powerful class of people in Virginia, and they were vulnerable in greater or lesser degree to use by whites. The great number of whites, the great number of blacks, and a sexual imbalance among whites in favor of white men set up powerful forces for miscegenation and the creation of a large mulatto population.

Sexual imbalance among whites in Virginia was a transitory thing. Probably its most persistent cause was an influx of indentured servants where the ratio ran three or four to one in favor of men. With the decline of the importation of indentured servants in the eighteenth century, balance quickly asserted itself. Probably by about 1750 white

Virginia had achieved numerical parity between the sexes. Certainly such was so in Maryland. While Maryland had been settled initially by both men and women, men predominated for about a century. By 1755, however, a seemingly very accurate count indicated that free white women in the colony outnumbered free white men 23,521 to 23,421 if 637 pauper men were excluded. That exclusion seems not unreasonable on the ground that these men were probably ex-servants who had failed to achieve either a livelihood, property, or a wife. Free white women in Maryland gained practical parity with free white men in spite of the continued importation into that colony of male indentured servants and male convict servants at a fairly high rate. Finally, Maryland in 1755 affords an example that closely parallels the British West Indian experience. The one county in which free white men greatly outnumbered free white women (by 613) was Fredrick, the frontier county. It seems fully possible that the female preponderance in the eastern counties was hastened by men following opportunity westward.[67] In the numerical sense Virginia and the rest of the upper South would ever remain solidly a white man's country, and that was true, in large measure, because they had early become a white woman's country.

In the Carolina world in 1703 the ratio of white men to white women was about the same as in Virginia. Officials in the colony counted 1,460 free white men and 940 free white women, along with 100 men and 90 women servants. In addition there were 250 Indian slaves, of whom 100 were men and 150 were women.[68] At the same time South Carolina was, also like Virginia, rapidly escalating the importation of slaves. If all white men in Carolina were to have mates, 540 would have to find mates of another color, red or black. One great difference between Carolina and Virginia was that Carolina had only 540 surplus white men and a total of about 1,000 black and Indian women, while Virginia had 15,000 surplus white men and perhaps 1,500 black women. Surplus white men and the presence of Negro women produced miscegenation and mulattoes in Carolina, but at a rate dramatically lower than in Virginia.

Proximity was the final physical ingredient required for a high level of miscegenation. People of one sex and race had to be within touching distance of the opposite sex and race. Amorous proximity is a quality not defined by statistics and difficult to estimate. However, what we know of plantations and slave patterns suggests that it was much more likely to occur in the upper South, given the one-to-one permanent mating system, than in the lower.

The pattern of early settlement in the upper South was one in which plantations and farms were much mixed. Plantations usually occupied the best locations along the waterfronts of the Chesapeake Bay and the large rivers, but there was sufficient room for farms in the interstices. Moreover, farmers away from the water often traded through the waterfront plantations, there being no significant number of towns or ports in which to trade. Thus the free white population of nonslaveholders in the upper South was in fairly close contact with Negroes on the plantations.[69]

This was one kind of proximity that prevailed in the upper South throughout the slave period, but for a limited time around 1700 there was another, very special kind of proximity that might account for the great numbers of mulattoes that appeared there. This was the time and place, alluded to previously, in which there was an overlapping of white servant and black slave labor. As noted, indentured white labor was the great labor supply in Virginia in the seventeenth century, the largest numbers coming immediately before and after the Restoration of Charles II to the throne in 1660. The authority on indentured servitude in the colonies estimates that during the 1670s there were always 12,000 to 15,000 servants laboring in the plantations, 6,000 of these in Virginia and 2,000 in Maryland. In 1681, of some 75,000 people in Virginia, Governor Culpepper thought that 15,000 were indentured servants and only 3,000 were slaves.[70] During the years around 1681 Virginia imported about 1,500 servants annually, the quantity diminishing after the Glorious Revolution in England in 1688 and 1689.[71] The number of people under indenture at a given time was a fraction of the number who had served their time and passed on into the hired-labor class and sometimes beyond either into property or paupery. Thus there existed a numerous underclass of servants and ex-servants in Virginia and in the upper South. Moreover, because servant men outnumbered servant women by about three to one, this underclass was heavily male, and that preponderance of maleness doubtlessly carried over into the underclass after servants had completed their terms.

Even before indentured servants began to decline in numbers in Virginia, the number of Negro slaves began a relatively rapid increase. Again as we have seen, the number rose from 2,000 in 1670 to 3,000 in 1681. By 1715 there were 23,000 Negro slaves in Virginia. Probably about 7,000 of these were African women new to America. At the same time there were about 15,000 surplus white men. According to accounts, the underclass of white men and women worked and lived alongside the Negro slaves on the farms and plantations. Proximity was at its maximum in Virginia in these years around 1700.

Maryland probably varied only slightly from Virginia, most notably in that the proportion of slaves was at first greater and later less than that of Virginia and in that indentured servitude had a longer life as a system of recruiting unskilled labor. Taken altogether, the mix of black and white was more intimate in those turn-of-the-century years in the upper South than it was at any other time and any other place in what is now the United States. Miscegenation was not only possible, it was probable.

As previously indicated, the Carolina world had a proper sex ratio for a large quantity of mixing; but it did not have the numbers, and only briefly did it have a propitious racial ratio. Similarly, only for a short time were the races sufficiently proximate to promote miscegenation.

The leading historian of the Negro in colonial South Carolina, Peter H. Wood, makes a great division between the first generation in the colony and the second. In the first generation the population was three-quarters white and rather thinly spread over the land. The Negro population of about 1,000, some of whom were mulattoes, had been brought from the West Indies. Negroes and whites lived close together. Men were numerically dominant in both races, but the numbers in both were tending toward a balance between the sexes.[72] There was intimacy and there was miscegenation, but the total population of each race was small and mulattoes were consequently few.

The second twenty-five years were a transitional stage in which Negroes were brought in from Africa in relatively large numbers. The Negro population increased rapidly, surpassed that of whites in 1708, and reached 64 percent in 1721. That special underclass of white servants and ex-servants, which probably accounted for much mixing in the upper South, was never large in the lower South and was almost lost in the inundation of African slaves. In 1703 there were only some 200 indentured servants in Carolina, of whom nearly half, 90, were women. The labor supply also included Indian slaves. In South Carolina in 1703 there were 350 Indian slaves, of whom only 100 were men; 150 were women and 100 were children. These worked and lived with Negro slaves in close intimacy. The result was the generation of an element of Negro and Indian parentage, locally called mustees. This population was never large and tended to merge into the mulatto group. Like indentured servitude, Indian slavery declined rapidly in the early eighteenth century. During this transitional second generation, whites of the master class and Negro and Indian slaves lived close together. The picture painted is of the frontier family with a handful of slaves. The situation was ripe for mixing be-

tween whites, blacks, and reds. But again the quantity was lacking. In
1721 there were only some 19,000 souls in the whole of colonial
South Carolina, and mulattoes could not have been very numerous.

In the third generation the picture changed yet again. In 1726 rice
planters began massive importations of blacks directly from Africa.
These moved rapidly through Charleston and out onto the plantations. Meanwhile rice cultivation had moved from the creeks down
onto the rivers to take advantage of fresh waters backed up by ocean
tides. Soon rice plantations stood crowding shoulder to shoulder
along the lowland rivers and streams of the tidewater. Because of the
systems of dikes, ditches, and floodgates required for rice culture, rice
plantations could not be small. They required large investments and
large gangs of slaves. A rice plantation might have 100 acres of flood-
able riverfront land and 1,000 acres in a strip behind it for support
functions. Thus rice plantations consumed the best lands and reached
well back from the rivers. Rice culture left little room for white
farmers in rice country. The few whites who existed in the tidewater
countryside were squeezed well back into the interior and away from
the now heavy concentrations of black slaves along the rivers.

With lands nearly perfectly suited for rice cultivation, with large
and profitable markets opened to them by imperial authorities after
1731, and with a seemingly endless supply of black slave labor,
planters in the tidewater who happened to possess that limited area of
ideal rice land grew suddenly and unwontedly rich. Increasingly, they
became absentee landlords, very unlike the planter gentry of the
tobacco world in the upper South. Planting families typically lived in
Charleston—and later in Savannah, Beaufort, Georgetown, and Wilmington—and traveled abroad. If they lived on the plantations at all,
it was only after the first frost in the fall, and they always fled the
miasmatic lowlands in the spring. Whites of the master class in rice
country were not often in proximity to plantation slaves. Even white
overseers were scarce, and black overseers not lacking.

Rice country, then, became uniquely a black man's country. A
young Swiss traveler spoke the truth in 1737 when he wrote that
"Carolina looks more like a negro country than like a country settled
by white people." [73] On the eve of the Revolution and for a century
afterward, the eastern littoral from lower North Carolina into middle
Georgia was indeed a black man's country, dotted here and there with
towns and cities populated by whites and mulattoes. In 1850, after all
of the hinterland had been settled, the Negro population in South
Carolina not only still outnumbered the white, it was also 95.7 percent black. [74] Newcomers to the area even in Reconstruction would

marvel at the blackness of the rural Negro population and notice the dearth of mulattoes.

The city of Charleston was the great exception. Charleston was the one place in the Carolina world where whites and blacks came together all through the generations. They did so with an intimacy unrivaled south of Baltimore. In the Queen City aristocratic households demanded Negro servants in numbers nearly equal to the city's total white population. Moreover, affluent whites wanted full and ready service, and they kept their slaves in their yards, in their houses, and, sometimes, in their boudoirs. Proximity became touching in Charleston, and it also became sexual intimacy and miscegenation. On the eve of the Revolution, Charleston was half white and half Negro, and its Negro half was more white than black.

In Charleston, another, more subtle factor worked, one not yet explicitly introduced into our scheme. That factor is time. Though whites who mixed in Charleston were small in numbers, they were persistent. They had begun to mix in the West Indies even before they began the first settlement at Charles Town in 1670. And they continued to mix in the city with highly visible effects. White men mated with mulatto women not only in one generation, but in successive generations, and begat children, boys and girls, who were lighter and lighter. By 1850, after two centuries of mixing, the mulatto community in Charleston District was not only very light but was also relatively numerous. In the lower South only in Creole Louisiana, where the history of mulattoes was not vastly different, were the Charleston mulattoes rivaled either in lightness or in numbers.

The rate of miscegenation was also influenced by inclination. Indeed, inclination on the part of one party, if not in some sense both, was the *sine qua non* of mixing. If Freud was only generally correct, it is safe to assume that the lines of lust in the old South ran continually and in all directions. Society as always, however, had its special preferences, and these often ran counter to the libidinous nature of individuals. In the upper South, apparently, the ruling class early set an adamant face against miscegenation, while the underclasses stubbornly practiced it. Yet by the middle of the eighteenth century the loose grains of Chesapeake society had sifted downward, and the ruling class had become fairly effective in working its will through the lower orders. In the lower South, in contrast, the Latin pattern prevailed. There the ruling class seemed relatively unaroused by miscegenation, and laxity was evident. Inclination fought mostly against lack of opportunity. In the cities of Charleston and New Orleans, where proximity afforded opportunity, inclination easily won. In these cities significant mulatto communities emerged even in the colonial period. They were enclaves in which free mulatto families were sufficiently close to one another to be mutually supportive, and they generated mulatto elites that were urbane, favored, and fairly free.

Respectable Virginia society might sympathize with the gentleman who lamented in 1757 that the "country swarms with mulatto bastards," and it might join him in denouncing those "wretches amongst us" who took up with Negro women and condemning white women who prostituted themselves to Negro men.[75] But of course Virginia was not a prison, and the ruling elite, there and elsewhere, could never make a total end of miscegenation by whites and a steady trickle of new additions to the mulatto population from that source. Miscegenation continued to occur among all colors and classes. However, by far the most dramatic and the most significant portion was between upper-class white men of the slaveholding class and mulatto slave women engaged in domestic service. Rather clearly, these men of the upper order surrendered willingly and repeatedly to the attractions of sex across the race line, and they did so in defiance of the rising inclinations of their society. Their affluence and their standing in the ruling class suggests a high degree of socialization in their lives, yet their mulatto children—and their often protective and promotive attitude toward those children—marked them as mavericks.

White men of the upper class who mixed apparently fell into two very uneven groups. A few were promiscuous, but a highly significant number established long-running relationships with a single mulatto woman. They were men of some degree of power. Most often, the man was a planter and the woman was a mulatto, a slave, and a domestic servant in his house. Occasionally the maverick was a son in the master family, sometimes a near relative. Without doubt such men did exploit their mistresses; ultimately he had a choice, and she did not. Yet one is often impressed by the depth of devotion displayed by both men and women in such unions. The relationship usually lasted until one or the other died. Most often there were two or more children born to the couple and maintained as a family. She was faithful to him, sometimes putting aside a slave husband and older children to live with the master and bear his children. He provided especially for her and their offspring in a material way. Often he arranged for some special education for the children and frequently for their emancipation. The latter was typically attempted by will, and involved resettling the children in a free state. Finally, he usually avowed the connection either publicly or to a friend or relative. In effect, the pattern was very much an Anglo-American version of the New Orleans "placage," though seemingly more permanent.

White men of the upper class of every marital category shared in such interracial liaisons. Some were married, others were not. Bachelors and widowers seemed simply to be taking a mulatto wife instead of a white one, almost to be taking the safe and easy path of mating with the mulatto maid at home rather than the less well-known single white woman at some distance. Widowers, in particular, seemed prone to take as mates the mulatto maids who had served their late wives, a phenomenon that paralleled a tendency among widowers to marry sisters of deceased spouses. Other than being unsanctioned cross-racial unions that society frowned upon and punished, these matings were very much like white marriages at the time.

Thomas Jefferson's father-in-law, John Wayles, is a good example of a widower who took one of his slaves, a mulatto woman, as *de facto* wife, in his case after the death of his third wife. Jefferson married Martha Wayles in 1772.[76] When her father died in the following year, Martha brought to the marriage 135 slaves, five of whom were her half brothers and sisters. One of the slaves was Elizabeth Hemings, Martha's father's mistress and the mother of these children. According to family tradition, Betty was the daughter of an English sea captain named Hemings and a black slave woman, probably a native African. Betty was born about 1734 in Williamsburg into the estate of John Wayles. Captain Hemings had tried to buy his daughter, but Wayles refused because, as his great-grandson related, "just about that time amalgamation [interracial mixing] began, and the child was so great a curiosity that its owner desired to raise it himself that he might see its outcome."

Betty Hemings's owner, John Wayles, was a lawyer, planter, and businessman. He amassed great debts and even more property, part of it by selling Africans straight off the boat four to five hundred at a time. He buried three wives, including Martha's mother, and then he took Betty Hemings, possibly his wife's maid, as his mistress. Having already had six children by a slave, she bore six more by John Wayles. After his death she came to Monticello along with ten of her children. At Monticello she mothered a son by an English immigrant employed by Jefferson, a carpenter named John Nelson, and a last daughter by a slave in 1777. Over a span of twenty-five years, Betty Hemings had two white lovers and two Negro. By them she bore fourteen mulatto children, seven of whom were three-quarters white. In 1807 when Betty died at the age of seventy-three, eleven of these had themselves moved into a prolific maturity.

Meanwhile, the light side of the Wayles family proved to be much less durable than the dark. Martha Wayles bore Jefferson six children in ten years, dying of complications after the last birth. Only two daughters, Martha and Marie, reached maturity. While Jefferson continued to be an interested, sometimes even an ardent lover, he never remarried. In 1787 he brought his youngest daughter Marie to Paris, where he was serving as United States minister. With Marie, as her maidservant, came her mother's half sister, Sally Hemings. Sally was the last of the children born of John Wayles and Betty Hemings. In 1787 she was fourteen or fifteen, "mighty near white," strikingly handsome, and known as "dashing Sally" back at Monticello. Later rumors, inspired by Jefferson's political opponents, had it that Sally became pregnant by Jefferson in Paris and would not come home until Jefferson promised to free all of her children as they came of age. Back on the mountain above Charlottesville she supposedly was delivered of a child named Tom. The child Tom is very elusive in the plantation records of Monticello. Indeed, there were at least two other Toms, and this child may have not existed. At least no such child appears in Jefferson's later records.

The Jeffersonian experience is inherently interesting because of Thomas Jefferson's ready visibility in the eyes of Americans. We know him well for other reasons, and in his story we have an easily accessible window through which we can look at miscegenation in Virginia during the Revolutionary generation. What becomes evident in such a study is that there were patterns of interracial mixing, and that the patterns persisted over generations.

Jefferson retired to Monticello in 1794, and in 1795 twenty-two-year-old Sally gave birth to a daughter. Subsequently she gave birth to four more children, the last in 1808. On each occasion Jefferson was home at the proper time to have been the father. The children were all very light. Political opponents of Jefferson in Virginia raised the charge that he had sired Sally's offspring. Whether Jefferson was the father or not is problematical and is still heatedly debated. The evidence for Jeffersonian paternity is purely circumstantial—his being home at the right times and the fact that one of the sons very much resembled the master. The argument seems to rest heavily upon the assumption that libido always wins and that something is wrong if it does not. The counterargument dwells upon Jefferson's character. That argument seems to rest heavily upon a rather insistent reading of nineteenth-century Victorian mores into a moral set that must have been formed in the middle of the eighteenth century—an era in which flourished such famous prudes as Ben Franklin and the fictional Tom Jones. Jefferson, in the heat of battle, tends to become lost. He was, of course, neither Victorian nor post-Freudian. If Jefferson came to love "dashing Sally," one can understand that; if he did not, one can understand that also.

Taking the material gathered in this study concerning planter men who mixed and applying it to Jefferson's case, it seems unlikely that Jefferson was the father of Sally's children. Up to a point Jefferson fits neatly the pattern of the widower as miscegenator exemplified by his father-in-law. One ought not to be greatly surprised to find that he had a mulatto lover among his slaves, but if he did, it probably was not Sally. If it was, he departed the role in two important respects: he did not avow paternity, explicitly or implicitly, for an array of five children or take very good care of them or of their mother; and he did not seem to maintain the relationship with the mistress until death did them part. If he was the widower father of these mulattoes, he was unwontedly careless about the children. Two were allowed to run away, disappear, and were left like orphans to find their way in the world. The modest care that he did take of the remainder was no more than would be expected for the nieces and nephews of a dear deceased wife and the children of a slave highly favored by his wife and daughters.

In the often revealing pattern of postmortem emancipations, Sally seems not so much the centerpiece as her mother. Sally herself was not freed by Jefferson's will, but by his daughter Martha two years after his death, and no special provision was made for her resettlement. By the will, Sally's two surviving sons were freed; but so were her half brother John, Jefferson's personal valet for many years, and two cousins, both of whom owed their kinship to Betty Hemings's union with a slave before she became John Wayles's mistress.

Jefferson's will emancipated five men and no women. Three of the men were middle-aged and well established in trades. One had been the President's valet, another an iron worker and blacksmith, and the third a skilled cabinet maker. Sally's son Madison was apprenticed as a carpenter at age fourteen, as were all of her children. Indeed, Jefferson seems to have put all of the Hemings children into training for some trade or service at that age. It is possible that he originally had ideas about freeing them seven years later when they had completed

their education and were prepared to go into the world as journey-
men. For hundreds of years in western society, apprenticeship had
begun at fourteen and ended at twenty-one. In 1822, when Sally's
oldest son Beverly was twenty-two, he ran away. His master entered
on the slave roll beside his name the comment "run away 22." Afterward his sister Harriet ran away, and Jefferson entered "run 22" after
her name. She was not yet twenty-two. Jefferson died in 1826, yet
Sally's children remaining at Monticello, Madison and Eston, were
not freed until 1829. Eston, the youngest, was twenty-one in 1829.

The golden threads tying all of Jefferson's emancipations together,
both before and after his death, are that all of the emancipated are
Hemingses, and each of the emancipated had a trade by which he
could support himself. Yet Jefferson did not emancipate all of the
Hemingses, and probably not all of those who could support themselves. He could free only a few of his more than one hundred slaves
because of the heavy indebtedness of his estate. Within the Hemings
clan the Wayles-Hemings children, Sally and her five siblings, were
specially—though not exclusively—favored. They were the slaves at
Monticello closest to the persons of the master family. Moreover, two
of these children, John and Sally, served the Jeffersons in France during the master's several years' residence there. Legally these children
could claim their freedom by dint of their years in France. However,
both voluntarily returned to Monticello. John, whom Jefferson had
apprenticed out to learn French cooking, was to remain in service
until he passed his art on to another slave. He was freed by Jefferson
in 1796. Sally was liberated much later, but each of her children
claimed their freedom either by running away or by will at about the
age of twenty-one.

Jefferson may have favored these children because they were his.
It seems much more likely that he favored them because they were
Sally's. She was free by reason of having lived in France, where
slavery was illegal, and if she were free so too were her children.
Moreover, Sally and her siblings were bloodkin to the Jeffersons and
deserving of special but not lavish consideration, which was precisely
what they got. Further, if Jefferson and Sally had been lovers, the
chances are that she would have had ten children instead of five.
Given good health, Sally could have borne children up until about
1817 rather than ending that career in 1808; and Jefferson was obviously still a very vital man through 1817. He had retired to Monticello from the presidency in 1809 at the age of sixty-five when Sally
was thirty-six or thirty-seven. If they had been lovers, most likely
there would have been a continuing string of children—or we might

have hints as to why not. The fact that he was at home at the proper intervals for the five births comes to mean very little when viewed in light of the fact that Sally had no children after Jefferson retired permanently to his home. Indeed, many planters were steadily at home while maids mothered whole flocks of mulatto children without the planters' being named their fathers.

Perhaps the best evidence that Jefferson was not the father of Sally's children comes from her side rather than his. Mulatto women who mixed, like planter men who mixed, conformed to certain patterns. Sally fits the pattern of the mulatto maid who had a number of lovers in sequence, not necessarily carelessly or promiscuously but sometimes in a sequence that was so loose that she herself could not be absolutely certain who was the father of a particular child. If Sally followed the example of her mother, she would have been available to her master, but if her master did not want her, would have taken such lovers as she chose. The great uncertainty about the Jefferson-Sally union is itself strong evidence against its existence and suggests rather that Sally had a number of lovers. Short-run affairs involving mulatto maids usually did not leave tracks. When long-running liaisons were made, the parties were usually known. Mulatto women with steady white lovers could not hide the fact and seemed not much to try, either during or after the event. Sex, even then, usually occurred in the sleeping quarters, and lovers had to enter and leave through doors, or at least windows. People saw and knew and talked, unless the meetings were sporadic, which would not have been likely with the widower Jefferson. Sally's quarters were near the big house, access was visible, and no one ever identified a certain man. On the contrary, the names of several men have been offered, including two of Jefferson's nephews. The chances are that Sally had lovers sporadically and in the same loose sequence as her mother, that her children like those of her mother had more than one father, that Jefferson probably was not one of these, being a widower and hence by inclination and training a one-woman man, and that Sally herself would not have been able to name the father of each child, did not feel especially immoral about her affairs, and did not feel much need to justify her motherhood by reference to a father—any father.

In the broad sweep of history it does not much matter whether Thomas Jefferson mixed at Monticello or not. Someone did, and the slave population on the mountain overlooking Charlottesville grew steadily whiter. When the Count de Volney visited Monticello in 1795, he was shocked to find children there as white as himself who yet were called black and treated as such. Apparently Betty's lighter

children—and the others too, if only by being mulattoes themselves—
were making their own contributions to the whitening of America.
Sally's children were themselves very light. One daughter ran away,
passed for white, married white, and settled in Washington. A son ran
away to Baltimore, passed, and, according to tradition, married into
one of the eminent families there. Two sons, Madison and Eston, remained on the plantation to be emancipated and married into mulatto
circles not unlike their own. Madison, so named by Dolly Madison,
who happened to be present at his birth, was apprenticed to his Uncle
John, a carpenter. John was Betty's son by the English carpenter John
Nelson. In a fantastic display of willfulness Jefferson died on July 4,
1826, precisely fifty years after the signing of the Declaration of Independence. Madison and Eston were among the five slaves freed by
his will in 1829. The brothers settled in Albemarle County near Monticello and took Sally into their home. In the census of 1830 they
were counted as white, probably because of that peculiar Virginia
law that drew the line at the quarter mark, even though Sally was in
fact one-fourth black. In 1834 Madison married Mary McCoy, whose
grandmother had been a mulatto and the concubine of her master.
The master freed both Mary's grandmother and mother. In 1836
Madison moved his family to Ohio, a road often traveled by the freed
mulattoes of Virginia. In Ohio Madison worked as a carpenter, and
the family grew to include ten children. Ironically, one of these children came south again as a soldier in the Union army and died in
Andersonville prison.

Sally Hemings's daughter was living in Washington and passing for
white when Francis James Grimké came there to serve as pastor of the
Fifteenth Street Presbyterian Church. Francis Grimké was the mu-
latto son of Charleston lawyer, planter, and businessman Henry
Grimké. Henry was the descendant of a long line of English and
Huguenot people of wealth, culture, and eminence. His brother
Thomas was famous as a persistent Unionist during the bitter Nullifi-
cation controversy in South Carolina in the 1820s and 1830s. His
sisters, Sarah and Angelina, were prominent abolitionists in the North.
Indeed, Angelina had married abolitionist leader Theodore Dwight
Weld. Henry Grimké had three children by his wife. When she died,
the widower—in a style not totally unfamiliar—had three more by the
mulatto slave maid Nancy Weston. These were Archibald, born in
1849, Francis, in 1851, and John, in 1853.

Unfortunately, Henry Grimké died before John was born, and the
small family fell upon hard times. Henry had made a careful will in
which he instructed his son Montague to take possession of and treat

kindly his half brothers and their mother in this second family. Montague turned them out without freeing them, and Nancy had a hard struggle to keep the family alive. When the boys were about ten years of age and beginning to be useful to Nancy, Montague took them away to use as house servants. Francis became a recurrent runaway. He was finally sold to a Confederate army officer to serve as a valet. After the war, Archibald and Francis were picked up by abolitionist educators and sent north. Finally they matriculated at Lincoln University, near Philadelphia, where they were discovered at last by their aunts, Sarah and Angelina, who undertook to promote their education. Francis entered Princeton Theological Seminary and eventually became the minister of the prestigious Fifteenth Street Presbyterian Church in Washington—a pulpit he held for fifty years. He married Charlotte Forten, a missionary to the Sea Islands of South Carolina during the war and daughter of a well-to-do mulatto clan of Philadelphians. Archibald finished Harvard Law School in 1874 and went on to become a distinguished member of the bar. Both Archibald and Francis were very active in the NAACP, taking key roles in preventing the segregation of the streetcars in Washington during Woodrow Wilson's presidency.[77]

In the same year, 1829, that Madison Hemings was emancipated in Albemarle County, John Mercer Langston was born in neighboring Louisa County. His mother was Lucy Langston, a slave on Captain Ralph Quarles's very prosperous plantation. Lucy was, as Langston later remembered, "the favored slave of the place." She lived in a very special small house next to "the Great House." Lucy was very light, being the daughter of a full-blooded Indian woman and a Negro man, perhaps mulatto. John's father was the master of the plantation, Captain Quarles, a hero of the Revolution and the seige of Yorktown. The Captain had acquired Lucy in settlement of a debt. He was a bachelor, and when he took her as mistress, her three previous children were set aside. In 1806 Captain Quarles freed Lucy and their firstborn child Maria. Eventually he purchased and freed Maria's husband; then he bought them a plantation and slaves. Maria and her husband prospered. She gave birth to twenty-one children, each of whom achieved adulthood. Late in life Captain Quarles fathered three sons by Lucy, the last in the line being John Mercer Langston. According to Langston's reminiscences, the Captain was the kindest of masters, using no overseer, whipping only one young boy in twenty years. He opposed slavery on principle, and his attitudes about his slaves led to his "social ostracism." It was natural, then, as Langston told it, that he chose a mate from among his slaves.

In 1834 both Captain Quarles and Lucy died after brief illnesses. By the Captain's will they were buried side by side on a site he selected on the plantation. Having already provided for Maria, he left the bulk of his considerable estate to his three youngest children. Executors were named from among Captain Quarles's more powerful friends, and elaborate provisions were made for the care of the three sons Lucy had given him. They too followed the well-worn path of the newly emancipated to Ohio. The two oldest boys were cared for by the children of Lucy's slave marriage, who had been freed some years previously and resettled in Ohio. John was given over to the guidance of Colonel William D. Gooch, a good friend of the Captain's from Virginia who had freed his slaves and moved to Ohio. John was sent to preparatory school in Cincinnati, finished Oberlin College, practiced law, and recruited Negro troops during the Civil War. After the war he became a Freedmen's Bureau officer and a founding dean of the Howard University School of Law. After Reconstruction he was an officer in the consular and diplomatic services. Before he died in 1897, he crowned his career by becoming the only Negro ever to hold a Congressional seat from his native state of Virginia. His name was carried forward into the Harlem Renaissance by his grandnephew, Langston Hughes, famous as a poet and writer.[78]

Some white men established passionate and lasting relationships with Negro women even while they were married to white wives. Because divorce in Virginia could be obtained only by petitioning the legislature and stating the full case, the existence of such circumstances in that state is easily documented. In 1848, for instance, a woman from Henry County charged that her husband had married her for the "large Estate of land and negroes" she possessed. She asked for a divorce on the grounds that soon after the marriage her husband had repeatedly taken a "negro servant girl" to bed and openly favored that girl over her in her own house. So great was his ardor for the girl that he "had not scrupled under the cover of night to introduce her into the chamber occupied by your petitioner." A witness for the wife asserted that the husband "frequently slept with her, the said negro servant girl—sometimes on a pallet in his wife's room and other times in an adjoining chamber. He often embraced and kissed her in my presence and invited her to a seat at the table at dinner with himself and family and appeared to be passionately attached to her." [79]

Often enough the married maverick reared a white family in the front of the house even as he reared a mulatto family in the back. Usually the mistress, the darker of the two mothers in the same household, would be a mulatto maid. This "shadow family" sometimes strikingly mirrored the white family, wife for wife and child for child, all touching a common husband and father.

A Virginia legend, perhaps very true in the essentials and exaggerated in the details, illustrates well the tangled lives that these people led and, incidentally, the irony of a Negro slavery that had to strain to distinguish its slaves by color. The story concerns the mulatto son of a planter family in central Virginia. The mulatto son was held as a slave by his white relatives. As he became a young man, he turned into something of a wastrel. Recurrently he ran off to Richmond, where he would carouse among those vaguely white, vaguely privileged people of mixed blood in the "bottom," a low-life section near the river at the base of the hill graced by Virginia's capitol. After a spree of gambling, drinking, and general debauchery, he would eventually run afoul of the law. The police would notify his relatives-cum-masters that he was in custody. With great trouble, expense, and no little embarrassment they would journey to the capital and retrieve the prodigal son only to have him repeat the performance again.

Ultimately the white family tired of the games of their black-sheep son, if such he might be called. They determined to sell him off as a slave to New Orleans and the Southwest. There, no doubt, he would soon be swallowed up in that great sea of harshest slavery and bother them no more. To take the rogue to New Orleans they chose his half brother, so close in age and appearance as sometimes to be taken for his twin. The young men, handcuffed together, embarked on a steamer in Norfolk and were assigned a cabin. Off Cape Hatteras the ship encountered a violent storm. In the noise and confusion of the storm the slave brother struggled with the free and succeeded in transferring the key to the handcuffs from his brother's vest pocket to his own. The next morning, emerging from the cabin, he stoutly proclaimed to all aboard that he was the master, and the white brother was his rascally and deceitful slave whom he was taking to New Orleans to sell away as a nuisance. All of the protestations of the white brother failed to save him from the auction block. After all, the owner was clearly white and a man of the world, and he had the key to the shackles firmly in hand. True to form, the wastrel used the money from the sale of his brother to celebrate yet again, this time on a new frontier of riotous living—New Orleans. And, doubtless, somewhere up the river there was soon an idiot slave who babbled incessantly that he was really a white man dragooned into bondage.

There were white women as well as men among the mavericks. In the upper South in the early and middle colonial periods, mixing by white women, primarily women of the lower orders, appears to have been frequent. After the colonial period, lower-class white women continued to mix with black and mulatto men. Charges were often levied that much of such mixing was closely kin to prostitution, but there were households all over the South, and especially in the upper South, in which census takers recorded white women as married to Negro men.[80]

In later slavery, mixing by white women appears to have been less frequent, but it clearly reached up to include middle- and upper-class whites. In Amherst County, Virginia, in 1809 a white man petitioned for a divorce from his wife. He had heard rumors in the neighborhood of his wife's infidelity and decided to set the trap. "It is now with painful recollection," he stated in his petition, "that on his return home, at a late hour of the night, on entering his house he found the said Elizabeth, undressed, and in bed with a certain Aldridge Evans, a man of color." [81]

Just as white men often chose lightly colored women for their mates, white women who crossed the line often chose light men. While Jefferson was living out his last years in Albemarle, in neighboring Louisa County the young wife of an elderly white man, a woman named Dorothea, had an affair of some six or seven years duration with a "white slave" who was "so bright in color . . . a stranger would take him for a white man." Dorothea showed a persistent passion for her lover, a sentiment not uncommon in such cases. On one occasion the slave patrol rousted her "out of one of John Richardson's negro houses . . . after midnight." Shortly thereafter "they went to the house of the said Dorothea, about the first day of the month of November last, a little after daybreak and found a mulatto man named Edmund, the property of John Richardson, in bed with Dorothea." During this lengthy affair Dorothea had apparently delivered two children by Edmund, one of whom survived.[82]

The great difference between miscegenation by white men and that by white women was, of course, that maternity could not be hidden with the same ease as paternity. The burden of racial purity, then, came to fall most heavily upon white women, and the penalty for failure to bear the burden faithfully was so severe as to occasion some very peculiar behavior. Again, oral tradition provides a revealing example. There is a story of a planter's wife in Orange County, North Carolina, who gave birth to a mulatto child, seemingly to the great consternation of everyone, including herself. Upon investigation it was found that a neighbor had been making a "run" in his liquor still on the day of conception, the fumes had wafted through the lady's house, and she, alas, had breathed too deeply. In a semistupor she had submitted herself to a slave, thinking, understandably, that he was her husband. Thus the unfortunate result was an accident on her part and wholly forgivable. Necessity is, of course, often the mother of invention. In this case, the necessity of rendering the mother not guilty of the compounded sins of adultery and miscegenation must have been no less than compelling to spawn such an invention. The society no doubt felt itself fully as relieved by the discovery of this "immaculate conception" as did the lady and her husband. Probably, however, it did not save the slave who had played the part of the husband from punishment.

Finally, there was an endless trail of mulatto children sired by white men who were, simply, more or less promiscuous. Some of these men were nonslaveholders—farmers, laborers, artisans, and overseers—but a significant number were of the slaveholding class, though not necessarily planters. Kenneth M. Stampp, a leading historian of American slavery, concluded that "unmarried slaveholders and the young males who grew up in slaveholding families, some bearing the South's most distinguished names, played a major role" in miscegenation. "Indeed," he asserted, "given their easy access to female slaves, it seems probable that miscegenation was more common among them than among the members of any other group." [83] The progeny of casual liaisons of this sort were the least favored children of the Old South, especially the boys. Waifs in rags and tatters, unwanted and often unloved, they struggled unaided between the white world and the black. Like Horatio Alger they sometimes rose. The two first great leaders of the Negro people in America sprang from such matings. Frederick Douglass was born on the Eastern Shore of Maryland in 1817. Later in life he asserted on the abolitionist stage that he was the son of a slaveholder, though he was uncertain which of several local slaveholders was his father. His mother never told him—if she knew—and even she was a very elusive figure in his life, being closely held as a slave on a plantation miles away. In his early years he was reared by his mother's mother, but as a child of six he was taken away like an orphan to a more arduous slavery from which he eventually fled north to freedom. [84]

Booker T. Washington, Douglass's successor as the spokesman for American Negroes, was born in the foothills of the Blue Ridge Mountains of Virginia, probably in 1856. Booker had less information about his father than Douglass, and he seemed to have even less curiosity. He refused to speculate on the identity of his father. "Whoever he was," he said, "I never heard of his taking the least interest in me or providing in any way for my rearing." His father, he generously concluded, was "simply another unfortunate victim" of slavery. Louis R. Harlan, Washington's biographer, after very careful research found that he could not definitely identify the man. He suggested that the place of Booker's birth was filled with small farms and small slave-holdings and described a closeness between whites and Negroes that could have led to a steady stream of mixing. Indeed, he said, mulatto children were common in the area, and no one was much interested in the paternity of the reddish-haired, gray-eyed child called Booker. Among several likely fathers was Josiah Ferguson, a slaveholding farmer "who lived and scattered his seed within a halloo of the Borroughs farm" where Booker's mother, whose name was Jane, served as cook and where Booker was born. "Si" Ferguson had a white wife and children, and he reputedly also had two slave mistresses by whom he had nine children. "He was capable," Harlan concluded, "not only physically, but by attitude and geography, of being the father of Jane's child." [85]

The slave children of these fly-by-night and backstairs lovers often lived in a quandary about who their fathers were. Looking backward, we can identify these men well enough even when we do not know the specific results of their ardor. Some planters of the Old South were notoriously promiscuous, sexually extravagant men who took advantage of vulnerable beings, black or white, women or girls, men or boys, and, yea, even the beasts of the fields. By its very nature slavery created commanding, imperious persons. Slaveholding planters saw themselves as the lords of their little earths, and of all the bodies that dwelt thereon. Slavery required the absolute mastery of masters, and of their agents the overseers. However much white society might denounce as wretches those who used their power to extract sex from their slave subjects, it positively defended their right to do so, even under circumstances that were blatantly outrageous. One morning in 1859 the overseer on a Mississippi plantation forced Charlotte, a slave woman, to "submit to sexual intercourse with him." Later in the day Charlotte told her husband, also a slave on the plantation, of the event, and the husband killed the overseer. The court recognized the clear necessities of the system when it declared that "adultery with a slave wife is no defense to a charge of murder. A slave charged with the murder of his overseer can not introduce as evidence in his defense, the fact that deceased, a few hours, before the killing had forced the prisoners wife to sexual intercourse with him." [86]

Slavery did indeed give to some people great power over the persons of others. It should occasion no surprise that some of these people abused their power to work their satyric will upon other creatures, or that a few passed from simple abuse into horrifying extravagance. Consider a case that occurred in New Kent, Virginia, about 1830, in which slaves Patrick and Peggy, lovers, murdered their master. One witness said that

> the deceased to whom Peggy belonged, had had a disagreement with Peggy, and generally kept her confined, by keeping her chained to a block, and locked up in his meat house; that he believed the reason why the deceased had treated Peggy in this way was because Peggy would not consent to intercourse with him, and that he had heard the deceased say that if Peggy did not agree to his request in that way, he would beat her almost to death, that he would barely leave the life in her, and would send her to New Orleans. The witness said that Peggy said the reason she would not yield to his request was because the deceased was her father, and she could not do a thing of that sort with her father. The witness heard the deceased say to Peggy that if she did not consent, he would make him, the witness, and Patrick hold her, to enable him to effect his object.[87]

Lamentably the planter as Portnoy was all too common in the Old South, and sexual exploitation, sadism, and even incest compounded the sin of slavery.

Unlike the fictional Portnoy, who fathered no children, the planter usually had to come to terms with the fruit of his passion, and often with that of his male relatives as well. The deep confusion of kinship across the race line, the tangled emotions that grew out of such familial connections could be appalling and indeed tragic. The agony seemed to increase as slavery evolved in its last generation. Witness a letter written by a father to his son in the late 1850s. The father was one of the wealthiest planters in the lower South, eminently well educated, cultured, and nationally famous. He was, indeed, a man of scintillating brilliance. He is explaining to his trusted son the peculiarity in the bequest of his slaves contained in his will:

> In the Last Will I made I left to you, over & above my other children Sally Johnson the mother of Louisa & all the children of both. Sally says Henderson is my child. It is probable, but I do not believe it. Yet act on her's rather than my opinion. Louisa's first child *may* be mine. I think not. Her second I believe is mine. Take care of her other children who are both of *your* blood and not of mine & of Henderson. The services of the rest will I think compensate for indulgence to these. I cannot free these people & send them North. It would be cruelty to them. Nor would I like that any but my own blood should own as

Slaves my own blood or Louisa. I leave them to your charge, believing that you will best appreciate & most independently carry out my wishes in regard to them. Do not let Louisa or any of my children or probable children be the Slaves of Strangers. Slavery *in the family* will be their happiest earthly condition.

Slavery was in truth a peculiar institution, and it did sometimes breed very peculiar family arrangements.[88]

The rate of mixing by slaveholding white men appears to vary from time to time. As one approaches the 1850s, however, it seems to be rising to a crescendo. Apparently whole families of planter men here and there surrendered sexually and fell over the race line. Whole clans of mulattoes, more slave than free, were created, to the almost inexpressible horror of their white neighbors. The response of the white South to the totally fallen was to ostracize them and isolate their plantations. Not a few communities were thus lost to miscegenation in the South in the 1850s.

A final important consequence of the mixing in late slavery of upper-class white men in the South with mulatto women was that the offspring were often well cared for in terms of property, occupations, and education. It was not so much the quantity of the new mulatto issue that was important as it was their quality. When freedom came, they were well prepared to leap to the fore in leadership, and did so. Mulattoes were especially prominent in education, politics, and business and the professions. Fully three-quarters of the top-level Negro leaders in Reconstruction were visibly mulatto, while the national proportion of Negroes who were visibly mulatto was about 15 percent. Moreover, these leaders were often the sons of the slaveholding class and young men, typically in their twenties. It was almost as if mixing of this special sort in late slavery had produced a new breed, preset to move into the vanguard of their people when freedom came.

The ultimate result of early colonial mixing was that in the upper South in the years around 1700 a strong beginning was made in the creation of a mulatto population, both slave and free. It built upon the earlier beginning that was made by the mulattoes who lived through the seventeenth century. The mulatto population reached that "critical mass," that "take-off point," whence over the next century and a half it grew into a wellspring of mulattoes, a "mulatto pool" that not only supplied slaves to the Southwest and emigrants to the Northwest but also greatly increased the numbers of those who stayed at home.

As masters moved west, they took their slaves with them, mulatto as well as black. Virginians were especially numerous in the West, filtering not only into Kentucky and then Missouri but also into Alabama and Mississippi and across the river into Texas and Arkansas. They brought with them both their mulatto slaves and their strong feelings against miscegenation and its results. Many masters who did not go west themselves sold off to the West numbers of their slaves, again mulatto as well as black. During and after the 1820s, when the domestic slave trade became an institution, tens of thousands of slaves were sold out of the older portions of the upper South southward and westward. Much smaller numbers, apparently, were sold out of rice and sugar country, where slave populations seemed to be comparatively stable. There were vast numbers of mulatto slaves on the evolving frontier, and their share in the total burden of slavery in the West approached astonishing proportions. In 1850 in Kentucky and Missouri there was one mulatto slave for every six black slaves. In that year the slave frontier was the trans-Mississippi South, and it was also preeminently the area of mulatto slavery. Arkansas and Texas, like Missouri and Kentucky, had one mulatto slave for every six black slaves. Closest to these four states in mulatto slavery were Virginia and Maryland, where the black-to-mulatto ratio was ten to one. Furthest away, predictably, was South Carolina, where this ratio was thirty to one.[89]

The presence of a relatively large number of mulatto slaves on the frontier might, of course, be explained by a host of hypotheses. It may have been, for instance, that white men in the west mated with slave women at a great rate, and that the laws against emancipation prevented them from freeing their children. Yet extending the demographic model used for the colonial East out into the postcolonial West suggests that a large-scale mixing of whites and Negroes did not occur there. Racial ratios favored miscegenation; sex ratios did not. Neither, seemingly, did the attitudes of the whole society.

But missing most was the vital element of physical proximity. White people in the mass were simply not close to Negro people in the mass on the plantation frontier. The economics and the culture of slavery in the southwest in the last decades of "the peculiar institution" militated against massive contact between Negroes and whites. High-priced slaves meant that owners had to command the richest land in order to profit from their investment. The richest land came in belts—in great river bottoms, in deltas, in strips of land with special attributes that stretched across broad areas. The result was that slaves poured into these certain, almost finite "black belts" to the exclusion of whites not connected with slavery. There were whole counties in central Georgia, in mid-Alabama, in the flood plain of the lower Mississippi, and up the Red River Valley where Negroes formed up to and more than 90 percent of the population. Negroes in the mass were fixed upon the plantations of their masters, and much isolated from the outside world. Indeed, planters cultivated the isolation of their slaves as assiduously as their crops. They did not want whites not directly under their control on or even about their plantations. White overseers and visiting artisans might seem a necessity, but they were severely circumscribed and often done without as masters and slaves filled the roles. Virtually all other white outsiders were excluded. If there was to be mixing, planters would have to do it. And do it they sometimes did. Small slaveholders, like Si Ferguson, who worked closely with their slaves probably sometimes mixed also. But social and economic pressures militated against miscegenation, slaveholders of any kind were not all that plentiful, and the progeny of those who chose to mix were not numerous.

The evidence we have from contemporary observers suggests strongly that the mulatto pool exported vast numbers of mulatto slaves into the southwest in and after the 1820s, the pool itself having by 1850 flooded westward into Kentucky and Missouri. The boom areas by that time were Arkansas and Texas, and most especially up the Red River as far as cotton could go. The statistics as well as impressionistic evidence suggest that mulatto slaves constituted an extraordinarily high proportion of the slave migration into the new frontier. It was almost as if the economics of an increasingly prosperous slavery was pulling into its vortex a supply of human material previously not fully exploited. Where slavery was strongest and getting stronger, it was also becoming whiter.

The mulatto pool supplied thousands of slaves to the Southwest, and it supplied hundreds of free mulattoes, such as the Hemingses and the Langstons, to the Northwest. Rather clearly the lodestone of freedom pointed nonslave mulattoes toward the Northwest Territory. By 1850 newly settled Western states outside of the South often had more mulattoes than blacks in their populations. In 1850 in the five states of Ohio, Indiana, Illinois, Michigan, and Wisconsin, mulattoes actually outnumbered blacks by 24,000 to 22,000, while in the older-settled New England and Middle Atlantic states blacks outnumbered mulattoes by about three to one.[90]

After the pool was established in the Chesapeake world about 1700, it is impossible to determine precisely whence came the increase in the mulatto population in America during the years before emancipation. Apparently, very few mulattoes were first generation, that is, born of purely white and black parents. In the South there were many conspicuous cases of slaveholding white men mating with mulatto women. Yet perhaps these seem numerous only because the records left behind by the relatively affluent are plentiful. Possibly mulatto men and women mating together account for much of the increase, especially among those who were free, both North and South. Finally, one would logically expect a great amount of mixing between mulatto slaves and black slaves because their labor and their living brought them steadily into contact under the most intimate conditions. Taken all together, later statistics support the logical choice. A great increase in mulatto slavery in the 1850s and the probability that by 1920 at least 70 percent of the Negro population was in fact mixed in some degree square well with a theory that mulatto slaves often mated with black slaves.

Thus the large pattern may be that the mulatto pool in the Chesapeake world was created in the mid-colonial period, proliferated as both slave and free, spread westward with slavery into Kentucky and Missouri and with freedom into the Northwest territory, was added to in some degree by new admixtures with the whites, especially slaveholding white men, but that ultimately—perhaps in later slavery— it served most significantly to lighten the great mass of black Americans, and especially those in the lower South, the black belt, as thousands of mulatto slaves were dumped onto the plantation frontier. Taking the economics of late slavery into account, an economics that set the shackles eagerly and firmly upon mulattoes as well as blacks, and considering the new intensity of white racial exclusiveness apparent in the 1850s, there were good reasons indeed why the mulatto masses should have looked back to their darker neighbors for wives and husbands and a sense of security and self. What emerged, beginning even in slavery, was not just a fusion of colors and features into a brown America but also a new people with a new culture that bore within itself both Africa and Europe plus layer upon layer of experience, physical and spiritual, in the New World. What was happening even in slavery was the genesis of a new people.

# CHAPTER II

# Changeover, 1850–1915

THE period between 1850 and 1915 marked a grand changeover in race relations in America. It was a time in which America switched from what might be called a slave paradigm of race relations to one that was characterized by separation and greater freedom. The changeover in race relations was a complex movement in itself, but it was tied to a larger and even more complex transition in the whole of American society and, indeed, in the western world. At the heart of the change stood the industrial revolution, pioneered in the first half of the nineteenth century by the textile industry in England, Belgium, and New England. In the seventeenth and eighteenth centuries the American South had developed plantation slavery to contribute significant quantities of tobacco, rice, and sugar to world commerce. Early in the nineteenth century it turned the vast productive power of plantation slavery to supplying most of the cotton that fed the mills of Manchester, Ghent, and Lowell.

Because of the climatic requirements of the cotton plant, the lower South in particular became the great cotton-producing area of the United States. Slaves from the upper South poured southward in and after the 1820s, and the lower South soon outstripped the world in cultivating the fleecy staple. The planter elite in the lower South came to presume that their place at the very fountainhead of the industrial revolution gave them great power. James Henry Hammond of South Carolina spoke well the sentiments of his class when he declared on the floor of the United States Senate in 1858 that "Cotton *is* king" and asserted that "no power on earth" dared make war against it. In 1850 American Negroes were integral to the industrial revolution through the institution of slavery. In 1915 they were excluded from direct and organized participation in the industrial revolution by institutions of segregation, disfranchisement, and proscription. In both slavery and freedom Negro Americans have been steadily and firmly excluded from enjoying an appreciable share of the benefits of industrialization. In the economic sphere the story of race relations in America in the twentieth century is the story of Negroes struggling to reenter the industrial revolution and to win a larger share of its abundant material rewards.

Culturally the story of race relations during the changeover transcends economics and is vastly more complicated. In its essence, however, that history is clear. In 1850 Negro Americans were pressing to enter the white man's world, while in 1915 they were beginning to build a world of their own. As race relations moved, so too did mulattoes. The position of mulattoes and the attitudes held by and about mulattoes were an index to the changeover in race relations. Perhaps more accurately than any other single feature, the story of mulattoes served to refract broad racial patterns in this transition.

Essentially, what happened in the changeover was that the dominant white society moved from semiacceptance of free mulattoes, especially in the lower South, to outright rejection. As mulatto communities in the 1850s confronted an increasingly hostile white world implementing increasingly stringent rules against them in the form either of laws or of social pressures, they themselves moved from a position of basic sympathy with the white world to one of guarded antagonism. In the movement the mulatto elite gave up white alliances and picked up black alliances. The change accelerated in the Civil War, took its set during the critical year 1865, and continued through Reconstruction, post-Reconstruction, and into the twentieth century. By the end of the period, roughly in the two decades between 1905 and 1925, mulattoes led by the mulatto elite had allied themselves rather totally with the black world. Meanwhile the white world had arrived at an almost total commitment to the one-drop rule. In white eyes, all Negroes came to look alike.

In the changeover the lines of power in the South underwent a revolutionary alteration. Involved in the process were three important groups of people: the white elite, the white mass, and the Negro mass. At the top of the triad, exercising continuing power, was the white elite. In 1850 the white elite, comprising large planters and slaveholders, had built a strong connection with the Negro mass through slavery. On the other side they maintained a rather tenuous, uncertain connection with the white mass. In 1915 they had abandoned the Negro connection almost totally and were busily bonding themselves to the white mass, economically and racially, of course, but also in education, religion, politics, society, and culture. The base line of power in the triad shifted over three generations from that which joined the white elite to the Negro mass to that which joined the white elite to the white mass.

During the changeover the number of mulattoes had grown prodigiously both in absolute and in relative terms. In 1850 the census counted 406,000 mulattoes among 3,639,000 Negroes. In 1910 it counted 2,051,000 mulattoes in a total Negro population of 9,828,000. In 1850 mulattoes were 11.2 percent of the total Negro population. In 1910 they were 20.9 percent of the total. Moreover, these figures represented only mulattoes whose mixed ancestry was visible to the census takers. Officials of the census estimated that actually some three-quarters of the Negro population in America was mixed in some degree.[1]

The great fact about mulattoes that emerges from a comparison of the census of 1860 with that of 1850 is a massive increase in the number of mulattoes who were slaves. During the decade of the 1850s slavery was becoming whiter, visibly so and with amazing rapidity. White people were enslaving themselves, as it were, in the form of their children and their children's children. While black slavery increased in numbers only 19.8 percent in the decade, mulatto slavery rose by an astounding 66.9 percent. The raw number of slaves visibly mulatto grew impressively from 247,000, to 412,000, and their percentage in the total slave population increased from 7.7 percent to 10.4 percent. Of the 165,000 added, the lower South consumed 93,000. Yet the upper South was not far behind with an increase of 72,000, a gain achieved in spite of its large exports to the lower South and West. In the upper South the percentage of mulattoes who were slaves swelled from 62.9 percent to 72.3 percent during the decade. For mulattoes, then, even the upper South was not getting any more free, but was becoming distinctly more slave. A very minor part of the overall increase came from "maverick" mixing, but probably most of it grew out of the mixing of lighter slaves with those who were darker. Almost certainly that mixing was accelerated by a domestic slave trade that disrupted older family and clan connections and imposed new ones. The domestic slave trade was very active in the 1850s and had been in relatively vigorous motion for three decades previously, moving slaves within the South from north to south and east to west. The conquest of each plantation frontier probably resulted in a new wave of internal mixing between blacks and mulattoes within the slave society.

Mulatto freedom was the other side of the coin, and the statistics there offered no encouragement. In the South the count of free mulattoes hardly grew at all, rising from 102,000 to 107,000. Without doubt, some mulattoes had gone underground and others had fled. In the North the mulatto population rose by only 15,000 to 72,000. Nearly a third of the increase appeared in Michigan and Ohio. The outmigration of mulattoes from the "mulatto belt" to the northwest, so conspicuous in the 1830s, continued, but at an unimpressive rate. The total number of mulattoes, rising from 406,000 to 588,000, was keeping pace with the increase of population in the United States as a whole, but the rapid rise in mulatto slavery and the less than average increase of free mulattoes portended a dismal future for mulattoes in America.

Statistically, the experience of free black Americans was very similar to that of free mulattoes. In New England, where three-quarters of the Negro population was counted as black, and the middle Atlantic states they barely held their own in numbers. In the Northwest they went precisely where free mulattoes went, increasing mostly in Ohio and Michigan. In the South free blacks came to share the plight of free mulattoes, and while the number of black slaves was not rising as dramatically as that of mulatto slaves, they nevertheless shared fully in that westward movement via the slave trade.

As in 1850, the really striking dichotomy in the areas of mulatto freedom and slavery was between the old slave South and the new slave South. In 1860, the new slave South held as chattels 94.2 percent of its mulattoes, an increase over the already high figure of 92.0 percent in 1850. Thus in a vast area of the South, including Georgia, Kentucky, Tennessee, Mississippi, Alabama, Missouri, Arkansas, Florida, and Texas, approximately nineteen out of every twenty mulattoes were slaves. Furthermore, mulatto slavery on the trans-Mississippi frontier continued to accelerate rapidly. In Texas in the decade 1850–1860 the mulatto slave population more than tripled to 25,000. In Arkansas it more than doubled to 14,000. And in Missouri there was one slave who was visibly mulatto for every four who were black. Slavery was moving west, and clearly mulattoes were not left behind.[2]

Mulatto slavery was gaining strength throughout the South in the 1850s, but publicly white people seemed unconcerned about white blood mixing with black and being held in slavery. On the other hand, they went into a rage against white blood mixed with black and being free. During the decade whites attacked the free mulatto population in the South with unprecedented virulence. As the lower South joined the upper South in the assault on free mulattoes, the line between the two, the line that had been formed by a Latin-like tolerance of mulattoes in the lower South, tended to dissolve.

In Virginia a storm of intolerance against free mulattoes and the continuing stream of maverick miscegenation had long been gathering. Popular opinion had seethed against the profoundly disturbing disjunction between social and legal definitions of blackness that bred a class of persons visibly black but legally white. The storm broke with a vengeance in the 1850s. A Charlottesville editor, writing within sight of the mountain upon which Monticello stood, posed the question bitterly. "What is a negro?" he asked. White and black made a mulatto, he recited, mulatto and white made a quadroon, quadroon and white made a mustee, and, by law, mustee and white made a white. But yet, he asked, how could one make a white person out of a Negro? If one looked closely, one could always detect "black and curly hair, nails dark and ill-shaped, feet badly formed, and much of the negroes [sic] propensities."[3] In brief, any black blood, no matter how remote, made one black, and endless mixture with pure whites would never erase that fact.

In the 1850s agitation against free mulattoes was virulent not only in Virginia but throughout the slave South. Most striking was the turnabout in South Carolina and Louisiana, states where traditionally mulattoes had been most esteemed. Marina Wikramanayake described the change in South Carolina. The white community in the Palmetto State had refused to turn against free mulattoes of substance after the Vesey affair in the 1820s or even during the drive to tighten the

bonds of slavery in the 1830s. With the sectional crisis of 1850, however, the governor asked the legislature to expel all free Negroes who
did not possess real or slave property. Between 1856 and 1859 no
less than seventeen grand juries saw fit to call attention to the danger
from free persons of color, of whom three-quarters were mulattoes.
"We should have but two classes," declared one grand jury, "the
Master and the slave, and no intermediate class can be other than im-
mensely mischievous to our peculiar institution." [4] O. Vernon Burton
has documented the rising rage for a two-part order in South Carolina
in his study of Edgefield District. There, in the early 1850s, some
whites created a vigilance committee that tightened surveillance of the
free Negro community—almost entirely mulatto. Largely by emigra-
tion induced by threats and whippings, the free Negro population in
the county fell from 251 in 1850 to 131 in 1860. [5]

Historian Henry E. Sterkx discovered a Louisiana in which free
mulattoes and whites lived easily together into the 1850s; then radical
agitation began against the "free people of color." He saw the whites
as activated by a new fear of abolitionism and insurrection. The great
fear of slaveholders "grew into unrequited hatred as the decade preceding the Civil War" progressed. [6] In 1856 the very influential New
Orleans *Picayune* urged the removal of all free Negroes from the
state as "a plague and a pest in our community, besides containing the
elements of mischief to the slave population." [7] Many whites pressed
passage of a bill before the legislature that would simply expel free
people of color from the state by a certain date and enslave those who
refused to go. But popular white agitation focused immediately and
actively upon concubinage and interracial connections of various
kinds. Vigilante groups arose, not unlike those in Edgefield District,
South Carolina, in the early 1850s and the Ku Klux Klans of the next
decade, to punish offenders. Activism reached a crescendo in At-
takapas, the region west of New Orleans where some of the richest
of the free mulatto planters lived. In the spring of 1859 Major Aurel-
len St. Julien led a campaign of organized intimidation and violence
in and around Lafayette. The purpose was to drive the free Negroes
out of the state and to punish immoral conduct, especially such as
that which occurred between white men and mulatto women. One
band of vigilantes, for example, called upon and whipped one Auguste
Gudbeer and his free mulatto mistress and warned them to leave the
state. Some Louisianians always decried the persecution and pled the
case for native mulattoes. Eventually the hysteria abated, and order
prevailed. But meanwhile the tide had shifted. Many free mulattoes
read the signals and fled the state. White people who were most

flagrant in the practice of interracial sex felt the lash of public opinion, if not of the active mob, upon their backs. Intimate association with Negroes had come more and more to mean certain contamination.

The passion to exclude free Negroes rose to a high pitch in other states as well. The exclusionists in Louisiana, for instance, argued for emulating Arkansas and Mississippi in passing laws that would absolutely prohibit any free persons of color from living in the state. Ultimately, Louisiana did not pass such a law, and other states did not perfectly enforce theirs, but the terrific pressure was indicative of the great anxiety extant in the white community.[8]

Mulatto freedom obviously outraged many Southern whites. Those who were most conspicuous in their opposition were men. Mulatto slavery, on the other hand, seemed to excite the public opposition of no one. Yet private papers make it abundantly clear that some white women of the planter class were outraged by certain aspects of that subject. The number of mulatto slaves as against black was undeniably gaining throughout the South in 1860. It was gaining in the upper South as well as in the lower; it was gaining even in the early-settled areas where the colonial mulatto population was strongest; and it was gaining massively in the newest slave states. It was everywhere evident that slavery was getting whiter and whiter, and that planter men themselves bore a significant part of the responsibility for that trend. The protest from women was not a loud one, but it was widespread and of fevered intensity. It came mostly from women on the plantations, from women whose families held mulatto slaves and who saw in those light-skinned women both sisters and rivals.

Consider, for instance, Ella Thomas, a young woman of the planter class who lived in central Georgia. One Sunday morning in January 1858 Ella fell into a discussion of mulatto slaves in her diary. Susany, a household slave and almost white, had just brought in her baby for the mistress to see. "A remarkably pretty child she is and as white as any white child," Ella observed. Susany obviously caused considerable consternation in the mind of the young mistress. Susany was "having children constantly without a husband," Ella complained, and the fathers were clearly not black men. Ella was reminded of Amanda, another mulatto servant who was reared by a prominent white family and grew up "knowing but little more of negroes than I do." Another was educated in *"mistaken kindness"* and then sold for debts, perhaps to masters "but one degree removed from the brute creation." This brought to her thoughts the whole subject of the prostitution of mulatto slave women. "I know that this is a view of the subject that it is thought best for women to ignore but where we see so many cases of mulattoes commanding higher prices, advertised as 'fancy girls,' o is it not enough to make us shudder for the standard of morality in our Southern homes."

Indeed it was. In her diary Ella Thomas told about a slaveholder's son who carried a mulatto slave off to the North with him and passed her off as his wife. The local community condemned his action, but when he went even further and attempted to marry the woman, his father tried to have him declared a lunatic. Ella was horrified that the father could more easily contemplate having a grandson in slavery than having the child free and bearing his name. But yet she knew that masters did sell their children into slavery. Indeed, her own family had bought such a child, she recalled:

> I once heard Susan (Ma's nurse) speaking of her respected father in a most contemptuous manner. Laughingly I said to her, why Susan, was not he your father? What if he was, she said, I don't care anything for him and he don't for me. If he had he would have bought me when I was sold. Instead of that he was the auctioneer when I was sold for 75 dollars. She was sold for debt, separated from her mother and has lived in the yard ever since she was three years old.

Ella felt that these "white children of slavery" were not to be blamed, and she revealed a profound ambivalence about the peculiar institution. "Southern women are I believe all at heart abolitionists but then I expect I have made a very broad ascetion [sic] but I *will stand* to the opinion that the institution of Slavery degrades the white man more than the Negro and oh exerts a most deleterious effect upon our children. But this is the dark side of the picture, written with a Mrs. Stowe's feeling, but when I look upon so many young creatures growing up belonging to Pa's estate as well as others, I wonder upon whom shall the accountability of the future depend." [9]

The trade in "fancy girls" to which Ella Thomas referred did indeed exist, and while it was not large, it was most conspicous. Abolitionists and antislavery people in the North did not miss the point. They focused with great effect upon the trade and upon the attendant idea that every plantation was a slave owner's brothel. In the jargon of the slave trade, a "fancy girl" was a woman trained for domestic service, but people generally understood that a "fancy girl" might also be offered as a prospective concubine. The historian of the slave trade in the South, Frederic Bancroft, asserted that New Orleans was the center for the sale of "fancy girls," and that next to New Orleans stood Lexington, Kentucky. Add to this his statement that Virginia slaves were favored in New Orleans, and it appears that it was out of the mulatto pool in the upper South that many of these highly desirable slaves came, along with a multitude of others.[10]

Fredricka Bremer, a widely read Swedish writer and traveler, crossed the path of the trade in "white" women as slaves several times during her journeys through America in 1850 and 1851. In a Washington slave pen she saw a "slave lady," a mulatto woman who had been reared to sew, read, make conversation, and so on. She had become too "uppity," however, and was being sold away to bring her down. In Richmond, in another slave pen, Bremer encountered a bevy of "fancy girls." She observed that "they were handsome fair mulattoes, some of them almost white girls." Among these girls she saw a small white boy, with "cheeks as red as roses." However, she soon learned that "he was indeed a Negro, had been sold away from his mother, and was being taken under the fair wings of these girls." In Lexington, Kentucky, another visitor saw more "fancy girls." These were kept in a "negro jail" where "the appointments are not only comfortable, but in many respects luxurious." In several rooms he found "very handsome mulatto women" whom the proprietor made "get up and turn around to show to advantage their finely developed and graceful forms." One of them could be bought for $1,600.[11]

In the lower South Fredricka Bremer saw these women nearing their destinations. In Augusta, Georgia, she visited a "slave mart" filled with young slaves twelve to twenty years of age, mostly from Virginia. "Many of these children were fair mulattoes, and some of them very pretty. One young girl of twelve was so white, that I should have supposed her to belong to the white race; her features, too, were also those of the whites. The slavekeeper told us that the day before, another girl, still fairer and handsomer, had been sold for fifteen hundred dollars." At that time a "prime hand" might have sold for about $1,000. "These white children of slavery," as Bremer called them in a phrase that grew famous, "become, for the most part, victims of crime, and sink into the deepest degradation. . . ." Ella Thomas, who lived on a plantation nearby, would certainly have agreed. Arriving in New Orleans, the Swedish traveler saw the ultimate in the white slave trade, the slave mart in the French Exchange in the St. Louis Hotel. That institution specialized in "superior-looking girls, varying from mulatto to octoroon" and sold one after another off of a block set among classical arches, pillars, and variegated marble floors under an elegant rotunda.[12]

Like Mrs. Bremer, women of the slaveholding class deplored the enslavement of beautiful women as a sin and a crime, but they could also hate the competition that such women represented—and hate, too, the men they lost in the competition. It was not, after all, the lower classes—the laborers, the plain farmers and tradesmen—who paid fancy prices for "fancy girls." "I hate slavery," wrote Mary Boykin Chesnut in her diary in August 1861. She was in Richmond at the time, in the very mouth of war. But she wrote during the lull after the first battle of Manassas, when it seemed as if slavery would surely win. Her husband was a highly political general, an ex-United States Senator, and a gentleman of the "old school." They were plantation people from central South Carolina, much given to cotton and slaves. After beginning with that stark and bitter line, she elaborated, suggesting a picture of Confederate women sitting around a Third Street parlor in the Southern capital, knitting socks for soldiers even as they tried in conversation to weave together the scattering threads of their lives. Inevitably they came to that most troublesome thread, their men—and the women loved by their men. "Are our men worse than the others?" was the question. "Does Mrs. Stowe know? You know what I mean?" For a time, then, the answer was repeated "No, our men are no worse," and explained by the common knowledge that everywhere "irresponsible men do pretty much as they please." A well-traveled lady whose husband had been a diplomat thought London possessed as many fallen women as the plantations of the South.

Mrs. Chesnut felt otherwise and offered the example of "a magnate who runs a hideous black harem with its consequences under the same roof with his lovely wife, and his beautiful and accomplished daughters." Meanwhile he posed as an absolutely noble gentleman. "You see," she said, "Mrs. Stowe did not hit the sorest spot. She makes Legree a bachelor." Mrs. Chesnut had touched the nerve, and conversation flew around the circle like sparks. One of the women said she knew "half a Legree." "He was high and mighty, but the kindest creature to his slaves; and the unfortunate results of his bad ways were not sold. They had not to jump over ice blocks. They were kept in full view, and were provided for, handsomely, in his will. His wife and daughters, in their purity and innocence, are supposed never to dream of what is as plain before their eyes as the sunlight. And they play their parts of unsuspecting angels to the letter. They profess to condone their father as the model of all earthly goodness." But again, as if the thought were too awful to discuss anymore, the threat was whistled away with the idea that the new generation, the current generation of plantation women, would not tolerate such treatment.[13]

But, of course, plantation women were tolerating exactly such treatment, and with ill grace. Privately Mrs. Chesnut stated the case precisely. "Like the patriarchs of old, our men live all in one house with their wives and their concubines; and the mulattoes one sees in every family partly resemble the white children," she wrote. "Any lady is ready to tell you who is the father of all the mulatto children in everybody's household but her own. Those, she seems to think, drop from the clouds." [14] Such bitterness, such outrage could not long go unassuaged, and when the drive for racial purity came women of Mrs. Chesnut's mind were firmly for it.

In the decades before the Civil War there was a curious refusal by thoughtful Southerners to put mulattoes into some kind of grand ideological order. There was elaborate philosophizing concerning blackness, and some thinking about whiteness, but only an awkward stumbling over mulattoness followed by a hasty flight from the subject. In particular were Southerners reluctant to justify the enslavement of mulattoes. Slaves were Negroes, simply by definition. In 1835, as we have seen, Chancellor Harper in South Carolina had carefully refused to define what made a free person white, then abruptly concluded that "it is hardly necessary to say that a slave cannot be a white man." Harper was not willing to define freedom by color, but he was willing, out of hand and without explanation, to declare slavery and whiteness incompatible. That a slave could not be white was a precept, it seems, that went almost without saying, much less explication. Governor James Henry Hammond of South Carolina, in 1843 defending the South against charges from the North and abroad that plantations were brothels for white masters, insisted that miscegenation was rare and that mulattoes on the plantations were actually very few. Hammond was himself a wealthy planter and slaveholder, and later as a United States Senator coined the famous phrase "Cotton *is* king." He thought it best not to talk about the topic publicly. "The number of the mixed breed in proportion to that of the black, is infinitely small," he declared in an effort to dismiss mulattoes, "and out of the towns, next to nothing." Those mulattoes in the towns he assigned to Northern and foreign fathers.[15]

Harper and Hammond were both early contributors to what soon came to be called the proslavery argument, a fantastic and rather weird flowering of intellectual development in the antebellum South. Whereas New England was giving rise to Hawthorne, Longfellow, Emerson, and Thoreau, the South was bending more and more of its intelligence toward the creation of an elaborate argument for slavery. Drawing upon literature, history, theology, law, medicine, biology, geology, and the incipient disciplines of economics, political science, and sociology, the South in and after the 1830s was generating and preaching a whole system of thought dedicated to the principle that Afro-American slavery was right because God had made the Negro to be a natural slave. The key object was to unlink the Negro from the great chain of humanity, to make of him a different creature somehow subhuman and specially fitted to slavery. The literature was, eventually, semicodified. In the late 1850s two massive volumes were published, each with an impressive array of authorities and each advertising itself as the "pro-slavery argument." And yet in the whole of this giant literature, one looks in vain for a fitting discussion of mulattoes as slaves. If whites be human and fitted only for freedom and blacks be somehow subhuman and made for slavery, what then is a mulatto? How does one justify the enslavement of white blood? The question is not even raised in the literature, and of course it is not answered.

If Southern advocates of Negro slavery could have surrendered their racism, they could have had slavery and miscegenation too. If they could have simply accepted the idea of white slavery, the problem would be met and solved. Bizarre as the idea now appears, it did exist—and conspicuously so—in the thinking of one well-published and often discussed advocate of slavery. That person was George Fitzhugh, a Virginia lawyer and polemicist, who argued in 1854 that because slavery was so great and natural an institution, its benefits ought logically to be extended to dependent whites as well as Negroes. Slavery, after all, he insisted, was the universal lot of humanity. Wives were slaves to husbands, slaves were slaves to masters, and masters themselves were slaves to others. It was much better to make it explicit, institutional, and humane—as the South was doing, rather than implicit, chaotic, and inhumane—as it was in the North. Northern wage slavery was simply one of the cruelest forms of slavery, Fitzhugh suggested. It used those workers who survived childhood and cast them aside when their labor was no longer profitable. The issue, he considered, was not whether a society would have slavery or not, it was simply what kind of slavery would it have. "Slavery, black or white," he declared, "was right and necessary." Fitzhugh himself slid easily around the possibility of white slavery in the South by being thankful that "we need never have white slaves in the South because we have black ones." [16]

Fitzhugh's argument for slavery, then, unlike that of his colleagues, did not rely on race and afforded easy relief from the problem of holding in slavery so much of the white blood of the South. Nevertheless, his Southern colleagues did not rise to the idea of white slavery, and Northerners were outraged. In effect by 1850 proslavery thinkers had no choice. They had already opted for slavery over freedom, and they had committed themselves to a racial defense of the slave system. A slave was a slave because he was black. Slaves, by definition, could not be white. The fact that slavery was getting whiter, that in reality many slaves were more white than black, was a fact with which the proslavery argument could not cope. Either it could ignore the problem, which it did explicitly, or it could brusquely dismiss it by applying the one-drop rule to persons in slavery, which it did implicitly.

The proslavery argument did not come to a formal recognition of the presence of mulattoes as slaves. It did, however, recognize the existence of mulattoes per se, and it explained them away rather easily using current scientific concepts. Contemporary scholarship differed on the matter of whether black people were or were not a separate species, but agreement seems to have run very high that each race of man was specially suited to its geographic region by a distinct physical and mental constitution. Africa was for blacks and Europe was for whites. Because it was in the temperate zone, most of the North American continent was also suited for whites. To mix the people of one region with another was to create an unnatural type, suited to no region. There simply could be no compromise between Africa and Europe in human form. The inevitable result of miscegenation would be that the offspring would die out within a few generations.[17] Mulattoes, then, were highly ephemeral persons whose white ancestry would be rendered irrelevant by their early disappearance, and whose presence was unimportant because they could not procreate as mulattoes beyond two or three generations. By creating a theory that erased mulattoes within three generations, the idea in effect disposed of them as a serious present problem.

Southern society in the decade of the 1850s suffered rising fevers of anxiety. It was these fevers that crystallized the one-drop rule in the

South. The members of the Southern elite were anxious not only about abolitionism and antislavery threatening from the North and abroad and troubles with slavery in the territories; they were profoundly anxious about dissent at home. They were fearful of a concert against them among the nonslaveholding classes. They were fearful of rebellion among their own women. They were fearful, too, of their slaves and insurrection, and of the possibility of conspiracy between slave Negroes and free Negroes. They were fearful, finally, of themselves, about their own determination, about their ability to hold their membership up to the challenges at home and abroad and to meet the fire when it came. Southern society in the 1850s was embattled. It was a tense, anxious, strung-out society. It needed a structure to meet its fears and overcome them. It needed an order, and the order would have to be as tight as the tensions with which it had to cope. In that decade the Southern elite was constructing such an order. The order stressed a role and a place for every person and every person in his place. The role of each fit neatly and naturally into the whole of what might be called "the organic society."

In the organic society everything had its place. There were roles for Negroes, roles for women, and roles for upper-class whites and those of the lower orders. This was a closed society in which individuals were assigned roles and the roles were fixed in a sort of societal firmament, each specially related to the other. The organic society of the Old South found an important part of its strength in the dichotomous nature of western civilization. Opposites were held in tight tension in the organic society—slavery was set against freedom, white against black, and men were strenuously balanced by women. Increasingly, the South grew furiously intolerant of anything that was not distinctly slave or free, black or white, male or female. There had been such fury before in the South, in the wake, for instance, of the Vesey plot and the Turner insurrection. But never had it been so widespread or so persistent as it became in the 1850s. The organic society was the ship; all else was the sea. No Jonahs allowed, no preaching of heresies to rock the boat. Those who did not fit must hide, or be thrown summarily into the stormy waters. In the pursuit of an ordered society, the upper South and the lower South came together. The lower South gave up its peculiar sympathy with mulattoes and joined an upper South already in place. Miscegenation was wrong and mulattoes must be made black, both within slavery and without. There was no middle ground in the organic society, no place for one who was neither white nor black.

The South came to the one-drop rule essentially because it came to accept slavery as its god. Slavery was the central and powerful institution in the South in the 1850s, and it bent everything to its will. Southern white racism was itself a slave to slavery, and racism took the shape that slavery imposed. In the world the slaveholders made, Southern whites were not allowed to believe anything about black people other than what served the purposes of slavery. So that, for instance, Southern racism came to see the Negro as a child, a "Sambo," to be cared for perpetually by paternalistic white masters. Also, slavery in the 1850s needed slaves for its westward movement, and it was almost as if it possessed an intelligence that deliberately decided that it would take slaves wherever it could get them—even if those slaves were nearly white. Slavery had the power, as Chancellor Harper's *obiter dictum* suggested in 1835, to make all slaves black regardless of their seeming whiteness. If slavery was strong enough to make Negroes seem children in the eyes of whites, it is not surprising that it was also strong enough to make lightly colored slaves seem black. Indeed it had even the strength to move beyond slavery and make all free Negroes, of whatever mixture, black also. Slavery in the South in the 1850s was a Leviathan, and its strength is indicated by the fact that it not only had the power to shape white thinking about Negro people to suit its ends but also shaped white thinking about white people for the same purpose.

During the 1850s and 1860s, the free mulatto elite in the South turned away from an alliance with the white elite into ambivalence and arrived, finally, at rejection. Before 1850 mulatto leaders, especially in South Carolina and Louisiana, had occupied a preferred position among the Negro population, essentially because whites chose to see them as allies helping to check the great mass of black slaves. The persecutions of the 1850s, however, could not fail to create great anxieties among leading mulattoes, anxieties that would ultimately bear bitter fruit for whites in the lower South in the form of the defection of their most powerful Negro allies.

One of the effects of the pressures against free persons of color was to drive many free mulattoes out of the South—particularly the more affluent who could afford to emigrate. Charles Chesnutt, the first Negro writer to achieve a national reputation without its being generally known that he was Negro, was born in Cleveland, Ohio, in

1858 instead of in Cumberland County (Fayetteville), North Carolina, precisely because his parents had responded to the pressure by
moving to a more liberal atmosphere in 1856. Chesnutt was seven-
eighths white. Both his parents were mulattoes whose white blood
went back several generations and whose kin were substantial yeoman
farmers in the Old North State. In a personal conversation in 1880 a
leading citizen of Fayetteville complained to Chesnutt about the departure of the better class of free Negroes from the area to the North
in the 1850s. Chesnutt replied that living in North Carolina had become impossible, probably thinking of the flight of his own family to
Cleveland. "You had taken away their suffrage," he said, referring to
the disfranchisement of free Negroes in 1835; "the laws were becoming more and more severe toward free colored people; and they felt
that their only safety lay in emigrating to a freer clime." [18]

In Louisiana several hundred mulatto farmers and artisans, some of
whom were wealthy and took their capital with them, moved to Haiti
at the invitation of the Emperor and in flight from the lash of public
opinion.[19] Where there had been eight mulattoes among the large
slaveholders in the state in 1830, there were only six in 1860 in spite of
a general increase in the population.[20] Mulattoes who were not slaves
were definitely losing visibility in the South during the decade. Quite
literally they were fleeing the country, or they were going underground where the mobs could not find them and not even the census
taker pursued.

As the war began, the mulatto elite was ambivalent. At first, almost
by reflex it seems, its members tried once again to join hands with
white leadership in the face of danger. Whites accepted that response,
this time with some evidence of misgivings. Shortly, however, the
mulatto elite turned against the white world. As it did so, it was
closely in step with the great mass of Southern Negroes. Invariably
in the South, when Union armies drew near, vast numbers of Negroes,
slave and free, black and mulatto, swarmed to their protection.

The changeover was rather dramatic in Louisiana, that richest of
the large mulatto communities. The approach of war brought from the
free mulattoes at least the appearance of a great rush to support
the state and the Confederacy. The free persons of color who were
veterans of the battle of New Orleans, now somewhat older but no
less brave, offered their services yet again in the defense of their state.
In May 1861 the governor accepted an entire regiment of younger
free *gens de couleur* into the state's military organization under Negro
officers. Shortly, the governor thought better of the idea and dis-
armed the regiment. A year later it was enlisted again—this time,

ironically, in the Union army it was originally designed to oppose. Indeed, under General Benjamin F. Butler three regiments of free men of color were soon enrolled and organized as the Louisiana Native Guards. The line officers (captains and below) in two of the regiments were Negroes, most of whom were mulattoes. The white officers were from older New England regiments. However, Yankee racism proved hardly less vicious than rebel racism. Shortly the conquerors squeezed the mulatto officers out of the service on charges of incompetence and reassigned the men to darker regiments where their lightness of skin lost its institutional focus. This was no isolated incident; Negro troops generally were horribly abused by the Union army in Louisiana. One can easily understand that when freedom came, the mulatto elite in Louisiana was more inclined to place their trust in black people than white, either Southern or Northern.[21]

Even before the war was over, the mulatto elite of Louisiana assumed its posture as defender of the freedmen. Through its two newspapers in New Orleans, the *Union* and the *Tribune*, mulatto leaders labored very effectively to maintain the self-image of the *gens de couleur* as cultured people, fight discrimination at the hands of the occupying forces, resist white slaveholders of the old order, and build an alliance with the freedmen to insist upon full rights of citizenship for all people of color.[22] One of these leaders was Louis Charles Roudanez, a well-to-do physician who had attended Dartmouth College and founded the *Tribune*, the first black newspaper in America to be published daily. In February 1865 his paper declared the independence of the Negro elite by asserting that "it is not the time to follow in the path of white leaders; it is the time to be leaders ourselves."[23] After the war, the mulatto elite of Louisiana steadfastly supported the causes of the black mass, at one point even opposing a measure called the "quadroon" bill pressed by the Democratic legislature that would have enfranchised only those of lighter color, specifically themselves, and would have defused pressure to enfranchise all Negro men.[24]

Just as 1865, the year of emancipation, was the crucial date in the life of every slave family in the United States, it was also the crucial year in the history of Negroes collectively and the history of race relations. Freedom for Negroes came simultaneously with the defeat of the South and the beginning of what, in its political phase, was called Reconstruction. In the study of American history we have come to accept the confluence of these two great events as natural: the North needed emancipation for victory. Yet for the future harmony of race relations the conjunction was hardly less than disastrous.

It happened that freedom came to the great mass of Negro people at the end of the bloodiest struggle that has ever occurred upon this continent. And it was wrested from a white people distressed by their great losses in the war, distraught, and seething with bitterness. Because they had proved their disloyalty to the South by helping the North to win the war, the association of Negroes with the Yankee victor was easily made in the Southern mind. Thus Negroes were left to make their way among Southern whites not as friends, nor even as dependents, but rather as enemies surrogate for the hated North. They would suffer a portion of the wrath that could not be heaped upon the head of the too distant and too powerful North. In addition, they would suffer a new racism. It is a tremendous irony that the emancipation of Negroes entailed the emancipation of racism. It had been black versus white within the bounds of slavery before; now there were no bounds. Unrestrained by the necessities of slavery, white people could believe anything they chose about black people . . . and racism ran wild.

Finally, the postwar conflict between black and white was made even more desperate by the fact that it took place in a land militarily conquered, materially impoverished, and in the process of being imperialized by a victorious North. With the least advantages, Southern Negroes were about to do combat with Southern white folk to determine which side would be chosen to serve the imperial North, and hence to wield the modicum of power over its destiny that would be allowed the South as a whole. Divide and conquer was a good strategy, divide the conquered was better.

It was in this time of great flux and a temporary eclipse of white power in the South that the mulatto elite engaged itself firmly with the Negro mass. The fusion between mulattoes and blacks that had begun in late slavery and accelerated during the war came to fruition during Reconstruction. The engagement was apparent in politics, and the political story has often been told—until recently with some distortion resulting from the assumption that blacks and mulattoes, slave and free, had no separate histories or interests, and that a rather perfect union of the two sprang full-blown from the head of slavery. The really significant story in Reconstruction, however, lies in the cultural realm. There began a melding of mulatto and black worlds, not only in politics but in the whole broad array of human endeavor.[25] By the end of Reconstruction the engagement had been made, and blacks and mulattoes together were well on the way toward the generation of a new people in America.

The alliance between black and mulatto Americans in Reconstruction occurred primarily in the lower South rather than in the upper South. Indeed, Reconstruction in the upper South was a rather pale thing both politically and culturally. The number of Negroes did not approach a majority in any state of the upper South, and any political movement by Negroes had to be made in concert with white dissidents whose interests inevitably differed significantly from those of the freedmen. Reconstruction in these states tended to be an abortive affair not running very long or very deeply. Missouri, Kentucky, West Virginia, and Maryland had been slave states and had significant numbers of Negroes within their bounds, but they had never left the Union. Reconstruction in Virginia proved short-lived and spotty, being essentially over by 1870 just as it was becoming deep and serious in the lower South.[26] Tennessee was readmitted to the Union in 1866 and never underwent so-called "Radical" Reconstruction. In the states of the upper South Negro leaders seem to have attempted political Reconstruction most seriously, not in the 1860s and 1870s, but in the 1880s and 1890s. In the upper South "black Reconstruction" came late, and it was weak, almost an afterglow of black Reconstruction in the lower South, where Negro majorities made Negro voting, for a time, very effective. In each state they were usually easily defeated by the conservative whites.[27] The one upper South state in which there was a second, very vigorous and briefly successful Reconstruction was North Carolina. There in the 1890s the Negro community joined Populists and white Republicans to win a significant share of power. But, as in the first Reconstruction, the reaction was more vigorous than the initial action, and there was soon a violent "Redemption."

The mulatto leadership that should have been active in the upper South during Reconstruction had circuitously migrated to the lower South. As we have seen, many favored mulattoes in the upper South had left their native lands before the outbreak of war. Those in the black belts of the lower South usually did not. The mass of mulatto migrants went north, and especially into the Northwest Territory. There they enjoyed a relative prosperity, both materially and culturally—for example, the Langstons and the Hemingses. When the war came, they returned south, joined in that migration by the children of the original mulatto populations of the mid-Atlantic and New England states.

The channels through which mulatto leadership moved from the North to the lower South are clearly visible. Many of the migrants, women as well as men, came as teachers sponsored by a dozen or so benevolent societies, arriving in the still turbulent wake of Union armies. Others came to organize relief for the refugees. Both teachers and relief workers first came under the auspices of the Union army and remained to work under the guidance of the Freedmen's Bureau. Still others of the Northern mulatto elite came south as religious missionaries, frequently serving first as chaplains in Negro regiments. After emancipation they too remained, and were joined by newly arriving missionaries of all persuasions. Together the missionaries poured into the black belts, organized numerous congregations, and then settled among the people they had organized. Some members of the mulatto elite came south as business or professional people seeking opportunity on this, as it were, specially black frontier. Finally, thousands came as soldiers. Specifically, some 2,000 young men, mostly mulattoes, came by way of the 54th and 55th Massachusetts regiments. Massachusetts was the first state to recruit Negro men into state regiments, and the state did so not only at home but all over the North and especially in the Northwest. The most ambitious sons of the upper South mulatto population that had resettled in the Northwest enlisted in these two highly select regiments. The 54th, as it happened, spent most of its career in South Carolina, and when the war was over, many of its young men remained there or returned after a stay of some months in the North to complete their education.

   Carter G. Woodson, the famous Negro historian, ascribed the curious lack of aggressive leadership among Negroes in the North during Reconstruction to the migration south of these young and vigorous people.[28] The "brain drain" of talented Negroes, usually mulattoes, from the North to the South occurred not only during and immediately after the war. It continued into the 1870s as young people who had not been in the war finished their education and saw in Dixie the land of opportunity. The black belt pulled these people like a magnet, and the area that was the blackest, the lower South, pulled the most. Indeed, the lower South attracted mulattoes away from the upper South as well as the North. It was in the lower South that able, educated, and ambitious mulattoes could find an abundance of students, congregations, clients, and sympathetic voters. It was there that they could, for a time, succeed in gaining not only a livelihood but status and dignity as well.

   Thus it was that the mulatto elite of the North and the upper South joined the mass of black freedmen in the lower South early in Reconstruction. The effect was most obvious in politics. In the states of the lower South the numbers of Negroes exceeded or approximated those of the whites. In 1867 under Congressional, or "Radical," Reconstruction Negro men were registered as voters in massive numbers by federal officials, while some white men were excluded on grounds of their demonstrated loyalty to the rebel Confederacy. In this imposed "federal" democracy the Negro majority had maximum impact. "Black power" soon reached an apogee in the lower South, as distinguished from the upper South and the North, and it persisted longest there. Reconstruction ended last in South Carolina, Louisiana, and Florida in 1877. Immediately prior to these, Mississippi and Alabama had fallen. It was precisely where Negro numbers were high and mulatto leadership most concentrated and aggressive that Reconstruction had its longest and most significant life.

The mulatto elite was strikingly effective in uniting itself with the black masses and black leadership. Southern-bred black leaders, naturally enough, tended to be ex-slaves from the black belts, and they represented the interests of ex-slaves. What their constituents most wanted was economic opportunity. In an agrarian society this desire translated primarily into access to the land and its produce. Mulattoes, on the other hand, were more interested in full admission to American society. Thus they stressed integration in all public facilities, from the schools through the common carriers to libraries, the theater, and even, in Atlanta, the opera. Mulatto and black leaders exhibited a ready ability to mediate their differences and join together in the pursuit of their goals. In terms of legislation, they were quickly successful in achieving their collective ends. In day-to-day life, however, success was achieved only slowly and very often was truncated by a violent end of Reconstruction.[29]

There was obviously a political fusion of mulattoes and blacks in the lower South during Reconstruction, but there was also a not so obvious and even more important cultural fusion. Clearly the life that free mulattoes had pursued as city dwellers in Charleston, New Orleans, and Philadelphia, as planters in Louisiana, and as farmers and artisans in Ohio was not the life that black slaves had been living in the lower South. The goals of political leadership of the two elements were simply the visible tips of large cultural bodies. There was a free Negro culture, and there was a slave culture. While they shared some things, they distinctly did not share others. In Reconstruction in the South, and especially in the lower South, the area of commonality rapidly expanded as differences melted. Freedom, for instance, very soon generated materially prosperous black individuals who swiftly narrowed the economic distance between themselves and the free mulatto elite. It was not long before successful blacks were merging with the mulatto world. Some blacks who rose had been slaves before the war, others had been free. Within the Negro community, as in

Latin America, in the first years of freedom, apparently "money lightened," and so too did power—power in politics, power in the pulpit, and the power of people in the professions.

In a very careful study of race relations in Richmond, Raleigh, Atlanta, Montgomery, and Nashville between 1865 and 1890, Howard Rabinowitz found the "black elite" well represented among Negro leaders and discovered "little evidence" that lightness of color was "a badge of special status." The importance of color did persist, but it lay primarily in personal matters. People did seem to marry consistently within the census categories of black and mulatto. Among 102 prominent Negro men in the latter four cities, only 11 married women not in their own color category. Nine of these were black men who married lighter, two were mulattoes who married darker. In Nashville there was a formally organized "Blue Vein Society" whose members were required to be light enough to make visible the blueness of the veins beneath their skins. Nevertheless, Rabinowitz found "enough blacks and mulattoes scattered throughout the social structure to make generalizations based on color unreliable." He concluded that "though more evidence is needed, it seems that wealth and cultural attributes were more important than color in gaining social acceptance or political leadership." Rabinowitz's study goes well beyond Reconstruction to cover the entire first generation of freedom, and it seems to have caught the changeover in full flight. Color within the Negro world still had meaning, and the meaning ought not to be ignored; but color was rapidly losing its significance in public life.[30]

Clearly more research is needed, but it seems highly likely that what is today black America began signally to take enduring shape in "black Reconstruction"; and when we do the deep history of the Afro-American in Reconstruction, what we will see is the coming together of a truly new people in politics, economics, religion, education, and social structure, and in those less tangible but highly important areas of language, music, art, entertainment, and the family. Moreover, it will be the story of a people in evolution, in growth, in a melting lessening of divisions, and in a rising integration of their lives and living.

South Carolina provides a good case study of how the mulatto elite responded to the Civil War and general emancipation. In South

Carolina, as in Louisiana, the mulatto community began the war outwardly maintaining its usual stance in support of the whites. The
guns that reduced Fort Sumter had hardly cooled before the free
mulatto community of Charleston had raised several hundred dollars
for the relief of women and children whose husbands and fathers
were in the Confederate States army. As Union forces occupied the
coastal islands, however, the defection of mulattoes proceeded. By the
end of the war large numbers of mulattoes, free as well as slave, had
not only fled to the Union lines, they had also joined the Union army
and were firing upon their erstwhile allies and masters. William R.
Jervay, for instance, was a mulatto and a slave servant to Gabriel
Manigault, a low-country rice planter. As a teenager he ran away to
occupied territory and joined the 128th United States Colored
Troops. He was a sergeant at age eighteen and at the end of the war
had saved enough money to open a store in Charleston. He soon be-
câme a carpenter, a minister, and a substantial farmer. At twenty-one
he was a state representative, at twenty-five a state senator, and he was
not alone in the rapidity of his progress.[31]

As the war came to a close, the mulatto elite in Charleston took the
lead in carrying its style of civilization to the mass of freedmen in
the state, some 95 percent of whom were visibly black. Members of the
elite began their labors in the city itself, and one of the first and most
effective efforts was in education. That movement drew upon teachers
not only from the mulatto elite of Charleston but also from those of
the North and upper South. In Charleston the largest effort was made
by the American Missionary Association, a benevolent arm of the
Congregational churches, under the leadership of, among others, Francis L. Cardozo. Cardozo was himself the mulatto son of a well-known
Charleston newspaper editor and economist. His father was Jewish,
and his mother was half Negro and half Indian. Cardozo had been
educated as a minister, primarily in Scotland and England. He returned to Charleston within weeks of the occupation to head a large
and excellent school on Morris Street. In addition to children lately
slaves, the school picked up pupils who, like Cardozo himself, had
been in the free Negro schools before the war, and he employed
teachers who had been trained in those schools. Indeed, the cream of
the free mulatto society in antebellum Charleston came forth to serve
as teachers under the AMA. What followed was in some degree a
continuation of what had gone before. The people who had been
eminent in the free Negro community before the war were also
eminent after, and they carried their leadership to the freedmen.
These educational missionaries included women as well as men. Typi-

cal of this class was Margaret Sasportas, whose family owned slaves and had made its first money as butchers, then branched out into real estate and banking. Her brother, Thaddeus, had pursued his education in Philadelphia before the war and returned to South Carolina as a soldier in a Negro regiment.[32]

Thaddeus's career as a teacher illustrates well the next step in the process, that of carrying the mission from Charleston into the hinterland. He moved deep into the interior of the state to teach the freedmen in the Bureau schools in Orangeburg District, and he persuaded his young friend William J. McKinlay to go with him. McKinlay was the scion of another eminent Charleston mulatto family. The McKinlays made their wealth first as tailors. Then they became slaveholders, and, on the eve of the war, landlords of considerable proportions in Charleston. Henry E. Hayne, also a freeborn mulatto, fled through the lines of opposing armies to become a soldier in the First South Carolina Regiment, a force organized in 1862 by the Union invaders in the Sea Islands. Afterward he too joined the move into the interior, becoming a Bureau teacher in Marion. The mission to carry education to the freedmen wherever they were was also shared by Northern mulattoes who had come south. Stephen A. Swails was born in Columbus, Pennsylvania, in 1832. In 1863, when he enlisted in the 54th Massachusetts, he was a boatman in Elmira, New York. Twice wounded, a man who exhibited exceptional courage and capacity for leadership, he was commissioned a first lieutenant shortly before the end of the war.[33] Eventually Swails went on to teach in Bureau schools in Williamsburg.[34] Northern women of mixed blood also enlisted in the educational crusade. Charlotte Forten, for example, was the daughter of a well-to-do Philadelphia mulatto family. She came south during the war to teach the freedmen in the Sea Islands. She ultimately married the distinguished Negro South Carolinian Archibald Grimké, in doing so personifying the union of the mulatto elite of the North with that of the South.[35]

The mission movement also had its religious component, and in this effort Northern and upper South mulattoes were prominent. Hezekiah H. Hunter, for example, was born in New York in 1838 and came south in 1865 as a Presbyterian minister subsidized by the American Missionary Association.[36] Benjamin F. Randolph was born in Kentucky in 1837, reared in Ohio, and educated at Oberlin College. He had trained as a Presbyterian minister and came to South Carolina in 1864 as the chaplain of the 26th United States Colored Troops. After the war he remained as a Bureau teacher and agent. In 1868 he became a minister on trial with the Northern Methodist Church. As a minister he traveled through the state. A forceful speaker, imposing in appearance and described as "a tall, stalwart mulatto," Randolph had charisma. In 1867 he turned highly political, only to have his career cut short by assassination while campaigning for the Republican Party in the interior in 1868.[37]

In addition to serving as soldiers, educators, and ministers, young mulattoes from the North and upper South served as relief agents and administrators of various kinds. Also some came without official portfolio. Benjamin A. Bosemon was a young New Yorker who was educated at Bowdoin College and came to South Carolina as a surgeon in the army. Afterward, he pursued his profession in Charleston.[38] Robert H. Gleaves was a Pennsylvanian who came to Beaufort District after the war to engage in business. He soon added politics to his interests and became one of the leading figures in the Republican party in the state.[39]

The motives that impelled those young emissaries of the mulatto elite into the black belts of the deep South were, of course, complex. Obviously they came at the first opportunity, as if some dam had burst, spilling its contents in upon the heels of fleeing slavery. The great majority of those who served in the South in Reconstruction came in this first wave. Surely there was an element of high adventure in their coming, and also there was the usual range of personal and pecuniary considerations. But they were also clearly moved by the ideal of doing good. Many would have agreed with Charlotte Forten, who said she came "for the good I can do my oppressed and suffering fellow creatures." [40] Francis Cardozo had happily left the South during the wave of oppression that preceded the war. He had worked hard to earn a comfortable Congregationalist pulpit in New Haven, Connecticut. But as the war closed, he thought of "so many of these boys and girls" in the South who were "just at that age when their whole future may be determined." To found a school for these children was why he gave up "all the superior advantages and privileges of the North and came South," he said, and "it is the object for which I am willing to *remain* here and make this place my home." [41] Among these would-be saviors inevitably there would sometimes be heavy condescension toward the freedmen. Hezekiah Hunter, freshly down from Brooklyn, thought that many freedmen on the plantations were "but a step above the Brute Creation." Even so, with God's help, he said, he would join in "the Great Work of Bringing these people to the standard of Man and Woman Hood." [42] It seems useful to emphasize that these were young people and their mission was marked by their youth. Only a few had known forty years, and most were in their twenties at the end of the war. They were energetic, intelligent, capable people, and their life thus far had led them to think that every door would eventually open to their knock. It was almost as if they had to be young, strong, and optimistic to face the odds they met, to deal with the whites on the one hand and to reach over to the disparate black masses on the other and embrace them. In some situations, inexperience is a blessing.

Initially, mulatto missionaries, in South Carolina and elsewhere, did not go into the hinterland to prepare Negro folk for politics. Indeed, they were already upon that ground before there was any conviction on the part of anyone that Negroes in the mass would be in politics. When politics came, however, it became still another major branch of missionary labor, and mulattoes leaped into the political vanguard and reaped rewards in power and office. In a very valuable study Thomas Holt has calculated that of the 255 Negroes who were elected to state and federal legislative offices in South Carolina between 1868 and 1876, at least 78, or 43 percent of those whose color is known, were mulattoes, whereas only about 7 percent of the total population was mulatto.[43] Even though they were a minority of the legislative delegation, mulattoes at first dominated the key positions. Four of the eight Negro Congressmen were mulattoes, while eight of the twelve Negro committee chairmen in the first House of Representatives organized by the Republicans were mulattoes.[44] The pattern continued through a range of other high offices in both government and party.[45]

Thomas Holt's count of leaders in South Carolina, even though it is limited to politics and does not encompass leadership in education, religion, and other fields, illustrates well the migration of the mulatto elite from the North and upper South into the black-belt lower South. Of the 196 Negro legislators whose place of birth is known, 13 were Northern-born, 8 were born in the upper South, and 3 were born in the West Indies. Only 2 were born in the lower South outside of South Carolina, and both of these were native to the neighboring state of Georgia. Thus the lion's share of the outsiders were from the North and the upper South. Significantly, there were not many of them, only 21 of 196, but about half of these rose to the top echelons in Carolina politics. Of the 13 Northern-born legislators, 9 were mulattoes; of the 7 born in the upper South whose color is known, 3 were mulattoes. Of the 13 Northern-born, 5 were from the old mulatto state of Pennsylvania. Each of these 5 came to hold very high state offices. Richard Gleaves became lieutenant governor. Henry W. Purvis, another young man out of the mulatto elite of Philadelphia and an ex-soldier, was adjutant general (administrator for the state mili-

tia) from 1870 to 1877. Stephen A. Swails was long the leading politician in Williamsburg County, a senator, committee chairman, and
president pro tem of the state senate. These three were mulattoes.
Two black men from Pennsylvania also held high office. Jonathan J.
Wright was one of three state Supreme Court justices from 1870 to
1877, and William J. Whipper was very influential in the legislature.
The upper South gave Reconstruction South Carolina one Congressman, one influential state senator, and Randolph, who might have become very powerful had he not been killed. The West Indians and
the Georgians did not achieve special prominence.[46]

Clearly mulattoes in Reconstruction South Carolina were political
leaders in numbers far beyond their proportion in the Negro population, and they occupied far more than their share of the highest positions in the Republican party and in state and national offices. There
were also black men in the top echelon of politics, but they were
usually out of the free Negro communities, especially those of the
North and the upper South. Apparently, slavery had left its mark in
a deficit of black leadership able to achieve high political office. While
some black freedmen rose rapidly in politics, they were usually young
men, and it would be many years before blacks would achieve general parity in high places. Meanwhile, however, prewar divisions were
abating. Black voters, after all, were casting the votes that gave offices
to mulatto men; and mulatto politicians consorted with black politicians day by day. In such a political climate they could not avoid
being affected by the lives of the black people even as they were
affecting them. As Thomas Holt asserted, "the freeborn mulatto,
bourgeois legislators by and large reached across the 'chasm' to embrace—sometimes belatedly and haltingly, often with vacillation and
quibbling at crucial moments—the political and economic agenda of
the black peasantry." [47]

The union of mulattoes and blacks in politics that occurred in Reconstruction South Carolina also proceeded in other Southern states.
Everywhere it was but a part of a larger cultural fusion. The white
community in the lower South in the 1850s had made clear its determination to have a biracial rather than a triracial society. The
whites had refused an option to continue to work at separating the
mulatto splinter from the Negro trunk. They chose instead to press

mulatto and black together. Mulattoes responded appropriately, at first hesitantly, and then, when emancipation became general, in a rush. A reporter for *The Nation* caught the movement in flood tide in the summer of 1865. In July he passed through Charleston and found mulattoes there very ready to make distinctions between themselves and blacks. Visiting Columbia, he found few such signs. Returning to Charleston in September, he discovered that "the old jealousy between blacks and mulattoes is disappearing." As he noted, "these wealthy slaveholding mulatto families of Charleston are fully identified in interest with the mass of colored people, and are becoming leaders among them. . . ." [48] The fusion in politics (and in the prelude to politics before 1867) proceeded not so much because mulatto politicians needed black votes as because they chose to ally themselves broadly with black people. They made that choice in 1865, and thereafter they were moving off on the course that would bring them to the meeting hall in 1928 in which Horace Mann Bond could observe a man apparently white soberly declaring the necessity of all black men standing together.

The union of mulatto and black in the lower South—and in the South and nation at large—was a partnership into which blacks entered as willingly as mulattoes. Faced with an outrightly hostile white population, North and South, and a grudging, parsimonious government, black people needed the help that sophisticated, resourceful, and aggressive mulattoes could give them. Confronting the necessity of moving away from the plantations and out into the broad world, they needed verbal and mathematical literacy, economic, political, and social education and organization, and people to teach their teachers. They were leaving the order of slavery, and they would have to cross over to a new order in their lives. The mulatto elite gave them bridges for the crossing. Northern white missionaries and a sprinkling of Southern whites also helped. Blacks themselves had not been asleep in slavery, and they had seen previews of freedom. They were eager students and fast learners. And they came not at all empty-handed to the union of light and dark. They brought with them out of slavery a rather full culture that was black—and beautiful. In it were vital and persisting elements of family and religion, and an ingrown, life-sustaining agrarianism. Black culture was not merely an imitation of whiteness or an imitation of mulattoes in their emulation of whiteness. It was rather a culture that was uniquely black, uniquely American, and invaluable for the survival of Negro America.

Interested observers during Reconstruction and afterward unanimously agreed that miscegenation between whites and Negroes greatly declined in frequency after the war. The evidence supports their impression. The dramatic reduction in the quantity of miscegenation was suggested in a study by Caroline Bond Day begun in 1918 during her senior year at Radcliffe College and completed in 1932. In that study she compiled a mass of information, genealogical and otherwise, on 346 families of mixed blood including 2,537 adults stretching back through history into the colonial period. She divided her subjects between those who had been born before 1861, Group I, and those born after 1860, Group II. In Group I there were 1,152 persons and 243 unions between whites and Negroes. In Group II there were 1,385 persons and only 3 unions between whites and Negroes. Even after taking into account the unrepresentativeness of her sample, the drop in unions between Negroes and whites after 1860 from 243 to 3 remains dramatic and represents a fundamental change in the history of miscegenation in America.[49]

In explaining this occurrence, it is useful again to talk of miscegenation in terms of opportunity and inclination. The war itself had a profound effect upon opportunity. It took tens of thousands of young Southerners away from their homes and their usual access to Negro women, and it outrightly killed a quarter million of them. The death of so many Southern men in the war caused a shifting in sex and racial ratios in Reconstruction. In the postwar South white women were in great surplus, and white men had little need to stretch across the race line to find willing mates.

On the other side of the sex line, white women were faced with a shortage of white men, a fact that produced a curious eddy in the usual stream of miscegenation in the South. White women had either to share the available white males, do without, or take Negro men as mates. In some areas white women took black men as partners, and the white world more or less acquiesced. John W. De Forest, a Union officer in the occupation forces in Greenville County, South Carolina, a semimountainous area, observed that several women of the poorer class took Negro mates immediately after the war. Further, the white community did not severely censure them for doing so. In fact, it seemed to excuse them. They and their children had to subsist in some way, and Negro husbands were sometimes good providers.[50]

That some white women in this time, like some white men previously, developed long-lasting liaisons across race lines was suggested by a farmer in neighboring Spartanburg County in writing to his brother in Alabama. "My dear Brother," he wrote, "as you have made several Enquiries of me and desiring me to answer them I will attempt and endeavor to do so to the best information that I have on the Various Subjects alluded to by you the first interrogatory is Relative to John H. Lipscomb's daughter having Negro Children, I am forced to anser in the affirmative no doubt but that she has had two; and no hopes of her Stopping. . . ." [51]

In New Orleans in the same postwar years John Blassingame has observed the power of sex ratios, along with other factors, to move white women across the race line in search of lovers. The prolonged proximity of white women to Negro men, the rising power of Negro men, and the fact that the war had killed so many white men as to leave many white women bereft resulted in an "increase in sexual contacts between white women and Negro men" in the Crescent City. "In many cases white females competed openly with Negro women for the sexual attentions of black males," he asserted. "Other white women had assignations with Negro men because the white man, by constant repetition of allegations of the black male's extraordinary strength, and exhaustless sexual desire and passion, had created a virtual black Apollo in their minds." By 1880 there were twenty-nine white women in the city married to Negro men, and nineteen of them were native-born. With its Latin flavor, metropolitan dimensions, and international ties, New Orleans was by far the most liberal of Southern cities in race relations. The record there indicates again, as in Piedmont Carolina, that white women did sometimes take black lovers, and, further, that they did marry across the race line. The phenomenon did occur; only the frequency of the occurrence is problematical. [52]

Emancipation also had a great effect upon opportunity. Simple freedom for Negro people resulted in a large measure of physical separation between the races. Throughout the South, as plantations fragmented into farms and slave gangs dissolved into Negro families, opportunities for miscegenation decreased. Moreover, Negro servants tended to desert the big houses, and Negro worshippers left white churches. Schools, too, were almost universally segregated. At work, at home, and in churches and schoolhouses Negroes early withdrew from whites to live among themselves. In Reconstruction the level of physical segregation between the races was vastly higher than it had been in slavery. Consequently, the relatively plentiful opportunities for bodily contact between the master class and slaves afforded by the peculiar institution diminished drastically in freedom.

More important, emancipation unleashed a latent and massive social antagonism against miscegenation, an inclination that existed among both blacks and whites. In freedom Negro women had more strength to resist the advances of white men if they so chose. Negro men had more power to claim their women and protect them. Rather clearly Negro men did both. For instance, Negro farmers took their women out of the fields whenever they could and confined their labors to the home, the yard, and the garden. Most of all, Negro women were given the paramount task of caring for the personal needs of the family. Seemingly, Negro males internalized fully the role of Victorian men and strove earnestly to create an environment in which their wives could be ladies. They largely succeeded. With the vote, Negro men could also protect their women at the legislative level, and they moved to do that too. Negro men in the legislatures voted to legalize interracial marriages, thus giving the concubine, at least officially, a possible path to a ring and a license. They voted for legislation that, in effect, made white men responsible for their off-spring by Negro women—responsible both in making them liable for the support of their children born out of wedlock and in making their property liable to inheritance by their mulatto children.[53]

It is possible that after slavery white feelings against miscegenation soon came to be fully as virulent as those among Negroes. At the very first, members of the defeated elite of the white South were gratified to find that upper-class mulattoes wished them no harm and seemed willing to fall easily into the old pattern of mannerly subordination. "Late arrivals from the city say the really respectable class of free negroes whom we used to employ as tailors, boot makers, mantua makers, etc., wont association [sic] at all with the 'parvenue free,'" a young Charlestonian wrote in her diary in May 1865, while a refugee in the upcountry. "They are exceedingly respectful to the Charleston gentlemen they meet, taking their hats off and expressing their pleasure in seeing them again, but regret that it is under such circumstances, enquiring about others, etc.," she continued, catching images of stylized figures on sunny Charleston streets, bowing and pirouetting like dancers in a ballet.[54]

These happy scenes of social intercourse between the races soon dissolved. Southern white society itself took stern measures to prevent miscegenation and came to frown severely upon mulattoes. When state governments were reorganized under President Johnson's guidance in 1865, legislatures hastened to pass laws outlawing interracial marriage. In South Carolina the black code enacted in the fall of

1865 contained the first law ever passed in the state prohibiting inter-racial marriage. The state also refused to bear the expense of providing for the mulatto children of white fathers. Before the war slavery had eagerly absorbed this issue; now the fathers of all children born out of wedlock were required to post bonds for their support in the considerable amount of $300.[55]

Shifting laws were indicative of a shifting mood in the white mind vis-à-vis Negroes. After the war the white elite turned against its ex-slaves as "ungrateful children" and seemed resolved to drive them from their homes and their protection. The willing alliance of the free mulatto elite with the great mass of black freedmen made it a target of similar denial. As the alliance between mulattoes and blacks began to win success in politics in 1867 and 1868, denial became vigorous hostility. Some whites took up the special idea that mis-cegenation was the basic sin of the antebellum South and the reason why God had forsaken them and allowed them to lose the war. "It does seem strange that so lovely a climate, and country, with a people in every way superior to the Yankees, should be overrun and de-stroyed by them," William Heyward, a low-country Carolina aristo-crat, wrote in 1868. "But I believe that God has ordered it all, and I am firmly of opinion . . . that it is the judgement of the Almighty because the human and brute blood have mingled to the degree it has in the slave states. Was it not so in the French and British Islands and see what has become of them."[56] For many whites, mulattoes became the living symbols not only of the defeat of the South but also of its great prewar sin—miscegenation.

As the alliance between mulattoes and blacks deepened and moved further into politics, native whites turned even more sour and very bitter. Instead of admiring the light elegance of the mulatto elite, they began to deride mulattoes as "neither fish nor fowl" and to heap upon them such epithets as "ring streaked and striped" and "yellow nig-gers." Mulattoes had no race, they taunted, and hence no identity. Whites now swiftly finished the work of mulatto proscription begun in the 1850s. By the end of Reconstruction, white Southerners were able to condemn the whole of the Negro community as a body, out of hand and without regard to variations in color. As the drama closed, a Northern-bred Negro leader testified that "they call every-body a negro that is as black as the ace of spades or as white as snow, if they think he is a Negro or know that he has negro blood in his veins."[57] The South had decided that it could, after all, lump all Negroes together. Over the next few decades, it perfected the insti-tutions that would implement its decision.

Even as the alienation of mulattoes from the white world rose and grew during and after Reconstruction, antebellum attitudes and practices persisted in some degree, especially in the lower South where the Latin influence had been strongest. In New Orleans, by the census of 1880, there were still 205 mixed marriages (made legal by the Reconstruction government), and as already noted, 29 of these involved white women. Of the 205 whites in these unions more than half, 107, were foreign-born. Also, all of the couples tended to be older people. In each of the four divisions by sex and race the average age was thirty-five or older. Thus interracial marriages in the Crescent City in 1880 appear to have often been antebellum in their origins, and the whites involved frequently were not totally rooted in the community.[58]

Another curious outcropping of antebellum looseness appeared in South Carolina in the Constitutional Convention of 1895. In that assembly it was decided that interracial marriage would be outlawed in the state. One delegate proposed that in such unions a Negro should be defined as a person possessing "any" Negro blood. George Tillman, aged sixty-nine and the brother of Senator "Pitchfork Ben" Tillman, the dominant political figure in the state and a racial extremist, argued for maintaining the very mild law of 1879 that defined as black a person possessing one-fourth or more of Negro blood. Otherwise, he declared, apparently to the astonishment of no one, some very respectable families of his native Edgefield County would find themselves proscribed. These families, he argued, had given soldiers to the Confederate army. Those men had served creditably, and it would be unjust and disgraceful to embarrass them in this way. Probably George Tillman's championship of this light fringe of the mulatto world sprang from the fact that he had matured in that earlier age in South Carolina in which, as Chancellor Harper had said, a man's status could not be decided by proportions of blood alone. Tillman was, in brief, a hangover from Carolina's racially loose and Latin past. The convention as a whole saw some merit in George Tillman's argument and finally settled upon one-eighth as the crucial fraction.[59]

Miscegenation never ceased, of course. There were always mavericks in every class who crossed the race line and found sex of some order on the other side. They would do what they would do regardless of laws or public opinion. From Hugh Davis on, somewhere in the South (and indeed, in America), one imagines that miscegenation ground on day by day, probably hour by hour, and perhaps minute by minute in continuous unrelieved and willing toil, beneath sun and moon, in heat and cold, white men with black women, black men with white women, a mass of arms and legs and torsos, ever writhing like some multilimbed, many-colored Indian goddess in a steady, rhythmic, and fluid copulation with herself, moving through centuries of time. Miscegenation was always happening; but after all, there were hot times and there were cool. The post-1865 era was distinctly less then torrid.

After emancipation some whites of the old order persisted for a time in their relative tolerance of mulattoes already present, but the great mass of white people rose in what amounted to a rage against miscegenation. Gary B. Mills observed that the Cane River Creoles of color were "soon abandoned by all but their closest white friends, and with the passing of years even these relationships withered." [60] And John Blassingame, surveying the New Orleans press in the postwar years, found feeling there against interracial marriage no less than "maniacal." [61] Throughout the South, the Ku Klux Klan and similar groups that presumed themselves to be the protectors of public moral-ity were notorious for punishing white men and women who crossed the race line for lovers. In Texas, as historian Lawrence D. Rice has observed, anti-miscegenation fever ran very high after 1879. In that year a white man named Emile Francois who was married to a Negro woman was sent to prison for five years under an act of 1858 which punished the white party in such a marriage but not the Negro. After Francois's conviction, the Texas press followed every incident of miscegenation with outraged avidity. During this time one Texan declared himself incompetent to serve on a jury hearing a mis-cegenation case by saying that he favored lynching any white man who so sinned. [62]

The animus against miscegenation and mulattoes seemed to reach a crescendo in the South about 1907. In May of that year citizens of Francisville, Louisiana, raised a vigilance committee to oppose the keeping of black women by white men. Simultaneously, in Vicks-burg, Mississippi, citizens actually organized an "Anti-Miscegenation League." [63] The delta country in which Vicksburg was located was reported to be infamous for the concubinage of Negro women with white men of means.

Along with an intensified pressure against miscegenation and mulat-toes, there burgeoned in the white mind a mythology about mulattoes. Whites came generally to understand certain things about mulatto character and behavior. For instance, "Mulattoes hold themselves care-fully aloof from blacks, considering themselves superior." "Mulattoes always marry light and never dark." "They cannot stand the heat of a summer sun." "Mulattoes are more intelligent than blacks, but they are also rather flighty and simply cannot and will not endure hard physical labor." Most important, Southern whites insisted, as before the war, that the mulatto was an effete being both biologically and, ultimately, culturally. Mulattoes, they frequently repeated, could not procreate among themselves beyond the third generation. Further, since mulattoes held themselves aloof from blacks, and whites shunned both blacks and mulattoes, there would be no new additions and soon no mulattoes at all. Whites finally could not save the mulatto, they concluded, and blacks despised him for his exclusiveness, even as both admired and favored him for his whiteness. Mulattoes, then, in the popular white mind were doomed to isolation and demise.

The myth of the mulatto demise functioned to relieve the Southern white mind of a great irritation. Whites chafed under the continued mulatto presence. Just as free Negroes and mulattoes *per se* before the war jarred the white man's conception of himself in a neat free white–black slave universe, the simple existence of mulattoes after the war militated against the white man's sense of identity. The dichotomy of free versus slave had died, but the dichotomy of white versus black lived on—and grew. Indeed, the white sense of self depended in part upon maintaining that separateness, and white "being" somehow lay close to the tensions involved in maintaining and refining the distinction. To merge white and black would have been the ultimate holocaust, the absolute damnation of Southern civilization. And yet that was precisely what the mulatto, by his very being, represented. He was the walking, talking, breathing indictment of the world the white man made. He rendered beyond denial the fact that white people had fallen, and white was therefore not totally right. It was apparent in his very person that white and black had interpenetrated in a graphic and appalling way. Life in the Southern world was not pure, clean, and clear as white people needed to believe. Whites who miscegenated were the fallen angels, and clearly it was they who pre- cipitated this evil upon the South—tempted of course, in the case of men, by the ample apple of the supersensual Negro woman.[64] But if one could believe that miscegenation was all but stopped, and that mulattoes were a dying people, in fact a people already dead by dint of their certain dying, then everyone was saved, both black and white.

In addition to a popular lore about mulattoes, there also arose a scientific lore. It was a part of a more general body of thought that worked like a continuing proslavery argument to keep Negroes in their subordinate role. The various ideas about mulattoes become tedi- ous after only brief study, but a good illustration of how the lore worked involved the new science of neurology. Neurologists decided that the electrical signals that control the body run in one direction in white people and in the opposite direction in black people. Mulattoes, obviously, were bound to be a highly confused people. Their signals were hopelessly mixed, and the slightest mixture—even one drop—was enough to upset the system and jangle the nerves. Small wonder, then, that mulattoes were sometimes imagined by whites to be a shallow, flighty, and fluttering people.[65]

For popular consumption, the whole complex of mythology of mulattoes was often translated neatly into the "muleology" of the South. The mule was the ubiquitous and important animal in the rural and premodern South. The mule was a hybrid, ordinarily a cross between a mare and a jackass. That mules had no ancestors that were mules and no descendants at all was common knowledge, and many jokes were built upon that theme. A few words associating mules and mulattoes instantly conjured up a rich and ready-built imagery in Southern white minds. Ultimately, the idea was that as the mule dies, so too dies the mulatto. The association with mules also carried the implication that the hybrid could be continued only by an artificial contrivance, by an unnatural act of mating that ought not and does not have to be, which, in fact, if we but know the truth, must be made to be by straining against the winds and tides of nature.

The rage against mulattoes and miscegenation did tend to reduce the new issue of mulattoes, and whites imagined the old issue would naturally die away. The last task was to exonerate even Southern white fathers and especially gentlemen from the original sin of producing the old issue. By the turn-of-the-century years the white mind of the South was much involved in that effort. One of the most intelligent, educated, and liberal men in the South, Edgar Gardner Murphy, declared in 1904 that "the present evidences of racial admixture are due not primarily to the period of slavery (for the old negroes are the black negroes), nor chiefly to the period of the present, but rather to the period immediately following the Civil War, when the presence at the South of vast numbers of the military forces of both sections—the lower classes of the Northern army demoralized by idleness, the lower classes of the Southern army demoralized by defeat— were thrown into contact with the negro masses at the moment of their greatest helplessness. . . . Among the great masses of the race, especially through the illimitable stretches of the rural South, the black people are still black." [66] Consequently, everyone could breathe a sigh of relief that the era of miscegenation had passed, and, with it, new issues of mulattoes.

The prevalence of such thinking among educated and intelligent

Southerners is striking. Sherwood Anderson, self-appointed mentor to young American writers in the 1920s, recalled hearing his friend and sometimes protégé William Faulkner testify to such beliefs. "I remember, when I first met him," Anderson later reported, "when he had first come from his own little Southern town, sitting with him one evening before the cathedral in New Orleans while he contended with entire seriousness that the cross between the white man and the Negro woman always resulted, after the first crossing, in sterility. He spoke of the cross between the jack and the mare that produced the mule and said that, as between the white man and the Negro woman, it was just the same." [67] Faulkner might simply have been entertaining his friend, or perhaps he later came to disbelieve the popular mythology. Certainly in his fiction he does not render mulattoes sterile. Nevertheless, in speaking on this subject for the benefit of his friend from Ohio, as in his later fiction, he rendered the spirit, if not the letter, of the South dramatically and nearly perfectly.

Even though miscegenation was probably minimal, Southern whites in power again after Reconstruction hastened to make mixed marriages illegal. Of the seventeen states whose territory comprised what had been the slave South in 1861, all but one had moved to outlaw mixed unions by 1940; West Virginia alone made no law prohibiting interracial marriage. Moreover, that most liberal of Southern states acted to punish white persons who cohabited with Negroes illicitly. Two states, Delaware and Louisiana, prohibited intermarriage without defining what made a person Negro. In actuality Louisiana, true to its Latin origins, remained relatively liberal. Even though it outlawed marriage between whites and "persons of color," the latter term was usually construed by the courts to mean visibly black. Furthermore, the courts were famously lenient in ruling that "children of mixed ancestry" were white.

Because they had to define the Negro person that white people could not marry, the fourteen remaining states felt constrained to describe exactly what constituted a Negro. Seven of these simply declared all persons with any black heritage at all to be Negroes. One of these was Virginia, where, until 1910, the highly bothersome one-quarter fraction had held. In that year the fraction was lowered to one-sixteenth, a proportion that made the presence of any Negro ancestry exceedingly difficult, if not impossible, to discern by eye. Finally, in 1930, Virginia cut the Gordian knot of fractional definitions and outlawed the union of whites with anyone with any Negro blood at all.[68] Seven other states resorted to the one-eighth rule. The use of that fraction constituted a comparatively liberal interpretation.

It allowed some Negroes to be legally white regardless of appearance
or reputation. There was no apparent pattern connecting the states
that established the one-eighth rule. They included Maryland, North
Carolina, South Carolina, and Florida and stretched across to Tennessee, Mississippi, and Missouri. Why legislators passed such laws when
they very well knew that in reality the one-drop rule prevailed can
only be imagined. The foremost author on legal definitions of white
and black, after taking his readers through an exhausting array of
fractions and phrases, ended his study with the simple dictum that
everyone knew that the social rule really prevailed: "If it is known
that an individual has the least modicum of Negro blood," he declared, "then he or she is considered a suitable mate of colored persons only." [69]

It would seem that the definitiveness of the one-drop rule ought to
have brought an end to Southern white difficulties in dealing with
mulattoes. In actuality, it only raised another and more subtle range
of difficulties around the central problem of "invisible blackness."
Well before one was down to the single drop of African blood, that
heritage was lost to sight. Centuries of miscegenation had produced
thousands of mulattoes who had simply lost visibility, so much did
color and features overlap between those who were mixed and those
who were purely white. John Blassingame noted that in Louisiana in
the late nineteenth century, for instance, racial intermixing had proceeded so far that it was simply impossible to tell on sight whether
many people were white or black.[70] In 1890 the census found 70,000
octoroons in the United States. Certainly this was an undercount because mixtures this slight were often lost to the eye.

The ultimate absurdity in America's attempt to draw a race line
with the one-drop rule was the fact that many mulattoes themselves
simply did not know whether they were white or black. Their African origins were lost to certain memory, and they were left only with
lingering doubts. David C. Rankin found at least three politicians in
Reconstruction New Orleans who were taken as Negroes but yet had
no certain knowledge of their Negro ancestry. Octave Belot confessed that "I cannot trace my origin to any colored family." J. B.
Esnard, asked if he were Negro, replied, "I do not know exactly
whether I am or not." And Blanc F. Joubert confessed that "I cannot
tell you whether I am a white man or a colored man." [71] William
Faulkner, with that transcendently complex and intuitive genius that
allowed him to represent precisely what it was in the South that was
unique and yet ultimately and universally human, caught the story of
the racially unknown, unknowing, and unknowable person perfectly

in the tale of Joe Christmas in his novel *Light in August*. Joe Christmas was the child of an errant Southern white girl and a carnival man, perhaps a Mexican, of darker hue. His father might have been partially Negro, or he might not have been Negro at all. The crux of the matter was that it was hopelessly impossible for Joe or anyone else ever to know whether he was black or white in a society in which everything began with that definition. Joe is intelligent and attractive, but his strengths only give power to his indirection, and out comes an awful, almost gothic character who stands out in Faulkner's world like some monster. Joe Christmas careens through life, disastrously, destructively, half out of control, a tortured body and a tortured soul, each tragically vulnerable to the use that others will make of it. And yet Joe Christmas will not destroy himself. He struggles to breathe, to move, to be. Like some Flying Dutchman he roves his world, driving through mists and storms, looking for a haven. In that strictly biracial universe of the early twentieth century he is led to flash white and black alternately—a brilliant indetermination that attracts literally scores of people to him to attempt to use him. They root him out of his hideaways and chase him flapping from one color to the other and back again. Ultimately, because he will not or cannot be what they want him to be in life, they crucify him and make of him in death what they need. At last, in killing him to serve themselves, they give him the life, the meaning he has been seeking. Joe Christmas, in the agony of crucifixion, like Jesus Christ, experiences finally what his life meant. He finds release, and he gives up the ghost of struggle for earthly being.[72]

At one level Joe Christmas illustrates yet again in literature the truism that individual humans feel the need to belong. Still, Faulkner upped the ante in the old game to a new and terrific height simply by taking a real historical figure, the man who did not know his color, and setting him down in the Southern universe where color was all-important, a universe that Faulkner, in his own Southernness, so totally compassed. Joe's not knowing was tragic; not ever being able to know was tragedy doubled; not ever being able to know in a universe where everybody else knew, and even inevitably knew, was tragedy squared. In the South everyone knew his color and, hence, his place. On that Southern stage all the actors were either white or black. They lived in two very real, very separate, and yet very interwoven worlds in an ultimately harmonious universe. Southern infants spilled onto the boards of that stage with lines already spoken, motions already made, feelings already felt. The child had only to note his nose and follow its color. Belonging was made easy. Everybody belonged. And if one slipped temporarily out of place, society nudged him back, sweeping him along with ten thousand tiny hairs. One needed, finally, only a simple faith in the harmonious universe and a physical persistence to find oneself comfortably a part of that great symphony. But in the South . . . in the deep South . . . in Mississippi, the longest journey began with the first step of knowing your color.

Invisible blackness also produced another phenomenon called "passing." Passing meant crossing the race line and winning acceptance as white in the white world. Now and again, light mulattoes would simply drop out of sight, move to an area where they were not known, usually north or west, and allow their new neighbors to take them as white. One of these was Thomas L. Grant, another member of that affluent Charleston mulatto community so often in evidence. Grant was a butcher and grocer in Charleston with at least six shops. He was also a landlord of impressive proportions. He not only managed his own property but also assisted in the management of that of the mother and sisters of his good friend Whitefield McKinlay. Whitefield was the son of the same William McKinlay who had gone off to Orangeburg to teach the freedmen in 1865. Whitefield had attended the University of South Carolina during its integrated years in the 1870s and then settled into a prosperous real estate business in Washington. After September 1901 he was Booker T. Washington's man in Washington, hosting his visits, arranging his appointments, calling on black and white editors to carry his subtle hints, and generally monitoring everything that could possibly be of use to the "wizard" of Tuskegee. Whitefield maintained a correspondence with his friend Tom during the turn-of-the-century years. In those letters one can see Tom Grant in Charleston managing his shops and real estate, escorting the aging Mrs. McKinlay in his carriage through the streets on a tour of her properties, serving sometimes as county chairman of the Republican party, and even attending the Republican National Convention in 1908 as a Taft delegate. And then, after November 1909, silence. On the last letter in the chain, a note was added in another hand—probably that of McKinlay or Carter G. Woodson, the collector of the manuscripts—that Grant had crossed the line and passed for white.[73]

Tom Grant was probably very light, but passing was not limited to mulattoes who were very light. Darker mulattoes could pass easily enough by moving to a proper locale and taking Spanish, Portuguese, or other Latin names that explained their color and features well enough.[74]

In reality there were many kinds of passing. There was, for instance, inadvertent passing. Charles Chesnutt earned his living primarily as a legal stenographer in the same Cleveland, Ohio, in which John D. Rockefeller and his lawyers were busily astir, assembling what soon became the Standard Oil Company. Now and again a lawyer would take Chesnutt for white and expound on the race question as if Chesnutt were another white man. Indeed, the Chesnutts—parents, one son, and two daughters—lived very much as if they were white in a Cleveland that was only marginally discriminatory. Chesnutt did not bother to deny his blackness, nor did he advertise it. He and his family like others were often *de facto* white from silence.

Frequently mulattoes passed only part-time. Sometimes they passed in order to have comfortable accommodations while traveling—on trains, in restaurants, and in rest rooms. Sometimes they passed for entertainment—to attend the theater, a musical performance, or a lecture from which they might otherwise be excluded. Sometimes they passed for simple revenge—to trick the whites. Walter White, a blue-eyed, blond-haired Negro from Atlanta who worked for the NAACP, passed for the purpose of investigating lynchings in the South—a very dangerous undertaking. Most of those who passed part-time, however, passed for the purpose of securing a better job. Sometimes the passer lived in the North as a white during a part of the year and lived at home in the South as a Negro during the remainder. Sometimes he worked up north as white, and became Negro again during vacation visits to his Southern home. In large Northern cities there were even mulattoes who passed as white during the day and became Negroes at night.

Alex Manly was a daytime passer in Philadelphia at the turn of the century. Manly was a journalist from Wilmington, North Carolina. In 1898 his newspaper had printed an editorial concerning mulatto men and white women that became the focal point for a devastating riot in the city. Soon afterward, Manly settled in Philadelphia with his family. He was also a painter and decorator, and, for a time, he tried to find work in that trade. Intelligent and industrious, allegedly the grandson of a Tarheel governor and very light, he had no difficulty finding jobs, but once he revealed his blackness he would lose his place. Finally, in desperation he allowed himself to be taken as white, found permanent employment, and even joined the all white union. Meanwhile, his family continued to live as Negro in the same city. After two years of sneaking in and out of his own home daily, he gave up the deception. He preferred to work, he said, as a poorly paid janitor and live openly with his family.[75]

Actually passing was relatively easy, but the emotional costs of passing were high. As Manly's case suggests, passing was often very painful. Not only was there the strain of maintaining the fiction of being white, there was also the necessity of cutting away one's roots. For those who passed permanently it was like a voluntary amnesia in which family and close friends, home, and all of the accustomed things of a lifetime were suddenly erased. Some found that they simply could not pay the tax. Others tried the white life for a while but returned to the dark side of the line. Some of these reported that life on the white side was simply too boring. They thought that whites were "stiff and cold," were not sociable, and did not laugh. Negro life was happier, they asserted, more humane and less confining than the stilted Victorianism of the great white way.[76]

Many mulattoes who could pass simply refused to do so, and many of these refused out of a sense of duty to their people. Charles Chesnutt, after some early temptations, came down firmly on the dark side. W. E. B. Du Bois, one of the two great Negro leaders in America in the first half of the twentieth century, seems never to have been tempted, and as a very young man married his spirit to the "souls of black folk." Often quite gifted, these mulatto leaders of the post-emancipation generation felt keenly the injustice of their ostracism from the dominant white world, and they frequently moved with, as one observer noted, "a spirit which expresses itself in the passionate defense of everything that is Negro." [77]

Passing, by its very nature, was a secretive affair, and no one can say how much of it occurred. Probably the rate varied with the severity of oppression. Passing seems very rare in Reconstruction when prospects were bright. As the level of discrimination escalated in the mid-1870s, the flight into whiteness became more attractive. John Blassingame estimates that in Louisiana probably 100 to 500 Negroes became white "every year from 1875 to the 1890s." [78] Ray Stannard Baker, a well-informed journalist who wrote about the color line in America in the first decade of the twentieth century, thought that it was a frequent occurrence, mostly by very light mulattoes going north or west. In those years of the "nadir of the Negro," Baker reported that Negroes not only seemed to accept passing, but actually encouraged it and protected those who passed. "Thank God, he is passing for white," Baker overheard one mulatto say to another about a mutual friend.[79]

Estimates about the rate of passing varied widely both in popular thought and among close students of the subject. Some put the number at over 100,000 yearly; others estimated that from 10,000 to 25,000 a year passed. Walter White thought that 12,000 went over the line annually.[80] Such figures seem exaggerated. White alarmists were prone to see great numbers. Some Negro leaders looked for great numbers as a quantitative indictment of the oppression of Negroes in America. Other Negroes wanted to see great numbers passing as a fitting revenge upon white exclusiveness. And, finally, social scientists, persuaded that America was well on the way to an assimilationist solution to the race problem, likewise welcomed news of large numbers of passers. The most recent careful calculation was made in 1946 by sociologist John H. Burma, who estimated the rate at between 2,500 and 2,750 a year, with some 110,000 living on the white side of the line at that time.[81] Probably the great age of passing began around 1880 and was over, practically, by 1925. Horace Mann Bond struck at the truth fairly closely in 1931 when he asserted that those who could pass and wanted to had done so, and those who remained could focus their energies "upon the immediate task of racial survival." [82]

It is not too much to say that Southern whites in the early twentieth century became paranoid about invisible blackness. In their minds blood, not environment, carried civilization and one wrong drop meant contamination of the whole. The identification of newcomers in a community was always important to them, but as blackness disappeared beneath white skins and white features, it became vastly more so. Marriage, for instance, became a much more crucial juncture in one's life. What if your son or daughter should, indeed, "marry one," all unknowing and unawares? The mistake becomes apparent only with the birth of the child suddenly and shockingly black. One never knew about antecedents, but one could try. The heritage of the potential spouse was subjected to scrutiny for generations past. Southerners had always looked closely at the origins of the would-be mates of their children. Now they had something to look for. The slightest suspicion could leave a willing mate waiting at the church, and figuratively it sometimes did. In the first decades of the twentieth century, even in the lower South, the Latin quasi-tolerance of the very light and cultured mulatto slipping quietly over the line to whiteness evaporated in a passion for racial purity.

The ultimate impossibility of the South enforcing the one-drop rule in the face of invisible blackness was evident in the mistakes Southerners made. For instance, in 1907 a newcomer from South Carolina was forcibly expelled from Albany, Georgia, by its white citizens, who accused him of being a mulatto attempting to pass for white. When the man returned some days later bringing with him a number of reputable white Carolinians to affirm his whiteness, the town was forced to apologize, with considerable embarrassment.[83]

About the same time just across the state line in Jasper, Florida, the mistake was reversed in color. Lillian Smith, a writer who became one of the pioneer Southern racial liberals in the 1930s, was reared in that small town. The Smiths were a large, eminent, and well-to-do family with deep roots in the area. One day while Lillian was still a child, it was discovered that a little white girl had been taken for adoption by a Negro family. Much exercised, the clubwomen of the town raised a furor. Finally, they went with the marshal and took the child, Janie, away from the distressed Negro woman. For three weeks Janie lived with the Smiths, and it fell to Lillian to take care of her—teach her prayers, share toys, and generally to ease her into the large and very comfortable Smith household. Janie slept in Lillian's bedroom. Then came a phone call from a Negro orphanage, a flurry of whispers and conferences behind closed doors. Janie was a Negro after all. It was quickly decided that Janie would go back to the poverty from which she had been rudely torn. Lillian tried to remonstrate; her mother grew cold and imperious. "You'll understand when you are older," she said. Janie asked Lillian why she had to go, and Lillian grew cold and imperious. Janie timidly searched for the solace that Lillian could not give. "Feeling lost in the deep currents sweeping through our house that night," Lillian later recalled, "she crept closer and put her arms around me and I shrank away as if my body had been uncovered. I had not said a word, I did not say one, but she knew, and tears slowly rolled down her little white face. . . ." Even though Lillian Smith was able to erase Janie from her thoughts for some thirty years afterward, the memory came welling up again and fed the feelings that led her to attack miscegenation and racial injustice with devastating effect in 1944 in her novel *Strange Fruit*.[84]

The confusion and embarrassment surrounding invisible blackness was continuous. It was frustrating for whites and tragic for Negroes. In 1931 Walter White's father was crossing a street in Atlanta when he was struck by a car so hard as to be knocked into the air. The car happened to be driven by a physician who hurried him, unconscious, directly to Henry Grady Hospital. Being light of skin and Teutonic of features, the stricken man was admitted to the white hospital and, for a time, well cared for there. Only when a son-in-law appeared did the hospital authorities realize that he was a Negro. They hastily bundled him up and took him across the street to the much less comfortable Negro facility where he died some days later.[85]

Under the pressure of invisible blackness, Southern whites squirmed still further out into an unreal world, writhing as if on the tip of a spear. William Watts Ball, the dean of newspaper editors in South Carolina, declared in 1932 that the days of passing were over in the South because "the South is on its guard." He joined others in whistling against their fears as they declared that their society was so sensitive to the single slight sign of blackness that it was impossible for a black person to pass.[86]

In the same decade in Mississippi, William Faulkner was asserting precisely the opposite—that white people often did not know a Negro when they saw one. In his novel *Absalom, Absalom*, Faulkner introduced a character who was one-sixteenth black, Charles Etienne De Saint Velery Bon. For twelve years before 1871 Charles was reared by his octoroon New Orleans mother, held in a "padded silken vacuum cell" like an incipient butterfly, reared to speak only French, and dressed in little Lord Fauntleroy suits, preserved in his innocence. When his mother died, his step-aunts, one white and the other mulatto, took him to Mississippi to rear. He was Negro, as the two women told him, but he looked white, a paradox that Faulkner captured neatly by linking "his sixteenth-part black blood and his expensive esoteric Fauntleroy clothing." The two women kept him suspended between the two worlds, a fate which Faulkner prefigured in the story by their having him sleep on the trundle bed while the white aunt, Judith, slept on the higher bed, and the mulatto aunt, Clytie, slept on a pallet on the floor. And both tried to protect him from the inevitable tragedy of confronting the outside world and his color, Clytie by isolating him, and Ellen and her white supporters by urging him, when he had become a man, to go away, pass, and "be whatever you will." Stubbornly he would not deny his blackness, and his attempts to be black led him to one violent encounter after another. Finally, he married the darkest woman he could find, became a tenant farming his aunt's land, fathered a child, and was mercifully killed in 1884 by yellow fever. And there was left, at last, his son, Jim Bond, "saddle colored" and clearly Negro, placidly, unknowingly at home working the earth he had been born upon and did not own.[87] Faulkner spoke the truth, but in the South he was as yet not much read and less understood.

Unable to cope with the problem at home, Southerners seemed to take comfort in seeing passing outside the South. They seemed to assume that an imagined massive passing and intermarriage in the North and West meant that it was not happening at home, and that the South was therefore a bastion of racial purity. Senator Hernando De Soto Money of Mississippi charged in 1903 that 2,000 interracial marriages occurred in Massachusetts every year. Ray Stannard Baker caused a count to be made. In Boston the actual number averaged about 30, ranging down from 35 in 1900 to 10 in 1905. About 90 percent of the whites were women, and most of these were immigrants.[88] W. E. B. Du Bois, investigating the Philadelphia Negro in 1897, found 33 cases of intermarriage in the Seventh Ward, 1.35 percent of the total number of marriages. These involved 4 white men and 29 white women, primarily from the laboring class. Projecting his figures, Du Bois concluded that there were only about 150 interracial marriages in the whole city.[89] A half century later another researcher found that "the City of Brotherly Love" still supported about the same number—141—of interracial marriages.[90]

In spite of the statistics available, Southerners persisted in seeing massive passing and miscegenation outside the South, and they dwelt upon it. During the presidential campaign of 1920, the rumor was widely circulated in the South that Republican candidate Warren G. Harding had black blood. The rumor had been launched against the Harding family in a political confrontation earlier, and probably grew out of a previous charge that they had been abolitionists.[91] A bizarre rumor spread in the South during World War II that a nationally famous and superbly talented young singer, herself Southern-born and Southern-bred, had given birth to a Negro baby, implying possibly that she too had Negro blood in her veins. Why that person should have been so chosen is beyond comprehension.[92]

Southerners increasingly were wont to see racial sins all around the world—and not to see those at home. They noted especially the fact that wherever the European went, he fell from racial and sexual grace. Ernest Sevier Cox, an amazing young Tennessean who was a student at the University of Chicago, undertook to study what he later called the "black belt around the world" by living and working in various areas heavily populated by blacks. He concluded that the real danger was white acceptance of mixing and the awarding of special status to mulattoes. Blood to Cox, as to many others, was the carrier of civilization, and to mix the blood and recognize the mixture was to destroy civilization. As he toured the world, he found that all the imperial powers except the Germans fell short. Germans had sex with natives, he admitted, but they wisely never recognized the legitimacy of the offspring. Where the spirit was willing, apparently, it could rule that the flesh did not count.

In South Africa, on the other hand, Cox found that the race problem was running wild. Living there in 1913, he reported to one of his professors that there were more rapes by blacks of white women in 1912 in the Transvaal alone than in the United States in the previous two decades. The worst of it was that the English were simply not sufficiently race conscious. He was appalled to learn that in the British portion of South Africa well-to-do mulattoes "may gain entrance to white society." On the other hand, in the Transvaal and the Orange Free State where the Afrikaners of Dutch heritage held sway, intermarriage was illegal and mixtures were not recognized. In those states, he said, the racial lines were firmly drawn in the minds of the whites, and they referred to the Cape Colony as the "land of the tar brush" and to Cape Town as the "Coffee Coloured Capital." He now saw the real danger. "The White race is in process of hybridization and it was knowledge of this that led me to return to the South," he declared.[93] Cox settled in Richmond and soon attacked the problem by urging the resettlement of American Negroes in Africa. He shared in the last revitalization of the American Colonization Society, then under the auspices of white racial extremists—a final and ironic turn in the history of that meandering institution.

Invisible blackness made one last and fantastic mutation in the mind of the white South during those turn-of-the-century decades when racial extremism reached its apogee. Whites became so fearful of Negroes that they insisted upon an absolutely "closed ranks" attitude among all whites. Lukewarm whites became objects of suspicion, and those who collaborated with Negroes in any way, for instance by becoming Republican leaders of Negro rank-and-file politicians, were singled out and labeled "white niggers." In the eyes of Southern whites, these people were Negro in their behavior, attitudes, and morals. Very often the immorality of the "white nigger" included a suggestion of sexual transgression.

The Hancock affair in North Carolina illustrates the point well. Hancock was a native white Republican of some local eminence during the Republican and Populist ascendancy in the state in the 1890s. As a reward for his political services, the party made him the president of the North Carolina Railroad, a line owned by the state. It was charged that he recruited his wife's niece, an unemployed schoolteacher, to serve as his secretary during that depression-ridden time and, holding her captive economically, took advantage of her sexually. The language used to discuss Hancock in this event in effect declared that this was Negro-like behavior. Hancock was, in brief, the black-beast rapist in disguise. His was a black soul covered by a white body; he was a "white nigger." [94]

By about 1900 it was possible in the South for one who was biologically purely white to become behaviorally black. Blackness had become not a matter of visibility, not even, ironically, of the one-drop rule. It had passed on to become a matter of inner morality and outward behavior. People biologically black in any degree could not openly aspire to whiteness; but whites could easily descend into blackness if they failed in morality. Thus there was created in the white mind a new and curious kind of mulatto—a mulatto who was in fact genetically white but morally black. In sum, "Negro" became an *idea*. Here in our very midst, the Southern white might say, there are unseen "niggers," men who might marry our daughters, who might thus in effect secretly rape them and spawn a despicable breed. Such men were the ultimate hidden enemies, and bound to raise fevers of paranoia. Faulkner caught this idea too, as he did so many other essences of the South, in his fiction. Joe Christmas, for instance, could possibly have been perfectly white in physical terms, but since he thought he was black, he was black and behaved black. In another story Faulkner ran the line the other way by having Lucas Beauchamps, a mulatto borne of the planter aristocracy, steadfastly refuse to accept the idea that he was a "nigger" and behave appropriately. His acting like a white man at first put his life in jeopardy from a lynch mob, and then it saved him. [95]

Thus by the early twentieth century the color line actually reached into the white world to include white people who behaved in a black way. The one-drop rule had attained an almost incredible extremity in white minds. Such was the terrific and continuing power of race in the South.

By 1915 white America had come to the one-drop rule. In the 1850s the South had embarked upon the course of creating a color-coded, strictly bifurcated social universe. The old order, as always, died slowly. In some places as late as the 1890s it was still skirmishing with fractional definitions of Negroes even as fractional definitions had little or no social substance. It was almost as if some people who had been adult men and women in the 1850s and reared to the old order had to die away and a new generation born to the one-drop rule come to maturity before the total changeover could occur. With very important and obvious exceptions, the North followed suit. Until 1915 the great mass of Negroes, roughly 90 percent, remained in the South, and the great mass of race relations in America were in that region. However, Southern attitudes about race had high power in the North; they were exportable and fully as capable of migration as the Southern Negroes who went north during the first decades of the twentieth century.

The Negro world too was in motion during this time, and in the mid-1920s it had also arrived at a new plateau. Free mulatto communities had responded to the close-out of the 1850s at first with ambivalence and then, in the critical year 1865, with firm acceptance. They turned to pick up the mission to their darker brothers and sisters, the vast majority of whom had just been freed from slavery. They continued that mission in Reconstruction and afterward. By the mid-1920s nearly all of the pre-1850 mulatto exclusiveness had faded, and Horace Mann Bond, as we have noted, could see a "blue-eyed Anglo-Saxon" stand up in a meeting and declare "the necessity that all of us black men in America and the world stand together!"[96] The task, the mission of leading Negro America to a better life, was one in which Horace Mann Bond, who was himself ten-sixteenths white, three-sixteenths Indian, and three-sixteenths black, would engage the remainder of his life, and one in which his son, Julian, would succeed him.[97] Insofar as Negroes accepted the blackness of the seemingly pure white speaker—and of others strikingly light—they too accepted the one-drop rule.

The situation of the mulatto is a fair index of the nature of race relations in America, and the central fact in that history is the evolution of the one-drop rule. The years from 1850 to 1915 are the time of a grand transition in race relations, the time when the whites of the South led the nation in turning from a society in which some blackness in a person might be overlooked to one in which no single iota of color was excused. During the same interval, the mulatto elite reached across to the black mass to effect an engagement that profoundly influenced the future of Negroes—and therefore of whites—in America.

# CHAPTER III

# Brown America

LANGSTON Hughes, in his novel *Not without Laughter*, paints Jimboy, an earthy, free-roaming Negro, singing in an early Kansas morning:

> I got a high yaller
> An' a little short black,
> But a brown-skin gal
> Can bring me right on back!
> I'm singin' brown-skin!
> Lawdy! . . . Lawd!
> Brown-skin . . . O, me Lawd![1]

In the Negro world after 1915 there was a rising awareness that blacks and mulattoes were melting together physically. This became evident in the works of the Census Bureau, which in 1918 accepted the estimate that three-quarters of the Negro people in the United States were indeed of mixed ancestry. Social scientists over the next three decades pursued the implications of this trend to its logical end. What they discovered was that a "New Negro" had been born. The New Negro was a new physical person on the face of the earth, and he was brown. Also, he was a new cultural person, a fusion of Africa and Europe in America. He was self-aware and proud of his race. While social scientists were making these discoveries, the mulatto elite continued its traditional mission of service to the race, and it continued to assimilate to its own ranks Negro leadership that happened to be black. Increasingly, it became less appropriate to speak in terms of a mulatto elite, and by midcentury the term hardly had meaning at all beyond the sphere of personal preferences. Whites, in both North and South, were largely disengaged from the Negro world and failed to record fully the significance of the new Negro even when they recognized his existence. The two peoples, Negroes and whites, existed side by side and yet, paradoxically, very much isolated from one another. Whites, most especially Southern whites, lived in a racial dream world, a world of the mind they fought tenaciously to preserve.

The censuses from 1870 through 1910 indicated a steady increase in the number of mulattoes, and a rise in the proportion of mulattoes to total Negro population. The number of mulattoes among Negroes in the nation at large increased from 12.0 percent (584,000) in 1870 to 15.2 percent (1,132,000) in 1890, and to 20.9 percent (2,050,000) in 1910. No listing of mulattoes was made in 1880 and 1900, but in 1890 the census takers were instructed not merely to count blacks and mulattoes, but to distinguish between blacks, mulattoes, quadroons, and octoroons. When the returns were in, they showed 6,338,000 blacks, 957,000 mulattoes, 105,000 quadroons, and 70,000 octoroons. Census officials readily admitted that those separate figures were not very reliable, and never attempted to make such distinctions again.[2]

In 1918 the Census Bureau published a survey of its work over the decades concerning Negroes. The compilations and computations for the collection were done by a "corps of Negro Clerks" under the direction of three Negro supervisors and a white chief, Dr. John Cummings. In his introduction to the results of the project, Dr. Cummings offered the opinion that whites were no longer adding significantly to the mulatto population. On the other hand, he felt that the extant mulatto population was already well into the process of absorbing all of the blacks. He conceded the probability that in 1910 three-fourths of the Negroes in the United States were of mixed blood, even though only about 21 percent were counted as mulattoes by the census, in which visibility was the test. Pure blacks, he thought, were on the way to extinction. "The black element in the population must decrease and tend to disappear," he predicted.[3]

Thus the grand cycle of mixing between the races had nearly run its course. The upper South in the middle colonial period had produced a large mulatto pool. Afterward, there had been a trickle of qualitatively significant miscegenation by upper-class whites. With emancipation, mixing by whites practically ceased. Meanwhile, probably in late slavery and certainly with emancipation, mulattoes and blacks commenced to mix at a high rate. By 1918 this miscegenation between blacks and mulattoes was rapidly generating a large Negro population and eroding the line between mulatto and black. Just as America was working as a melting pot for whites, so was it working as a melting pot for Negroes. Moreover, the task had been made easier for Negroes by the prohibition of further importations of slaves from abroad in 1808. Much as the National Origins Act of 1924 virtually stopped the flow of white immigrants into America after that year, legislation in 1807 virtually halted the influx of black immigrants. For more than a century while white America struggled to absorb wave after wave of alien immigrants, Negro America was quietly merging its own. It was perfectly symbolic that by 1920 a higher percentage of Negroes in America had been born in America than of any other race, including Indians. In that year 99.3 percent of the Negro population was native-born, whereas only 97.4 percent of the Indian population and 85.5 percent of the white population had been so born.[4]

The census of 1920 indicated that the number of mulattoes in the total population had decreased only slightly over the last seventy years, from 1.87 percent to 1.57 percent. It also indicated that the proportion of mulattoes in the Negro population had dropped from its peak of 20.9 percent in 1910 to 15.9 percent in 1920, not greatly above the 11.2 percent of 1850. The percentage of mulattoes who resided in the North and West remained in 1920 at 14.0 percent, precisely where it had been in 1850. The really dramatic change was that the mulatto belt had slipped from the upper South to the lower. Whereas 60.6 percent of the mulatto population in 1850 had lived in the upper South, seventy years later 63.3 percent lived in the lower South.[5] Seemingly what slavery had begun, freedom had finished. The great mass of mulattoes who were sold off from the upper South to the lower during late slavery had mated with blacks in bondage and continued to do so after emancipation. The result was that the black belt had also become the mulatto belt. The heartland of Negro life had settled in the deep South, and the deep South operated like a magnet to draw the ambitious and adventurous to it. The movement of the mulatto elite from the North and from the upper South to the lower South during Reconstruction was but a following of the mass movement of slaves, mulatto and black, that had occurred in the previous generation. And the coming of Booker T. Washington from Hampton Institute in Virginia in 1881 to found a school at Tuskegee in central Alabama was more of the same.

The census of 1920 was the last count of mulattoes made in the United States. Thereafter, insofar as the Bureau of the Census was concerned, all Negroes did look alike. On the one side there were simply Negroes, and on the other the melting pot was busy making everyone simply white. Obviously the Bureau was quite willing to add its strength to the effort to create a simply biracial America. In 1935 when it updated its superb 1918 compendium on Negro population, it not only omitted entirely the section on mulattoes but apparently avoided even the use of the word on any of its 845 pages.[6] There was, of course, much to justify the omission. No one could be very certain what the numbers meant. Those persons who had been counted as mulattoes were people whom the census takers perceived as mulattoes. They had been counting mulattoes "visible" to themselves. Moreover, "visibility" probably changed over the generations. A person whom the census taker in 1850 might have judged as a mulatto in 1920 might be judged as black. In brief, as the entire Negro population became lighter, both what was thought to be black and what was thought to be mulatto became lighter and mulattoes were counted as blacks in increasing numbers.

It is revealing that officials of the census ceased to count persons of mixed white and black ancestry after 1920 and began to count "half-breeds" of another sort—the children of the native-born and the foreign-born, designated by such labels as Irish-American, or German-American, etc. Seemingly the foreign-born replaced the Negro as the most important unassimilated minority in America. In some respects the parallel was appallingly precise. Just as mulattoes were not allowed to remain a separate category in the white mind, neither were "half-aliens." The National Origins Act of 1924 excluded from the country all but a trickle of immigrants, and most of these were northern Europeans. Soon there would be very few aliens to marry the native-born. All white Americans, like all Negro Americans, would look alike to the Bureau of the Census, a consummation obviously devoutly desired, both within the Bureau and out. (Of course, the government simply reflected the passion of Americans to have the "melting pot" complete its task. *The Abstract of the Census of 1920* is replete with information on the "foreign born." One table, for example, traces out the progress of immigrants in seventy-three major cities, counted first as "aliens," then as "having first papers," and finally as "naturalized"—in itself an interesting word choice.)

In effect social scientists took over the study of miscegenation and mulattoes where the census left off. In the very same year, 1918, that the Census Bureau was giving birth to its great volume on Negro population in the United States, sociologist Edward B. Reuter published his book on the mulatto, *The Mulatto in the United States: Including a Study of the Role of Mixed-Blood Races throughout the World.*[7] Reuter was a student of Robert E. Park of the Sociology Department of the University of Chicago. In the second decade of the twentieth century Park was concentrating a great amount of his own energy and that of his students upon the study of race and Negroes in America and around the world. Simultaneously another center of interest in race and culture evolved around Franz Boas of Columbia University. His most famous student in the area of Afro-American studies was Melville J. Herskovits, who published his study of the physical traits of American Negroes in 1928.[8]

Black social scientists were also very important in the study of Negro society. W. E. B. Du Bois, with the publication of his work on the Negro in Philadelphia in 1897, was, of course, the pioneer in the field and the first Negro American formally prepared as a sociologist. In the 1920s two other young men, both trained in the Department of Sociology of the University of Chicago, appeared on the scholarly scene to make very impressive marks. E. Franklin Frazier, among many other things, did the first really significant work on the Negro family. Charles S. Johnson became not only an eminent sociologist but also one of the key leaders and organizers of social action among the Negro intelligentsia, first as a magazine editor in Harlem during the 1920s, then as a research scholar at Fisk University in Nashville in the 1930s and the 1940s. Each of these scholars and a host of others less well known were concerned in a greater or lesser degree with miscegenation and mulattoes, and some were close students of the subject. The whole effort of the social scientists in the area of race and the Negro came to a special culmination with a vast cooperative study headed by the Swedish sociologist Gunnar Myrdal.

The results were published in 1944 in Myrdal's massive volume *An American Dilemma.*[9]

Who was mixing with whom was a major area of interest to these scholars. They concluded very early, as did interested observers and officials of the census, that the rate of mixing between whites and Negroes was almost nil. It was thought that a few mavericks from the upper class might have continued to mix up into the 1890s, but even that small trickle had all but ceased. Kelly Miller, a professor at Howard University in Washington, wrote in 1914 that out of 1,500 students in Howard, probably not 6 had a white parent.[10] Melville Herskovits studied some 1,551 Negro subjects, many of them students at Howard. He found that only 2 percent of the students had a white parent, and only 10 percent remembered a white grandparent, while a higher percentage knew of a white great-grandparent.[11]

Clearly there were social attitudes that fed the phenomenon of a drastic reduction in miscegenation between Negroes and whites.[12] One of these sprang from an intense hatred by the mulatto elite itself of mixing between white men and Negro women. It associated such mixing with a pernicious pattern in slavery in which white owners exploited Negro women, especially women lighter in color. There grew up among the mulatto elite a tremendous social pressure that deterred its women from marrying white or becoming the mistresses of white men. Caroline Bond Day, who was herself a mulatto, a child of the mulatto world in Atlanta, and a graduate of Atlanta University and Radcliffe College, made a study of several hundred racially mixed families between about 1918 and 1932. She concluded that her subjects were moved by "an artificially exaggerated animus against interracial unions." The mulatto elite had very good reason to believe that the white world was mean and vicious; and it was easy for some members of the elite to go from there to a rejection of their own white ancestors. Caroline Day recalled meeting an old gentleman, a quadroon in Atlanta, who had refused aid from his white father in spite of his early poverty, and who had risen to become one of the wealthiest Negroes in the city. He told the researcher "that as old as he is he cannot think dispassionately of his father and the wrong done to his mother."[13] Negro society, like white society, wanted no further sexual relations across the color bar and no new-issue mulattoes. Day found only 3 mixed couples among 568 postwar matings. The white men involved were, interestingly, "still of the aristocratic class." One was the president of Georgia's Negro Convict Board. These men persisted, she said, risking the censure of a crystallizing public opinion against such unions. On the other side, "the women in question were

likewise violently tabooed by the better class of colored people."
Whites would have been astonished to learn that the Negro world
was as much opposed to miscegenation as they, and, further, fully as
anxious about the sudden appearance of a light baby in a dark family
as whites were about the appearance of a child too dark. On one
occasion the birth of "a blond child in an otherwise swarthy family
gave rise to the common supposition of the infidelity of the mother"
and created a scandal around the twin sins of adultery and mixing. It
soon appeared, however, that the family genealogy afforded full opportunity for such an occurrence and the entire community breathed
a sigh of relief.

Mulattoes themselves could sometimes be bitter about the white
blood in their own veins, but all Negroes could deplore new infusions
of white blood under degrading circumstances. They came to assume,
and with good reason, that such mixing as persisted involved the lower
classes on both sides. Carter G. Woodson, the Negro historian, for
instance, declared in 1918 that social pressures restricted miscegenation "to the weaker types of both races. . . ."[14] There emerged a
popular, persistent, and grossly unfair idea that the offspring of such
unions were marked by special colors. Often they were designated as
"yellow niggers."[15]

The idea of the light mulatto as a low type also appeared in Negro
communities in the North. E. Franklin Frazier, in a close study of
black Chicago in the late 1920s, was surprised to discover a mulatto
community of disproportionate size, but not on the border between
black and white areas as expected. Rather, they were located in a third
zone of the ghetto between fringe and core. Frazier concluded that
they were there in concentration because they had settled themselves
in and around the sin street in the ghetto. "It was the headquarters of
the famous 'policy king'; the rendevous of the 'pretty' brown-skinned
boys, many of whom were former bell-hops, who 'worked' white
and colored girls in hotels and on the streets; here the mulatto queen
of the underworld ran the biggest poker game on the South Side. . . .
To this area were attracted the Bohemian, the disorganized, and the
vicious elements in the Negro world."[16]

Light mulattoes in Harlem were also sometimes associated with
pandering to salacious if not criminal tastes. The Cotton Club, probably the most popular of the night spots in Harlem in the 1920s, was
reputed never to hire any but light mulattoes for its famous chorus
line. The white patrons to whom the club catered obviously preferred
their Negroes light, and so too did the owners. Lena Horne, the
singer and actress, joined the club's chorus at age sixteen in 1933. She

later recalled that the older girls were sometimes pressured to enter-
tain friends of the all-white, gangster-like management after work.[17]
In the next decade Harlem sprouted as one of its minor but highly
ambitious hustlers a tall, light-skinned, carrot-topped lad known as
"Detroit Red." Among other enterprises, Red steered white cus-
tomers from downtown Times Square to various "specialty" houses
in Harlem where they could buy the kind of sex they preferred. Red's
real name was Malcolm Little. In the 1960s his name was transmuted
yet again into Malcolm X.[18]

Social scientists saw a great diminution of mixing between whites
and Negroes on the one side, but they saw a great amount of mixing
between mulattoes and blacks on the other. To the latter they applied
the term "internal miscegenation." Mixing within the Negro world,
they thought, was rapidly melting an already small black population
into the Negro mass. Whereas the census statisticians estimated in
1918 that only about 25 percent of the Negro population was black, a
leading American anthropologist, Ralph Linton, asserted in 1947 that
the "steady infiltration of white blood into the Negro group" had
proceeded so far that "most scientists believe that not more than 10
per cent" of the Negro population was purely black. No scientist, he
added, estimated that the black proportion amounted to over 30
percent.[19]

Sociologists working in the 1920s and 1930s thought that they had
discovered the mating scheme within the Negro community through
which this internal miscegenation proceeded. A central tenet in the
scheme was that Negro men, especially those who were successful,
generally married women lighter than themselves. Melville J. Herskovits in samplings derived from Howard University students and
Harlem citizens found very similar color combinations in marriages in
both places. In each survey exactly 56.5 percent of the women were
reported as lighter than their husbands, while about 14 percent were
the same and about 29.5 percent were darker.[20] When Gunnar Myrdal
made his grand summation of the study of Negroes in America, he
concluded, in rare harmony with his American colleagues, that "dark
males who have distinguished themselves in any way tend to take light
mulatto women as wives." [21] The marriage pattern among Negroes was
like a ladder on which the mating rungs were always slanting upward
toward the female side. On the female side, the darkest women at the
bottom were left without mates, while on the other side, the lightest
men at the top tended to seek white brides. Thus assimilation was expected to proceed rapidly as darker women were left out and lighter
men passed over the race line into whiteness.

With the color progression toward whiteness, social scientists also saw a cultural progression that left out less talented blacks. As a result of this marriage selection, Edward Reuter indicated, "whatever talent there is among the mulattoes remains among the mulattoes; whatever talent there is among the black group marries into the mulatto caste. In either event the talent of the Negro race finds its way into the mulatto groups." [22]

Scholars were fascinated by what became of the darkest women in a mating scheme that passed them by. Herskovits suggested that they married widowers and older men generally. Linton thought that "the very black girls marry later, if at all, and have fewer children." [23] Gustavas Steward, in an article entitled "The Black Girl Passes," argued in 1927 that young black women were simply being erased from the society—economically, socially, and sexually. Occupationally they suffered because employers wanted what Negroes called "the pink type" for maids, elevator operators, etc. "Pinks" were girls who were light but still visibly Negro. In sexual terms Steward found that "rarely does the Negro man mate legally with a black woman." Instead, a black woman had to rely for companionship upon a male prostitute, usually called "the sweet back." These men were "well-dressed, well fed, well satisfied," Steward observed. "Not unusually will he boast of how he is supported, conceiving himself, where he is devoid of the saving grace of self-examination, both as virile and compelling Lothario and as shrewd and unsurpassed financial genius." Steward thought that black women who avoided the male prostitute found a substitute for sex in intense religion, where again they were often exploited. The ultimate result was that "the black girl is vanishing." [24] If the black girl vanished, so too, of course, would black people.

At the other end of the mating scale were the very light men who could only marry lighter by marrying white. Social scientists surmised that it was these men who were the passers, and it was clearly true that many more men passed than did women. There was also the curious statistical fact that again and again in any fairly large census of Negro people, mulatto women outnumbered mulatto men by a slight margin. Experts often took this as one indication that very light mulatto men were moving into the white world, and they concluded that passing was frequent. Most Negroes of the upper class knew some people who had passed, sometimes fifty or more. In 1921 one writer estimated that between 1900 and 1910 about 25,000 Negroes had passed yearly. A few years later Charles S. Johnson and others guessed that some 10,000 to 20,000 mulattoes had crossed the color bar annually between 1900 and 1920. If true, these figures meant that a large element had defected from the Negro world and were then living, with their progeny, among the whites. Looking to the future, Johnson envisioned a time when men would "ask for the Negroes" and be told, "There they go, clad in white men's skins." [25]

In retrospect it seems that the mating pattern envisioned by the social scientists had both strengths and weaknesses as an interpretation of the facts. It probably overemphasized the importance of color in marriage. Without doubt a preference for light color existed, but a question remained as to its strength and effectiveness. In finding that 56.5 percent of the women in his samples were lighter than their husbands. Herskovits was not, after all, presenting a very striking majority. If, indeed, Negro women all over America were lighter than their husbands, one might still ask how much lighter. Obviously the choice of mates rested on a complex array of factors, of which consideration of color was but one. Writers probably also greatly exaggerated the rate of passing. The excess of mulatto women over mulatto men in the census figures was often used to estimate the number of men who had passed. No doubt that differential was related to passing, but it was probably much more consistently related to what seemed to be the fact that mulatto men were simply more heavily pigmented than women.[26] Furthermore, the differential seems to exist even when passing probably is not occurring. It exists in the 1755 Maryland census and in the censuses dealing with mulattoes in slavery, where passing was virtually impossible.

Finally, social scientists were hustling the black girl to the vanishing point much too rapidly. The black girl—and the black boy too—never vanished. It seems as if there were always feelings of warm human attraction in mating that prevailed over more calculated considerations of color, status, and economics; and black women did find mates, both black and mulatto. Apparently, few scholars gave much thought to the fact that although a large majority of Negroes had inherited some white genes, they had not inherited many of them. Thus visible mulattoness lagged considerably behind real, "genetic" mulattoness. Analogously, the same was true of the Indian heritage of the Negro community. Herskovits found that more than a fourth of his subjects had Indian blood, but a random look at that heritage exhibits a great range of quantities in individuals from, for example, one-eighth to one-thirty-second and even to one-one-hundred-twenty-eighth. Many Negroes were indeed part Indian, but the part was not large and diminished rapidly over the generations. Over time, of course, as internal miscegenation proceeded, purely black Americans did tend to decrease in numbers, but the black girl and the black boy did not merge into the mixed population with the rapidity that scholars in these decades seemed to expect.

In their haste to melt blacks into mulattoes, social scientists seemed to underestimate pressures within the Negro community that retarded the process. In the personal sphere, blacks had a pride and exclusiveness all their own; and rank-and-file mulattoes, no matter how much some might hate the white world, did not suddenly and totally forget or despise their lighter skins and Caucasian features. Indeed, a part of their interior strength and exterior power derived from their lightness and the fact that they were the carriers and translators of the white world into the Negro community. Separate churches and clubs consisting of browns and blacks persisted into the twentieth century. There were churches, it was said, where the front doors were painted a certain shade of brown, and no one could pass who was darker than the door. There were still "blue vein societies" where prospective members had to be light enough to show blue veins at their wrists. Such exclusiveness was under attack and diminishing, but older attitudes persisted and had some effects.

It appears likely that social scientists in this era, and later, were led astray in part by an underlying assumption that assimilation was the near and inevitable end of race relations in America. It was a happy assumption and one that, in a sense, solved a very perplexing race problem in the present by assuming its automatic end in the future. Probably Robert E. Park of the University of Chicago was the person most responsible for the prevalence of that assumption. Park, a Pennsylvanian who earned his master's degree from Harvard University in 1899 and his doctorate from Heidelberg University in 1905, greatly admired Booker T. Washington and spent seven years teaching and studying at Tuskegee before beginning his career at Chicago in 1914. Park conceived and taught that whenever two races meet, a four-step process ensues as each race acts and reacts according to its innate nature. First there is contact, which inevitably gives rise to conflict. Over time conflict yields to accommodation, and as the exchange proceeds accommodation gives way to assimilation, the final phase in which the two races merge culturally and, ultimately, physically. In the end society becomes "homogeneous." In Park's view the Negro in America had already lost, primarily in slavery, virtually all of his African heritage. In his estimate the races in America had already passed through contact, conflict, and accommodation, and were well into the assimilation stage.[27]

Park's highly important assumption that assimilation was well underway stuck, and that assumption undergirded the structure of conceptualization, research, and conclusions in the disciplines that addressed the race question in the decades that followed. Three of Park's students, Edward B. Reuter, E. Franklin Frazier, and Charles S. Johnson, provided many of the data and much of the direction for the field in the second quarter of the twentieth century. They were wont sometimes to see assimilation whether it was occurring or not. For instance, in his study of the Negro community in Chicago, Frazier fully expected to find the darker people in the center and the lighter on the fringe "assimilating" with the whites. When he found a large, conspicuous, and seemingly vigorous mulatto neighborhood not on the fringe, he explained it away as an aberration, the habitat of the criminal and marginal element in the mulatto population.

The mating ladder seems to represent the same kind of insistence upon an omnipresent assimilation on a vast scale. It was a very powerful engine working for assimilation, and its greatest errors probably lay at those precise points where assimilation would be maximized—the vanishing black girl, the steady marrying of darker men to lighter women, and, finally, a large amount of passing of light men into the white world. If it were perfectly true, the black girl would vanish with one generation, the next darkest girl with the next generation, and so on until the entire ladder would disappear into the white heavens and perfect assimilation.

The first great dissenter from the assimilationist consensus was Gunnar Myrdal. When one reads Myrdal's *An American Dilemma* after reviewing the history of miscegenation and mulattoes and the history of the work of social scientists upon those subjects, one is struck by the number of times the Swedish sociologist criticizes the scholarship of his American colleagues and the acrimonious tone in which he does this. Again and again he attacked their data, their methods, and their conclusions. Myrdal's is a vast and complex work, but at least one strong theme seems to consist of discounting, in effect, the assimilationist schema. Another theme stressed instead the contrary tendency of the Negro world to persist and strengthen itself as a separate entity and to generate a rising race pride. He did agree with the Americans that the mating ladder was skewed and produced a lightening effect physically, but he was scathing in denouncing the assumption that mulattoes were appropriating the best talent from the black world and moving steadily up while leaving the remnant to decay. He also absolutely refused to put any serious numbers on passing and demolished the work of others in that connection with a sharp and busy scalpel.[28] In the 1940s an increasing number of social scientists either criticized the assimilationist schema or rejected it outright. Theirs, however, does not seem to have been the majority opinion, and the meaning of Myrdal's dissent seems not to have been understood.

Ralph Linton, Sterlin Professor of Anthropology at Yale University and president of the American Anthropological Association, recorded the persisting dominance of the assimilationist attitude in a series of talks and an article in the mid-1940s. ". . . most anthropologists agree," he wrote, "there will be no Negro problem in another two hundred years; by then there will not be enough recognizable Negroes left in this country to constitute a problem." Thus Linton predicted the early demise of color; and he assumed there was no Negro culture at all to serve as an obstacle to that end. "The Negroes have no distinct religion or culture to set them apart from the rest of the population." he declared.[29] One could hardly imagine a more imperfect conception of the reality—or a more hazardous one.

On the other hand, one of the great strengths of the work of the social scientists in the early decades of the twentieth century was that it noted the apparent end of mixing between whites and Negroes and focused intensively upon the physical mixing of mulattoes and blacks. Moreover, in studying such institutions as the Negro family and church, social scientists began to line in the details of the total and viable way of life that Negro people were constructing. Inevitably, if slowly, this scholarship filtered into the popular world to lead both whites and Negroes away from the grossest misconceptions. For instance, social scientists faced the popular opinion that mulattoes could not recreate themselves beyond the second or third generation. The power and persistence of the myth were no less than astounding. Whereas the journal *The Cotton Planter* in 1860 had said that mulattoes were short-lived and that white people did not realize that mulattoes were short-lived, they came to believe this in the next half century under a bombardment of "scientific" evidence. It was only in 1909 that Franz Boas raised the charge that scientists actually knew nothing about mulatto fertility. In the very next year a writer in the *American Journal of Sociology* asserted that hybrids had a "smaller chance of survival, both because they are either sterile or relatively infertile and because departure from type is not conducive to the favor of their fellows." [30] It remained for E. Franklin Frazier in 1939 to establish to the satisfaction of most scholars that mulattoes were as fecund as other people in similar situations.[31]

Social scientists concluded, then, that the mulatto was not dying, but rather was mixing with the remnant of the black population and evolving into what came to be celebrated as "the New Negro." The New Negro was both a physical and a cultural type.

The direction that social science took in regard to the Negro was a part of a larger movement of social science into environmentalism. Generally, nineteenth-century science and social science had stressed the innate and largely unchanging character of man. In the early twentieth century, the still very youthful disciplines of social science began to stress the mutability of man under the influence of environment. Race came to be seen as constituted of clusters of traits, overlapping and changeable. Types of peoples within the races, ethnic groups, were similarly composed and also mutable. Thus races and peoples flow over times and places, always changing. Franz Boas, the Columbia University anthropologist who perhaps did more to propagate this idea in America than any other academician, encapsulated the concept as "a decided plasticity of human types." Boas himself did studies of immigrants to America that suggested that important changes occurred even in the first generation born in America. The structures of human bodies changed; consequently the manner in which bodies operated internally changed also, and so too did the style in which bodies performed externally. What began as a physical matter ended as mental, psychological, and social, and the very quality of human thought and behavior was offered as basically mutable. Applying his hypothesis to the Negro in America, Boas concluded that the passage of laws "cannot hinder the gradual progress of intermixture" and that the real task was to study the mulattoes to determine "their physical types, their mental and moral qualities, and their vitality." [32] In retrospect it is clear that the new social science, the rising passion of native Americans for the reconstitution of "aliens" into "natural" Americans, the specific questions asked of the populace by the census, the National Origins Act, the assimilationist schema as applied to the study of Negroes and race relations, and the New Negro himself were all parts of a piece. That piece was a hard-driving effort by the ruling elite to melt down the ethnic mix in America and to render the substance in a single mold.

On the physical side, social scientists in the 1920s undertook large projects in the classification of American Negroes. They compared the results with studies made of white Americans and others. They measured and described what came to be a fairly standard list of about thirty anatomical traits. Some were obvious, such as skin, eye, and hair color, nasal width, height, and weight. Others were curious, such as "sitting height" and the size of earlobes. Whites tended to have larger earlobes and be significantly taller sitting than Negroes, who tended to have proportionately longer legs and shorter torsos.

Boas's student Melville J. Herskovits made the first fully professional efforts in this field in the mid-1920s, examining some 1,551 people in Howard University, Harlem, and a rural community in West Virginia. In his opinion, the most remarkable of his findings was the fact that there was a high degree of uniformity in the physical characteristics of American Negroes. Taking more than thirty traits into account, Herskovits found that "the variability of the greatly mixed American Negroes I have measured is as low as, or lower than, that of the unmixed populations from which it has been derived." [33] The single trait in which there was great variability was the most conspicuous one, skin color. But Herskovits was well into the stream of thought then flowing strongly through the social sciences that asserted that race involved a broad range of physical traits of which skin color was merely one, that color and each of the other traits overlapped racial boundaries, and that it was better to think in terms of clusters of traits when thinking of race. Herskovits concluded, and others accepted his conclusion, that America had bred a new physical type, a type that was neither African nor European, neither Negro nor Caucasian. At the physical level, America had given rise to a strikingly homogeneous person, the "New Negro." [34]

Herskovits and other researchers as well combined the physical examination of their subjects with questions concerning racial background. The answers to these questions produced very interesting indexes into the nature of miscegenation, past and present. Herskovits found that 71.7 percent of his subjects were of mixed white and black ancestry and, further, that more than a quarter, 27.3 percent, claimed Indian heritage as well. Only 22 percent were black. His findings seemed accurate enough for such samples as he used and reinforced the conclusion of the Census Bureau in 1918 that roughly three-quarters of the Negro population was mixed black and white. Also it was not greatly surprising that many Negroes were part Indian in view of the facts that the mixture had begun so early and diffusion was always a function of time. [35]

In the twentieth century, when the great majority of Negroes were actually mulattoes, it became increasingly less relevant to talk about mulattoes and blacks and more relevant to talk about gradations of mixture within the Negro community. That was precisely what Caroline Bond Day did in close detail in her 1932 study of more than 2,500 individuals belonging to families of mixed blood over several generations. First, she found that Negroes who were more than half black were clearly so. There was a significant shift, however, at the halfway point, and it became impossible to approximate fractions on sight. Mulattoes proper split into three groups. Some exhibited an array of black characteristics that made them apear more purely African than they actually were. These she labeled "recessive," not in the Mendelian sense, but in the sense that there seemed to exist a natural tendency, she thought, toward whiteness. A middle group carried a more or less balanced array of traits. A third group exhibited a preponderance of white characteristics. These she labeled "dominant." Dominant mulattoes, she thought, were sometimes almost white in appearance. Some dominant mulattoes were even blonds. Moving on to examine those of her subjects who were five-eighths white, she found them "surprisingly light." She compared some of these with American Indians, Italians, Japanese, Chinese, Syrians, and Greeks, and found "the hair form and skin color identical in many cases." Quadroons never combined in one person all three of the most important "negroid" traits—"swarthy skin, frizzly hair, and heavy features." Finally, octoroons were simply white. In the few octoroons she studied, she asserted, "I have been able so far to see no traces whatever of Negro admixture." [36]

The Caucasian features of mixed bloods on the white side of the middle line were such as to make passing possible for some people whose ancestry was in a large measure black. "Dominant mulattoes and 5/8 individuals are frequently mistaken for foreigners of various nationalities, or for white Americans," Day observed, "and . . . I know of no case of a quadroon who could not easily 'pass for white.' " As an illustration she indicated that those in her study who had "crossed over" included sixteen people who were quadroons, fifteen who were five-eighths white, and four mulattoes of the "dominant" white type. These had passed permanently, and most had married white people. Another score passed periodically to secure "lucrative employment." She felt that any three or four individuals out of the mixed families studied could produce the names of several hundred people they had known who had passed within the preceding two generations. She thought it a "grim joke" that while popular writers were discussing whether or not the Negro ought to be absorbed, some of the passers "are constantly rubbing elbows in daily life with some of the very ones who are discussing them." [37]

White people might well be terrified that under the one-drop rule they could unwittingly marry Negroes passing for white, but they could take great comfort from some of the conclusions that Caroline

Day's mentor, Professor Earnest A. Hooton of Harvard University, drew from her data. He asserted, first, that there was no indication that miscegenation "produces anthropologically inferior types." He declared that "there is nothing mysterious or unnatural in the mixture of races and nothing very extraordinary in the physical results of such mixtures." Whites could also find relief in his conclusion that as long as one parent was white, really white, a couple could not produce a child who was darker than the darkest parent. In brief, no one would marry a passer and get a black child. Finally, both Day and Hooton felt that "white features seem to gain over Negroid features," and that over generations people with the same fractions of white and black tended to become lighter. Even without miscegenation, *mirabile dictu*, there would be a whitening of America and, presumably, an automatic assimilation![38] Obviously, both professor and student moved easily with the assimilationist current.

In the 1920s Negro America was becoming, quite literally, "brown America." In 1927 Gustavas Steward asserted that assemblages of Negroes had become noticeably lighter in the preceding twenty-five years. Now, he thought, "brown is the predominating hue. . . ."[39] Steward, apparently, had good vision. In the early years of the twentieth century very few Negroes were marrying or mating with whites, but Negroes were marrying Negroes from the lightest to the darkest and of all shades in between. Negroes were marrying Negroes and producing children in such a way as to diminish significantly the proportion of Negroes who were either very dark or very light. Thus the black girl and boy were gradually disappearing, but so too were the light girl and boy as the mass of Negroes tended toward a middle ground on the color spectrum.

Historian Laurence Glasco has made a close study of the photographs of students graduating from Howard University during the years from 1912 to 1972 to determine the degree in which colors changed. One of his salient findings was that "in particular the 1920s witnessed a sharp drop in representation among both the light and black students." Specifically, "between 1923 and 1931 the percentage of light men dropped from 14 percent to 4 percent and among women the percentage fell from 39 percent to 18 percent." Black students exhibited a similar pattern. "The percentage of males fell from 60 percent in 1923 to 38 percent in 1931, while among women the corresponding decline was even more drastic—from 29 percent to only 8 percent. As both groups declined, of course, the number of brown students increased correspondingly." In nine years the proportion of brown men increased from 26 percent to 58 percent, and brown women rose from 32 percent to 74 percent. Thus by 1931 two out of every three Howard graduates were brown. Interestingly, a generation later, between 1947 and 1953, light women followed light men in one last steep decline from 17 percent to 3 percent. The declines had permanence. After 1931 the number of light men trended downward from 4 percent to 2 percent; and after 1953 the number of light women rose to 4 percent in 1963 and fell to 2 percent in 1972. While the percentage of black graduates fluctuated more widely, the proportion never again rose above the 1931 figures of 38 percent for men and 29 percent for women. It seems clear enough that the "melting pot" within Negro America was working and sending a fair sample of its children to that very prestigious Negro university.[40]

The same sort of color dynamic was operative in the city around the university. In the early 1950s Gilbert F. Edwards studied the colors of Negro professionals in Washington. He found that 20 percent of those over fifty years of age were dark while only 2 percent of those under thirty-five were dark. Not only were the dark men disappearing from the professions, so too were very light men. Professional Negroes in the nation's capital, like the students at Howard, were becoming vastly brown.[41]

Negroes soon began to see themselves as "brown" and to relish their "brownness." In a remarkable survey, the results of which were published in 1941, Charles S. Johnson asked some 2,200 rural black-belt children by questionnaire what was "the best color to be." By far the preferred color was "light brown." Of the girls 46.5 percent and of the boys 38.3 percent chose light brown, while "brown" ran second with 20.1 percent and 23.5 percent. Moreover, most dark children saw themselves as brown, and darker browns saw themselves as a lighter brown than they were. They also saw popular figures in their midst, such as well-liked teachers or principals, as light brown even when they were darker. Colors on either side of brown met disfavor. It was easily possible to be too white or too black. When asked what was "the worst color to be," 34.9 percent named black, 32.1 percent white, and 28.2 percent yellow. When asked by interviewers why not white, some suggested that white was "too mean." When asked why not black, answers often indicated that blacks suffered too much abuse, from lighter Negroes as well as from whites. Yellow was often in disfavor because, as one youth phrased it, "Yellow is mixed bad blood." [42] Black was unfortunate, but yellow and white were frankly bad, and as whiteness became less attractive in the Negro world it became less powerful in its influence upon Negroes.

Not only were Negroes in the 1920s losing both their lighter and darker coloring, they were also coming to idealize the middle ground of brownness. American Negroes were generating in the brown person what the Dutch scholar Hans Hoetink has called a "somatic norm image," meaning a "complex of physical (somatic) characteristics which are accepted by a group as its norm and ideal." "Norm" refers to the use of the image as a measure of "aesthetic appreciation"; "ideal" refers to the fact that no one embodies that image perfectly.[43] The idealization of brownness was a phenomenon among the young, as Johnson's study testifies. Similarly, Gunnar Myrdal encountered a tendency among student teachers in Alabama to look to the middle ground when he asked them to fill out a questionnaire. They insisted upon describing themselves as "pure Negro" although they were clearly mulattoes.[44] The movement toward brown also prevailed among their literate elders. The most popular contemporary description of Negro culture was a book entitled *Brown America*. Written by a white man long active in the civil rights movement, the volume first appeared in 1931 and went through eleven printings in eleven years.[45] Finally, the idea achieved a popular consummation in 1936 when boxer Joe Louis became the heavyweight champion of the world and was proudly dubbed "the Brown Bomber."

In America in the early twentieth century it could be said that there were three mulatto groups. There were a great number who were "genetic" rather than "visible" mulattoes. Visible mulattoes, in turn, could be divided into two groups, based primarily upon status rather than color. Most conspicuous among visible mulattoes were the members of the mulatto elite. In this period they were clearly the scions of that element we have been tracing from the colonial period, through slavery, and into freedom. They continued to profit from the advantages vested in them by their whiteness over the generations.

Wherever they were, members of the mulatto elite remained conspicuously in the vanguard. In rural areas they were well represented among the most prosperous of farmers, professionals, and merchants. In urban centers, such as Atlanta, New Orleans, Nashville, Charleston, Chicago, and New York, they formed clusters of affluence and influence in business, in the professions, and in the trades. In 1918 Edward Reuter published his finding that 3,820 of 4,267 Negroes who had "made any marked success in life" were mulattoes.[46] Greatly numer-

ous and scattered across America, they and their black allies were
providing, by example as well as by precept, a kind of leadership that
pointed ultimately toward the ideal world that whites of the same class
pursued. What they wanted was full participation in the good things
of American life—material, civil, and cultural. They themselves were
better able than others to pioneer in the achievement of those ideals,
and they were doing so. In the pursuit of whiteness, the mulatto elite
was of course seriously hobbled by segregation; but its members knew
better than most what was happening in the white world. They
could read, they could travel, and they could sometimes even pass
into and out of the promised land. They were still the link, still the
great carriers of whiteness into the Negro community. They were the
prime leaders, as they had been early in Reconstruction, against exclusion from the white world and for the uplift of the race.

In their labors for the race there seemed to be little color exclusiveness among members of the mulatto elite. They were not at all adverse to joining hands with leaders of a darker hue for the common
cause. As the mulatto elite evolved over time, it took into its ranks
darker people of talent and industry, not necessarily by marriage, but
by openly and, seemingly, freely sharing power with them. Significant numbers of rising black leaders were not at all lacking. Slavery
had indeed bound Prometheus down to Mt. Caucasus, and out of the
ranks of the unbound there emerged darker men and women, usually
young, who pressed their way upward in the Negro world—in the
ministry, in business, in politics, and in education. There were people
like Colonel Charles Young, a graduate of West Point and the highest-
ranking Negro officer in the U.S. Army before World War II, who
collected objects of African art in his Atlanta home and studied
African folklore.[47] The mulatto elite was gradually becoming simply
the Negro elite.

Carolina Bond Day's study of 1,385 individuals born after 1860 and
belonging to mixed families, principally in Georgia, Alabama, and
Texas, yields a rare and revealing picture of where a selected group
of mulattoes had been, where they were, and where they were going
in 1932. "So far as the behavior patterns and mores of this group are
concerned," she declared, "there seems to be no difference between
them and those of any other American people of the same class."
Much of her evidence warrants such a conclusion, but some, as we
shall see, does not.[48]

The mulatto past was clearly reflected in the occupations of Day's
subjects. The movement of the mulatto elite into education in Reconstruction had left a lasting mark. Out of 839 persons whose occupa-

tions were known, by far the most (188) were teachers and professors. The next most populous occupations were those of housewife (163) and student (127). After these came 54 doctors and dentists and 32 postal employees. There were remarkably few ministers (14) in view of the fact that teaching and the ministry were the two great professions open to Negroes. Presumably, the pulpit was often left to darker Negroes. The mulatto elite obviously continued to value education highly and to achieve it. One quarter of this group had finished college, another quarter had finished normal school, and nearly a quarter had graduated from high school. An additional 5 percent had managed to complete a professional education without finishing high school.[49]

Among the mulattoes in Day's study, Methodists were most numerous (34 percent), but Congregationalists (25 percent) had come to outnumber Baptists (17 percent), and Episcopalians (14 percent) were running a strong forth. The rise of the Congregationalists had much to do with the number of people in the study associated with Atlanta University, a Congregationalist-affiliated institution, but the strength of the Episcopal Church among mulattoes had a historical basis and was widespread. In slave times mulatto children had often joined the church of their white fathers, and for decades the Episcopal hierarchy had made a concerted effort to reach Negro leadership by pressing mission churches and schools into Negro communities under educated and attractive ministers.[50] Day thought that the younger people in her study were moving into churches featuring "decorum and dignity." After visiting one Baptist and one Methodist service, she suggested that informality was the dominant tone in these evangelical churches and that the membership in each seemed older. "The hymns when sung by the congregation," she noted, "were punctuated at intervals with a suggestion of rhythmic motions by some of the older women."[51]

In looking at the families and homes of these people of mixed ancestry, Day found patterns very much like those of other Americans of the same class. As among whites, the average number of children per family dropped markedly in the twentieth century. Her figures showed 5.07 children for each set of parents born before the Civil War, as against 2.86 for those born after 1860. The tendency to marry was very high. Only ten women remained unmarried at the age of forty, and five of these were college-educated. The fact that there were limited places in the society for educated Negro men reduced the chances for an educated mulatto woman to find a compatible mate. There was a tendency to marry somewhat later than was ordinary. Six of the women married after thirty-five, and most of these were teachers. Of the grooms, five were much older, and one was much younger. Only the wife of the younger man gave birth to a child. As among their Victorian white contemporaries, divorce was a disgrace. Day discovered only one separation and no divorces among 565 matings in which both parties were Negroes.[52]

A few people in Day's study were rich, and a few were poor, but the great number were solidly in the middle class and rising. In spite of the fact that many were teachers and ill-paid, she concluded that "the standard of living among the subjects of this investigation has been raised during the past thirty or forty years in just the same manner as among the families of white Americans." Visiting as many homes as she could, she considered them "attractive outside as well as within." Moreover, she judged that 75 percent were furnished "in what I think the average person would call good taste." About 40 percent of the families owned automobiles. Only 16 out of 268 contemporary families observed rented their homes, and the average value of the homes owned was a very considerable $7,600.[53]

Day's conclusions were countered in some degree by her own materials and statements. The very fact that mulattoes, like all Negroes, were substantially excluded from the white world meant that their life style would be different in important ways. First, they would be forced to develop a culture of their own, somewhat in emulation of the dominant white culture by which they were surrounded, but also in part out of materials which whites could never know. Second, they would bear a "mark of oppression." There would be special psychological taxes to be paid and resulting nonwhite behavior ranging from self-hate to withdrawal to protest. A revealing symbol of just how Day's subjects were different from the great mass of white Americans was the fact that only 1 of 2,537 individuals in her group was ever known to be arrested. His name was Edward Franklin Frazier, and he was a young sociologist when he was arrested in 1921 for picketing the Capitol Theater in New York City to protest the screening of D. W. Griffith's film *The Birth of a Nation*.[54] The mulatto elite, apparently, could not even afford to generate an average number of criminals, and only one of a political type.

Negro cultural life, Day concluded, was "really only southern," intensified by "unique racial situations." Negroes could not attend the opera, art exhibits, concerts, or lectures. In the theaters they were relegated to the rear seats in the second galleries so that many opted not to attend. "It is not to be wondered at then if, shut off to themselves, a group within a group," Day observed, "they have retained a few remnants of an older and less desirable social order, not being allowed opportunity to benefit by the progressive new order." One result was that some small communities were given to "lavish hospitality which is considered as extravagance and attributed to characteristic Negro laxity, when in reality it is only an outlet for sociability which dares not assert itself in any other way." Larger communities were apt to exhibit "two extremes of behavior among persons of this group, namely a great deal of lighter entertainment (especially card-playing and dancing) on the one hand, particularly among the younger groups, and an unusual amount of seriously organized club work both for self-development and community betterment, on the other." [55]

There was a special intensity in the style in which members of Day's mulatto elite in the twentieth century carried on its tradition of service to the Negro people at large. Not only were they engaging in the work professionally in teaching and medicine, but more than a sixth of them devoted their leisure time to uplift projects among their darker brothers and sisters. Mulatto women were especially active in this effort. In Atlanta they belonged to such organizations as the Gate City Free Kindergarten Association, which worked with children in the slum districts. In Birmingham they did survey work on sanitation and the schools and reported to the authorities. In Houston they worked with young women with special needs through the YWCA. Mulatto men belonged to the Business League and fraternities, and they urged young Negroes to go to college and to "Study Negro History." All of this they did in the face of an always menacing white world.[56]

The conditions under which the mulatto elite labored produced, Day thought, peculiar psychological effects. "This over-developed seriousness of purpose produces in some individuals a kind of super-racial consciousness and zealousness," she observed, "which appears to those unacquainted with their mental background as bordering on the neurotic. I am quite sure that the abandon with which many ignorant Negroes relinquish themselves to song and dance is only a swing of the pendulum from endurance of injustices and the throes of thwarted desires, since they are not intelligent enough to function on the psychological level of the majority of the people in Group I or Group II. This interest in race improvement on the part of educated Negroes is perhaps a safety-valve for emotions which would otherwise mean devastation to themselves and to society." [57]

In order to function, the Negro—including the mulatto elite—had to be shrewd. "He is down, outnumbered, and bested, and the time is not ripe with him for foolish, desperate actions." He had to be crafty and sometimes play the buffoon. "The individuals represented here are by no means unmindful of the real status of affairs, although they turn a smiling face to the world," she insisted. "Seldom is there assembled a group of intelligent adults that some phase of 'the problem' does not arise for discussion." But yet overt action was hazardous, even in the realm of conventional politics. Day's data on politics was, she admitted, "the most meager of those collected on any subject." The questionnaire might have been at fault, she thought, or else "the status of the Negro in politics in various places is in such a state of metamorphosis that many people dislike to commit themselves." Of the 221 who answered her question on politics, 194 were Republicans, 12 independents, 9 doubtful, 3 Democrats, and 3 Socialists. Nearly everyone believed in the NAACP but "only a few are active members," primarily because of the organized pressures against it—for instance, those emanating from the Ku Klux Klan.[58] Actually Day's rather thin closing was prophetic. Within a generation there would begin a "Negro Revolution" in which the NAACP, Negroes as Democrats, and various civil rights organizations would be prime movers in the fight for equal rights in America. In that revolution there would be virtually no mulatto elite.

The basic response of the white world to brown America was simply to maintain as much ignorance about it as possible. This was true in the North as well as in the South. With the exception of the special and exceedingly important contacts established between white and Negro intellectuals in the aura of the Harlem Renaissance, whites in the North, as in the South, had already arrived at the one-drop rule and stopped all Negroes abruptly at the thresholds of their lives. There was little contact, either physical or social, between whites and Negroes in the North. Precisely because there was so little contact, Northerners could easily imagine whatever they chose about Negroes.

Often enough they chose badly. One of the most popular "scholarly" books by a Northerner on the subject of race to appear in the first half of the twentieth century was *The Passing of the Great Race* (1916) by Madison Grant. Grant was a New Yorker educated at Columbia and Yale, a lawyer by profession, and an avid zoologist, traveler, and writer. His passion was for a pristine America, and he turned his energies freely into such things as saving the redwoods, the bison, and the white race. Grant's central argument, drawn from Darwinian science, was that the white race had recently passed into a higher stage of specialization that rendered it superior to others. White bodies had literally evolved to a new, high level of intricacy and complexity that allowed great mental, moral, and social organization. This fragile new structure, however, could be easily destroyed by a mixture with other races. "Whether we like to admit it or not," he warned, "the result of the mixture of the two races, in the long run, gives us a race reverting to the more ancient, generalized and lower type. The cross between a white man and an Indian is an Indian; the cross between a white man and a Negro is a Negro; the cross between a white man and a Hindu is a Hindu; and the cross between any of three European races and a Jew is a Jew." [59] By 1944, when Gunnar Myrdal published his *magnum opus*, the great majority of social scientists believed that mixing simply bred an intermediate type. But Myrdal himself recognized the strength of Grant's style of thinking in the popular mind and referred to him as "the high Priest of racialism in America." [60]

In the South, by the time of World War I whites had lost all real communication with and much control over the internals of Negro life. Looking at both blacks and mulattoes, they perceived only the smiling face they chose to see. They concluded, from this and from the relative powerlessness in which Negroes at large lived, that if the South were left to itself, there would be no race problem. Whites not only lost communication with Negro people, they all but lost awareness of the existence of Negro people as a people. In the mass white mind the Negro past all but disappeared. Negroes, the school books said, had been good slaves. The Yankees had made a great error with Negroes in Reconstruction, but that was all over. Young white people born into an era of deep segregation came easily to understand that there was a white world and a black one, that Negroes found happiness in their own separated "nigger heavens" and in serving whites, that God had made things that way, and that it was the way things had always been and always would be unless man in his unwisdom interfered. It was only with great unease and often for personal and highly arcane reasons that individual Southerners ever thought anything else. In the mass, the Southern white mind worked itself out into an unreal world in which whites established as racial realities what suited their fancy. If a Negro stepped out of the role that the dominant white society prescribed, he became, to use Ralph Ellison's perfect phrase, an "invisible man." [61]

Mulattoes shared fully the oblivion to which the white mind consigned black people. There was no denying, of course, the persisting presence of mulattoes in the twentieth-century South; nor could one deny the continuing small trickle of concubinage and the occasional birth of a child lighter than it ought to be. But even in these obvious circumstances, the Southern white mind was able to imagine itself out of all embarrassment. For example, in 1936 Georgian Margaret Mitchell, in her very popular novel *Gone With the Wind*, quickly reduced to nearly naught Southern responsibility for the extant mulatto population with the suggestion that it was the Yankee soldiers of the occupation forces who caused "an enormous increase in mulatto babies" in the South.[62] No person generally visible to the white world raised an eyebrow at this explanation, and everyone applauded the book and the film that followed. The idea that the mulatto population was the offspring of Yankees and scalawags was one that appeared prominently in the turn-of-the-century years. It carried with it the suggestion that if the Yankees and scalawags were gone, so too in effect were mulattoes. They were simply to be lumped with blacks and dismissed.

The Southern white elite was most disturbed when its own members deserted the racial ranks. A few lower-class white men going with Negro prostitutes was not a great bother. A few upper-class white men keeping Negro concubines was a nuisance, but the cure of social ostracism was easily effected. It was upper-class white men and women steadily engaging in pro-Negro good works that drove the white elite to a sense of outrage. A few dozen highly respectable men and women persisted in going into such things as the Southern Regional Council and making such studies and writing such books as were coming out of the Institute for Research in the Social Sciences in Chapel Hill and the University of North Carolina Press. These endeavors were executed in Southern institutions under the direction of leaders, such as Will Alexander and Howard Odum, whose credentials as Southern aristocrats and totally moral persons were impeccable. The only defense left to the white-supremacy South was not to shut the liberal mouths of these people, however much they might have wanted to do that, but rather to close the ears of potential listeners. In the 1950s the Southern white elite was very effective in that endeavor simply by holding up the myth that "there is no race problem in the South." Don't bother to listen, urged the leaders, because there is nothing to hear.

One of the most powerful assaults on the Southern racial establishment to occur during the first half of the twentieth century came in

1944 in the form of Lillian Smith's novel *Strange Fruit*. Lillian Smith's memory of racial injustice, latent since childhood, came vividly back in the 1930s. She chose as the point of her attack the sexual reduction of mulatto women by upper-class white men—by then a rare occurrence but perhaps the most vulnerable point in all the considerable armor of the white-supremacy South. In choosing the novel as her weapon, she found the means of opening the ears of the literate South. *Strange Fruit* is the story of Tracy and Nonnie. Tracy is the crippled, weak, and unambitious son of a leading family in a small Southern town. He loves and seduces the beautiful and well-educated mulatto maid Nonnie. After an affair of years, Nonnie becomes pregnant. A tortured Tracy is driven by his mother to decide to marry the white girl with whom the white community has always paired him. Tracy pays his Negro servant to marry Nonnie. The tangle ends, appropriately, in emotional disaster, violence, murder, and a lynching.[63]

In Boston they banned the book because it was explicit about sex; in the South they railed against it because of its indictment of the racial system. Georgia Senator Eugene Talmadge called it a "literary corncob," presumably referring crudely to the fact that corncobs were sometimes used for toilet paper in the rural South. Southerners publicly denied that *Strange Fruit* was true to life, but they knew in their hearts that it had been true and continued to be true in some degree, however small. As long as every community was able to see its exception as the only exception, euphoria could be perserved. But the local cases were universalized in the Tracy and Nonnie of fiction, and every real situation—always known, never stated—was replicated and raised to view through them. Moreover, the story could be taken by the more sophisticated as a metaphor for the exploitation of Negroes in every realm, including the sexual. As such, it was a powerful indictment. Ultimately, Lillian Smith's message could not be squelched. The book sold 3 million copies, and the story was produced as a Broadway play directed by José Ferrer and featured Jane White, the daughter of Walter White, the eminent NAACP official, as a very convincing Nonnie.

With the appearance of *Strange Fruit*, storms broke over Lillian Smith's head. Efforts were made to dissociate her from Southern society, to deny in effect her Southern credentials and ability to know whereof she spoke. They charged that she was in the pay of Yankees, and they made over-much of the facts that she was unmarried and lived apart on top of a mountain in the wilds of northwestern Georgia. It was all very frustrating to the racially conservative South because Lillian Smith was so very much and undeniably Southern, and a

Southern Christian lady at that. If she did not flee, she could not be beaten. Finally in 1955 two young men—in what was later labeled merely a boyish prank—burned down her house. She happened to be absent, but lost most of her papers and belongings. Still she would not leave, and the Southern white mind did what it always does when forced to cope with a persistent irritant; it lacquered her over as the oyster does the intruding grain of sand and made of her a pearl. The pearl is alien to the body, but it is made smooth and round and beautiful . . . and, other than being there and occupying a space, it has nothing to do with the body. The rhetoric ran that "Mis Lil" was a "deeply Christian woman," a fine lady, and the book was something that the Yankees made.[64] Really, people meant, she didn't do it, and it had never happened.

It remained for Mississippi Senator Theodore Bilbo to give the *coup de grâce* to Lillian Smith's indictment of Southern white gentility. Bilbo was probably the best-known spokesman for Southern white supremacy in the nation's capital during the second quarter of the twentieth century. In 1947 he published a book entitled *Take Your Choice: Separation or Mongrelization.* Even though he conceded that white men had "poured a broad stream of white blood into black veins," Bilbo insisted that white racial purity was not impaired. "Southern white women have preserved the integrity of their race," he declared, "and there is no one who can today point the finger of suspicion in any manner at the blood which flows in the veins of the white sons, and daughters of the South." [65] In other words, Southern whites are all safe because mother was safe, never mind father. White men could fall from grace every minute of every hour into the arms of thousands of Nonnies, sire a massive progeny, and no one need be alarmed. Such mixing was wild seed sown to bear a withering and wasted fruit. White women untouched and above suspicion were the key to racial purity and moral salvation. As long as white women were strictly separated from black men, no one need be alarmed.

It should come as no surprise that white women in the deep South were idolized, pedestalized, and that they took to angelhood naturally. It was as if a bargain had been struck in which they exchanged a portion of their humanity to become goddesses. It was no accident that five of the ten Miss Americas named between 1951 and 1960 came from, not just the South, but the deep South, two of them from Mississippi, the most Negro state. Nor should we be astonished that Southern women even now are overly represented among those who are most reluctant to descend from their pedestals. Recently, eleven of the fifteen states that had not ratified the Equal Rights Amendment were Southern. Southern women, like the subservient and smiling Negro, have had a special role to play in the South, but unlike the Negro they have often become internally very much what they played outwardly.

Thus, in the Southern white mind in midcentury mulattoes did not mean anything, miscegenation did not mean anything, Lillian Smith did not mean anything, the NAACP did not mean anything, and Negroes were still smiling. All of the warning signals were beyond the sight and sound of Southern eyes and ears. When the crash came in May 1954, with the Supreme Court desegregation decision, the white South went into shock. In the following year, just as it seemed that Southern judges might delay the enforcement of integration indefinitely, came the Montgomery bus boycott, then in the early 1960s the sit-ins, bringing with them a rapid escalation of agitation and chaos. Southerners could hardly believe that it was happening there, and when they did believe it, they reacted in furious outrage—as if cheated. Their fantasy world had suddenly tumbled, and they had no viable structure for dealing with the real world of nonviolent, Christian Negro protest. Through the television eye the scrutiny of the nation was fixed upon them. For the first time since Reconstruction, initiative passed in a significant degree to Negro leadership. What brown America was to do differed essentially from anything it had ever done before. The difference had been in the making for more than a generation, and it had its genesis in the Harlem Renaissance.

# CHAPTER IV

# Harlem
# and After

"WHAT is it you love about Harlem?" the writer asked his friend Jesse B. Simple over drinks at the bar.
"Its so full of Negroes," said Simple. "I feel like I got protection."
"From what?"
"From white folks. . . ." [1]

Beginning in the years around the turn of the century, there was an outflux of Negroes from the South to the North. The migration included people of all levels and all colors. During World War I the need for labor in Northern industry accelerated the movement. By the 1920s writers realized that Negroes were no longer just a Southern people; they were a national people. They were also a people whose culture was in rapid flux. A part of the flux sprang from the fact that Negro culture, which had been in the mass so rural, now had moved into the great and growing metropolitan areas, especially those of New York, Chicago, and Philadelphia. The urban ghetto added new elements to Negro culture—material, medical, political, religious, artistic, recreational, and familial. It was in the urban ghetto—in the new black belts of America formed in Harlem, in South Side Chicago, and elsewhere—that Negro culture reached the new and high plateau upon which it is still deployed. Nowhere, perhaps, were the new elements so richly present and the effort to attain a synthesis of old and new so striking as in what came to be called the "Harlem Renaissance."

Harlem was that portion of New York City, first established as a Dutch village early in the seventeenth century, into which numbers of Negro migrants began to move in the 1890s. By the second decade of the twentieth century, with 70,000 people, it was already the largest Negro community in the world. It was a city within a city and intensely segregated. Harlemites often worked outside of Harlem, but within Harlem, Negroes served Negroes, and, at least in the 1920s, Negroes often owned homes in which Negroes lived. Harlem was the new magnet of Negro life, displacing the lower South, and it pulled in Negro folk of all kinds from everywhere. Its constituency included people not only from North and South, but from the islands of the Caribbean and the coasts of South and Central America as well. Harlem streets sounded with not only Afro-American English, but with the clipped accents of Jamaica, Puerto Rican Spanish, and lilting island French. By 1930, with more than 200,000 dark people crowded into a bit less than 2 square miles above 110th Street, Harlem was the center of Negro life, not only in America but in the western world.[2]

Harlem was where things were happening for Negro people. It was perfectly symbolic of Harlem's rising leadership in the Negro world that three very influential Negro magazines came to find their homes there. In 1910 W. E. B. Du Bois had moved to Harlem from Atlanta to edit *Crisis*, the official magazine of the National Association for the Advancement of Colored People. In 1915 Booker T. Washington died in Tuskegee, and no one person was powerful enough to fill his place. By the 1920s, however, Du Bois in Harlem was probably the best-known Negro leader in America and *Crisis* the best known of the Negro journals. In 1914 Du Bois had been joined in Harlem by James Weldon Johnson. Johnson, a very light mulatto, had been reared in Jacksonville, Florida, was educated at Atlanta University, and had succeeded in a broad range of careers. In 1916 he became the executive secretary of the NAACP, the first Negro to hold that position.[3] In the same year A. Philip Randolph began publishing the *Messenger*, a magazine originally intended to represent the most radical positions but eventually transformed into the organ of the Brotherhood of Sleeping Car Porters. In 1923 *Opportunity*, a third magazine, began publication in Harlem. Edited by the young sociologist Charles S. Johnson, *Opportunity* was the journal of the Urban League, an organization formed by Negroes designed to help their people cope with the problems arising from the great migration to the cities.[4]

Just as the lower South had been the land of chance for talented Negroes in and after Reconstruction, Harlem became the land of opportunity, the magnet, for the young and ambitious in the 1910s and 1920s. With the same certitude with which Du Bois traced a path from Atlanta to Harlem, the center of gravity of Negro life in America shifted from the lower South northward to the great urban centers, and especially to Harlem. Langston Hughes was one of those who came to Harlem like Moslems to Mecca. He arrived in New York in 1921 at the age of nineteen. Even though he was born and reared in the United States, he, like several others in the vanguard of the Renaissance, arrived by ship. He came from a year of living with his father in Mexico, and he hastened to Harlem. "I can never put on paper the thrill of the underground ride to Harlem," he later recalled. "I came out onto the platform with two heavy bags and looked around. It was still early morning and people were going to work. Hundreds of colored people! I wanted to shake hands with them, speak to them. . . . I went up the steps and out into the bright September sunlight. Harlem! I stood there, dropped my bags, took a deep breath and felt happy again." [5]

Indeed, Harlem drew talented young people from all over the New World and, sometimes, the Old. Claude McKay, the writer and poet, and Marcus Garvey, the leader of the "back to Africa" movement, came from Jamaica. The young Sydney Poitier came, in the late twilight of the Renaissance, from Trinidad, and the poet Eric Walrond came from British Guiana on the coast of South America. And lastly, to illustrate the far range of Harlem's appeal, Andy Razaf drew his roots from the African island of Madagascar and came to Harlem to contribute to the Renaissance one of its most luscious fruits—the lyrics for the everlastingly charming, so American song "Honeysuckle Rose." [6]

The Harlem Renaissance was well named, if only because in its essence and within its own universe it was so much like the Renaissance that occurred in Europe early in the second millenium. In its broadest sense, it touched virtually every aspect of Negro life—politics, religion, economics, personality, and culture. In its narrowest sense, it was high culture—literature, painting, sculpture, music, the dance, the theater, and social philosophy. Just as that earlier Renaissance occurred elsewhere than in its original and prime center of Italy, so too did the Negro Renaissance of the 1920s occur outside of Harlem. The Renaissance reached out to Chicago, Washington, Nashville, New Orleans, Atlanta, and every other city where the Negro population was of any size. It happened, too, in all the white world that people in the black Renaissance touched. Finally, the Renaissance was a white as well as a Negro creation. It was white people talking, writing, and publishing about Negro people, Harlem, and "Catfish Row." It was, at one level, no less than all-American, and at another it was indeed international.

As in the European Renaissance, the protagonists of the Harlem Renaissance were elitists. They were numerically few, and the people they touched were also relatively few. But these men and women were the dynamic vanguard, the wave of the future, a wave that would still be moving the waters generations after its prime movers were lost from sight. They were extremely energetic and able people, literally "Renaissance men" who consciously turned their talents to amazing rounds of achievement. James Weldon Johnson, for example, was a schoolteacher, school principal, and lawyer in Jacksonville, Florida; a songwriter, musician, performer, playwright, poet, and novelist in New York; a politician, a diplomat, and, finally, the executive secretary of the NAACP. And he performed impressively in each of these roles.

Like earlier Renaissance people, the Harlem elite looked to universals. They were aware of being akin to people engaged in the "Irish Renaissance," the "Czech Renaissance" in Czechoslovakia, and other contemporary awakenings in the 1920s in which the cultural nationalism of oppressed groups struggled for life within larger polities. It was an age when people were seeking ethnic clarity all over the world, and the Harlem elite consciously shared the spirit of that age.[7] They also discovered Africa again for American Negroes, and they began to identify themselves with colored people everywhere. As universalists they were able to transcend whiteness—either in the sense of considering it the key to the only life worth living or in that of seeing it as evil incarnate. There was bitterness in the Renaissance, to be sure, but there was much, much more—including a rejection of simple bitterness. Renaissance people could see themselves as Americans, and they could positively appreciate America and what Negro people had been in America. Again like the artists and intellectuals in that earlier Renaissance, they were, at the very least, different from what had gone before in their sharp awareness that they were different. They felt passionately that they were newly embarked on a great and promising enterprise. And so they were.

The Harlem Renaissance of course drew black leaders as well as mulatto. Yet it was precisely the children of that mulatto elite whose history we have been following who manned most of the positions in the vanguard. For example, of the four writers who were probably most eminent in the literary phase of the Renaissance, three—Langston Hughes, Jean Toomer, and Countee Cullen—were mulattoes. The fourth, Claude McKay, was black, Jamaican by birth and rearing, and very British in his cultural orientation. Of the most eminent Negroes in the NAACP, three out of three—Du Bois, Johnson, and Walter White—were very light mulattoes. A quick sampling of other phases of the Renaissance and second- and third-tier activists suggests that a substantial majority were visibly mulatto.

The mulatto elite in the Renaissance—like so many elites in America, appearances to the contrary notwithstanding—did not start from scratch. Du Bois, Johnson, Walter White, Langston Hughes, Jean Toomer, and Countee Cullen did not suddenly spring from Harlem's head full-blown. They were not the awakening children of submissive and ignorant freedmen barely fifty years out of slavery. On the contrary, their ancestors had been free well before 1865. Many of these ancestors had been eminent themselves as leaders in the Negro community, and, while they may have sometimes been poor, they were by no means ill-educated and never unaware. The mulatto elite in the Harlem Renaissance was clearly the effective heir—either by birth or adoption—to that long-running mulatto tradition that we have thus far traced. They were the next legitimate generation in a continuous line, and they were there ready to define and to do the next task implied by that tradition. Renaissance leaders came well prepared for the work. They brought to Harlem not simply raw gifts of mind and heart to be shaped to a happenstance end. They brought three generations and more of experience in the special mission of their class to the people they had embraced as their own. Finally, not only were they the *de facto* heirs of a tradition of leadership and mission, they were often enough the direct, bloodline descendants of people who had led previously in the labor of marrying together black culture and white culture within the Negro world. The intimacy of the connection was not accidental, and it is important.

Langston Hughes, perhaps the most prolific and persistent of the writers of the Renaissance, illustrates well the mulatto antiquity of the vanguard. His antecedents traced out precisely the classic line of mulatto children born to white planter masters and mulatto mistresses.

On his mother's side, Langston Hughes was the great-grandson of Captain Ralph Quarles and Lucy Langston, a hero of the Revolution and his mulatto slave mistress. He was the grandnephew of their son John Mercer Langston. John Mercer Langston followed the usual path of the mulatto elite in the upper South. Born a slave in 1833, he was freed by his father's will and resettled in Ohio. He received an excellent education, taking a degree at Oberlin College and qualifying at the bar. In and after Reconstruction he found his land of opportunity in the South, crowning his career by becoming the president of Virginia State College and a Congressman from Virginia, the only Negro to date to bear that title. John's brother, Charles, was Langston's grandfather. Charles was an active abolitionist. He married the first Negro woman to enter Oberlin, Langston Hughes's grandmother, Mary. Her first husband, Lewis Sheridan Leary, who had escaped from slavery in North Carolina, was killed while fighting with John Brown at Harpers Ferry. Charles and Mary eventually settled in Lawrence, Kansas, where he engaged in farming, storekeeping, and politics. At his death Charles left his wife and daughter very little money. His daughter, Carrie Mercer Langston, had attended the University of Kansas for a time but was forced to withdraw to help earn a living. Soon she married Langston's father, James Hughes, and in 1902 Langston was born.

Two of James Hughes's four great-grandfathers were white. One was a Jewish slave trader and another a planter, allegedly one of the Kentucky Clays. Hughes had been reared in Joplin, Missouri. He was trained as a lawyer, but so rejected America that he exiled himself to Mexico, where he became successful in ranching and mining. His wife refused to live in Mexico and eventually divorced him. Like a number of other ambitious and talented young people of the first generation born after slavery, James Hughes rejected and scorned American Negroes for their lack of pride. His son later remembered his scathing denunciations of "niggers." Langston was reared by his grandmother in Lawrence, Kansas, and then by his mother in Cleveland, Ohio. During the early years they were terribly poor, but Langston derived from his grandmother a high appreciation for the worth and eminence of his ancestral kin, and a deep commitment to his people. In Cleveland he attended Central High School, where he received an excellent public school education and, by dint of his intelligence and literary ability, the respect of fellow students and faculty. At his father's insistence, after graduation he spent more than a year with his father in Mexico. James Hughes urged his son to desert America, to take a European education and prosper in a culture relatively tolerant of people only slightly brown. With great difficulty Langston finally prevailed upon his father to send him to Columbia University, which in 1921 brought him to New York and straight to Harlem. He was already a published poet and, after suffering a year as an underachieving freshman, dropped out to devote all of his attention to writing. In 1925, when he was well established as a young writer, he enrolled in Lincoln University in Pennsylvania and took a degree.[8]

Jean Toomer, considered by some eminent authorities in Afro-American literature to have been the first Harlem intellectual to break the molds of the past, illustrates again the fact that the mulatto elite in Harlem was the direct and legitimate heir to a long tradition of mulatto culture in America. His story is worth telling, first, because it reaffirms the importance of the antiquity of the mulatto tradition in the Renaissance, and, second, because Toomer's path to Harlem commenced in the purlieus of the mulatto elite in New Orleans and proceeded in the turn-of-the-century decades through the home ground of the most exclusive and persistent mulatto elite in America, that of Washington, D.C.

Jean Toomer's maternal grandfather was P. B. S. Pinchback, a very light mulatto and onetime acting governor of Louisiana. Born in 1837, Pinckney Pinchback, like many other "new" mulattoes in the lower South, was the son of a wealthy white planter and his mulatto mistress. Pinckney's father, Major William Pinchback, was a white Mississippi planter and large slaveholder. His mother had been his father's slave in Virginia and bore him several children there before the family moved to Mississippi in 1836 and 1837. By the time Pinckney was born, his father had freed his mother. During his early years, Pinckney lived on a Mississippi delta plantation with his father, his mother, his siblings, and a host of slaves. In 1846 his father sent him to a boarding school in Cincinnati. When his father died in 1848, Pinckney's mother, fearing vengeance from Major Pinchback's white relatives, fled with her children to Cincinnati, where Pinckney came of age. Always independent and adventurous, "Pink," as he was called, soon took to life on the riverboats, first as a servant, then as a valet to a set of gamblers, and finally as a gambler himself. As a young man, Pink knew what it was to slip overboard and wade ashore to save both his winnings and his life. He also had his full share of physical combat, with and without knives, and he bore the resulting marks. In 1860 he married a sixteen-year-old Memphis belle of light color named Nina Emily Hawthorne. Early in the war, Pink fled to the Union forces in New Orleans. Shortly he was commissioned a captain in the free-person-of-color regiment raised by General Butler. After a year he, along with all the other officers, resigned his commission in protest against the discrimination shown his color. Soon he slipped into Republican politics in "liberated" Louisiana—that southern portion of the state occupied by the Union army. After the war he rose easily in party ranks and won election, finally, as lieutenant governor. For forty days during Reconstruction Pinchback was the acting governor of the state. During the remainder of his life he carried as a courtesy the title of "Governor."

Pinchback was elected to the United States Senate by the last Republican legislature in Louisiana, but the Senate refused him a seat. Soon he was appointed to a sinecure in the federal service in New Orleans. With his salary and a personal income of $10,000 a year derived from various investments, he was a rich man and could afford to engage in a variety of political, social, and philanthropic enterprises, and did so. For well over a decade, with the beautiful Nina, he thrived at the very peak of light society in the Crescent City, mixing freely with the persisting prewar mulatto elite. In the early 1890s the Pinchbacks moved to Washington, where they settled comfortably in a house on Bacon Street and entered the social life maintained by one of the most affluent and sophisticated mulatto communities in the nation. With the exception of an interlude in the customs house in New York, Pinchback and Nina spent the last three decades of their lives in the capital city. "The Governor" held a minor position in the federal service, but his real role was that of political broker. His special function was to line up Negro delegates for one or another of the always available politicians seeking the Republican presidential nomination. He prospered as a political broker, moving around town in summers under a Panama hat (made popular by Teddy Roosevelt in visiting the "big ditch"), impressing visiting Negro politicos with his *savoir faire* in important offices and Pennsylvania Avenue bars, and attending Republican celebrations, including inaugural balls, with *la belle* Nina.

Elegant, sophisticated "Governor" Pinchback and his wife and daughter were a part of the "Four Hundred," as the Negro elite in the nation's capital during the turn-of-the-century decades came to call itself. After the end of Reconstruction in the South large numbers of prominent political refugees, most of whom were mulattoes, had fled to Washington. There they easily joined a preexisting aristocracy of business people—such as the Wormsleys of hotel fame, old abolitionists like Frederick Douglass, who himself took a white bride in 1884, and the often lightly colored faculty of Howard University. After Reconstruction and before the Harlem Renaissance, mulatto Washington was at the very top of the Negro world, and it was notorious in its exclusiveness. Its eyes were steadfastly fixed upon the white clouds, and it hardly deigned to notice what it was on top of.[9]

Pinchback's daughter married a mulatto of light complexion from Georgia named Toomer. Toomer's background remains vague; possibly he was a minor politician somehow in exile. Shortly, in 1894, a very light child was born to the couple. The new father deserted his family, perhaps driven away by the overbearing and superior attitude of his father-in-law. The child, Nathan Eugene "Jean" Toomer, grew up in his grandfather's house in Washington, in the very bosom, as it were, of the whiteward-aspiring Four Hundred. In his early youth Jean hardly even understood that he was Negro, so white was that world, and, paradoxically, so separated was it at important points where the cutting edge of prejudice might have hurt. Brilliant, attractive to women, charming when he chose to be so, he engaged people on all sides. But he was also erratic and vain, and he often hurt those who loved and befriended him. He dropped out of a remarkably long succession of schools and in 1917 came to New York. In 1920 he returned to Washington to the Bacon Street house to care for his ill and aging grandmother and grandfather. Nina passed away first, then, in 1921, "the Governor." Jean took his grandfather's body to New Orleans for burial. Pinchback's old friends met the train and attended the ritual that saw his body sealed in the family vault in beautiful Miltairie Ridge Cemetery. Shortly afterward Toomer took a teaching position in rural Georgia. There, near his father's roots, he rediscovered his blackness. For Toomer it was a spiritual revolution, and out of it came the great work of his life, the book *Cane*. *Cane*, dedicated to Nina, was published in 1923. What Toomer did in *Cane*, in essence, was to lay his blackness alongside his whiteness and, however imperfectly, beautifully join the two. With that single work he won sudden and lasting fame as the groundbreaking writer of the Harlem Renaissance.[10]

The poetry of the sequence is almost too perfect as an illustration of the transition from the Reconstruction generation to that of the Renaissance. "The Governor," so white in every way, dies in 1921 just as the decade of the Renaissance commences. He is laid to rest in the New Orleans where he led the mulatto elite in Reconstruction, with a corporal's guard of his old fellows about and with the whole of that next generation missing. He is buried by a man so light as to be white, his grandson, who is about to go from light New Orleans to his father's dark Georgia, and then to Harlem to write a book that is black in every way and that will signal the beginning of the literature of the Renaissance.

If Langston Hughes was a steady star, Toomer flashed first and shone like a meteor. He never achieved so well again. His next significant act after completing *Cane* was to have an affair with the wife of Waldo Frank, the writer who had arranged for the publication of the book and wrote an introduction for it. Toomer lived until 1967 and never published nearly so successfully again. Indeed, his strength seemed to come from his brief embrace of his dark Southern roots. His grasp there was not firm. He lost those roots often, and when he did so, he seemed to lose direction. Not unlike Joe Christmas, he ricocheted between whiteness and blackness like a bullet angling down a dark and narrow alley. Sometimes he married white, sometimes figuratively he married black, and sometimes he did not marry at all. But by evoking the blackness of his past and joining it to his whiteness in that one bold, broad, and single swing, Toomer pioneered in what was probably the most significant labor of the Renaissance.[11]

Like Langston Hughes and unlike Jean Toomer, Countee Cullen, the third person in the mulatto triarchy of Renaissance writers, never lost his hold upon blackness. Unlike both Hughes and Toomer, however, he did not have a line of illustrious forebears. Countee Cullen was born Countee Porter in New York City in 1903 and early orphaned. It was generally understood that his folks had come from Kentucky, and his mulatto ancestry was inferred from his appearance, it being said that he had reddish, or "mariney," colored hair. Until he was eleven years old he was reared by his grandmother. Upon her death, he was adopted by the Reverend Frederick Asbury Cullen and his wife, a childless couple. Cullen was a Methodist minister and an extraordinary man. He had been born into a very large and very poor family in Maryland. He had brought himself up to be a schoolteacher and then had worked his way through seminary. Thereafter he quickly rose to become the pastor of the Seventh Avenue Methodist Church. Under his ministry the church became one of the largest and most important in Harlem. He was a well-educated man with a substantial personal library, living, at the time of Countee's adoption, in a spacious parsonage next to his church on Seventh Avenue.

Countee Cullen was not born with a silver spoon in his mouth, but he was offered one in middle youth, and he accepted it with grace. Thereafter he handled being privileged well—better, indeed, than most who were born privileged. The Cullens gave Countee every advantage that loving, affluent, and eminent parents could give. He was a very bright, strangely tractable lad who repaid their kindness with devotion and a steady succession of achievements. He was a storybook boy—bright, mannerly, and very attractive in his sturdy brown-skinned body. Unlike his three literary peers—Hughes, Toomer, and Claude McKay—Countee progressed pliably and brilliantly through his studies, first as prestigious De Witt Clinton High School and then at New York University. While he was a senior in the university in 1925, he published his first book of poems, *Color*. As a man and as a writer, Countee Cullen, rather incongruously, combined smoothly a buttoned-up elegance of mind and manner with rich and deeply passionate poetry. His book won for him instant acclaim. In the next year he was welcomed as a student at Harvard University, where he took a master's degree in literature. In the year of his graduation, the congregation of the church made a gift to his father of a grand tour of Europe and the Holy Land. Still his father's good son, Countee was an eager companion. In Italy he visited Shelley's memorial and the grave of his idol, John Keats. He was ecstatic, and, in the manner of poets, he wrote a sonnet in celebration. Back home, he worked for a time as assistant to Charles S. Johnson on *Opportunity*, won a Guggenheim fellowship, and married, briefly, Yolande, the only daughter of W. E. B. Du Bois. The fellowship took him to Europe, where he lived for two years. Returning in the midst of the great depression, he settled down to teaching English in a Harlem junior high school. He continued to write until his untimely death in 1946, most successfully still in poetry and always in the clear, predictable forms of the nineteenth-century Romantic poets he so dearly loved.[12]

In retrospect it seems clear that the mulatto elite in the Harlem Renaissance was perfectly true to its tradition of leadership in not simply following the course set by its predecessors, but profoundly altering that course to meet the age. Confronted with the rock-hard exclusiveness of the white world, the mulatto leaders of the Renaissance turned back to the black. They changed the mission of the mulatto elite from one of carrying white culture to the Negro mass to one of picking up black culture within the Negro world and marrying it smoothly to the white culture that they knew so well. This was the next logical step in responsible leadership and one of the most critical turns that Afro-American history has taken. It meant that Robert E. Park's ultimate end of assimilation would not be attained either culturally or physically during any future with which we must be concerned. It meant that the young vanguard of the mulatto elite was about to dissolve itself as a vanguard based on color. It signified the essential acceptance by the Negro world of the one-drop rule, a rule that was virtually the antithesis of assimilation. Finally, and most important, it meant that Afro-Americans would begin to build a separate culture—one that was neither white nor black, but both. The result would be a new Negro culture and a new Negro person. The heirs of the mulatto elite were in the vanguard that led Negroes into that labor, and it is a labor in which they are yet engaged. "It was a beginning and not an answer," as Nathan Huggins has so cogently concluded. "And we have worked from that moment ever since." [13]

What most distinguished the members of the mulatto elite in the Harlem Renaissance from their parents and grandparents was that they turned back to discover, study, describe, and exalt the blackness that was within themselves. It was almost as if three generations of freedom had to pass before mulattoes would be able to appreciate their blackness—a loose weave of cultural strands derived from Africa, Southern slavery, the rural peasant life of the South after emancipation, and, most recently, the urban ghetto. It is probably significant that the artists and writers of the Renaissance were young, most of them in their twenties. They were the third generation to live in freedom and the second to be born after slavery. Their grandparents and parents had operated upon the assumption that the achievement of white culture would bring Negro people, one by one, into acceptance in the white world. Yet even as those earlier generations eagerly learned white culture and diligently taught it to their children, they found themselves rejected. They beat more and more loudly, frantically, and futilely upon the closed door of the white world.

The people of the Renaissance rejected that single-minded pursuit. In the words of young Wallace Thurman, they considered irrelevant these "alarmed and angry Jeremiahs spouting fire and venom or else weeping and moaning as if they were either predestined or else unable to do anything else." As he phrased it, "every chord on their publicist instrument had been broken save one, and they continued raucously to twang this, unaware that they were ludicrously out of tune with the other instruments in their environment." [14] If the white world was determined to reject the society of Negro people—from the darkest to the lightest and regardless of wealth, cultivation, or individual merit—then the most accomplished, the most aspiring Negroes, including mulattoes, would turn back to the Negro mass and discover there the materials for a broad cultural construction in which they could find meaning. In brief, if one could not be white, then one would be, in some way, satisfyingly black.

Even as their parents were saying, "We done got away from all that now," meaning the ways of the slave and peasant past,[15] young people in the Renaissance were returning to precisely what their elders were fleeing. Jean Toomer is an excellent example of the switch. Himself so white, born of a mother and grandparents who were so white and so much a part of fashionable New Orleans and Washington societies, he was inspired to write *Cane* by going back to the dark Georgia world from which his father had sprung. Toomer rediscovered his blackness and raised it almost to a mystery, to a source of awe and power more felt than analyzed. *Cane* is not really so much a story, or several stories, as it was a book of images, sometimes in prose, sometimes in poetry, sometimes in Southern settings, and set sometimes in the North—in Washington, Harlem, Chicago, and Madison, Wisconsin, where Toomer had spent parts of his life. The people in the book are offered with great sensitivity and deep humanity. But what is even more interesting was the tone. It is a vivid, highly emotional, impressionistic interweaving of black and white— the real black postslave Georgia of Toomer's long-gone father and the rather ideal and pristine whiteness of Pinchback's precious Washington. *Cane* is like a tapestry woven in two strong colors, each strand definably one or the other, the strands brought together skillfully to make a compelling image. Romantic, lyrical, dreamy, almost ethereal, the mood of the book reflected the color complexity of the author— perfect whiteness at times, followed by a sudden, complete, and willing surrender to Georgia blackness. Clearly, Toomer raised the standard of "black is beautiful" in a compelling way, and the most alert among both whites and Negroes almost intuitively recognized its worth. In 1925 critic William Stanley Braithwaite pronounced him "the very first artist of the race" and "a bright morning star of a new day of the race in literature." [16]

In the Renaissance one of the most assiduous and astute of the seekers after blackness was Zora Neale Hurston, herself a person very light in color. Everyone in the Renaissance, in his own way, was involved in that labor, but Hurston's efforts merit detailed attention here because she was so superbly perceptive, because her pioneering contribution has gone underrecognized, and because her efforts illustrate concretely the kind of work Renaissance people were doing in bringing up blackness. She was a native of Eatonville, Florida. She had striven painfully up through academia to become a student of anthropology with Franz Boas at Columbia University. One of her fellow students was Melville Herskovits, and many of those measurements of Harlemites upon which he based his conclusions in *The Anthropometry of the American Negro* were taken by Hurston during the summer of 1926.[17] In addition to walking around Harlem measuring the heads of willing subjects, Hurston did extensive research isolating and defining precisely how Negro culture in America was different from any other.

Among many things, Hurston concluded that Negro culture was "angular." Angularity was obvious in painting, sculpture, and dancing, she insisted. It was even present in the positioning of furniture in Negro homes. For instance, pictures would be hung slanting away from the walls at exaggerated angles. It was also evident in Negro music, where one saw sudden, surprising changes in key and rhythm, and where the lyrics began with a low-key, almost innocuous statement, then cut swiftly to a sharp and telling end. Such occurred, for instance, in these lines of "St. Louis Blues":

> Woke up this morning, feeling blue as I can be
> Woke up this morning, feeling blue as I can be
> Cause that no good woman
> Took my man from me.

Negro culture often went beyond simple angularity into asymmetry. It was not that one simply moved smoothly from one line to another at an angle where the two were joined. It was as if there were a space between the different lines, leaving them unjoined and seemingly disjunctive. But when the whole pattern was displayed, the audience filled in the spaces and knew that the parts did indeed fit into a broader, never explicitly stated whole. Satisfaction always required a "stretch" by the individual in the audience, a performance by himself complementary to that of the principal. Thus in ragtime the music not only changes directions, it suddenly stops and as suddenly starts up a different line in another key. Keys change frequently, and so does the rhythm. In black music anything can happen, and it always does. Lyrics exhibited the same proclivity toward asymmetry—for example, this verse by Langston Hughes:

> I aint gonna mistreat my good gal any more,
> I'm just gonna kill her next time she makes me sore.

Hurston saw the same phenomenon in the Negro dance. She thought that "the white dance attempts to express fully." A white dancer not only makes the suggestive motion but follows it out as well. The Negro dancer, more provocatively, offers the "dynamic suggestion" and seems to promise that "much more" is to come. The effect is to force the watcher "to finish the action the performer suggests." [18] Small wonder that Negro music, song, and dance were almost inimitable by whites, whose whole culture hungered for the full, complete, and smoothly rounded statement.

Hurston was also impressed by the importance of mimicry in Negro life. There were dances, for instance, that did animals (the buzzard lope), people in certain rituals (walking the dog), and even machines ("seabord," which was probably inspired by the performance of a locomotive on the Seaboard Coast Line, a railroad which ran squarely through the black belts of the east coast). Negroes, Hurston declared, also liked adornment and embellishment that whites would often consider chaotic and absurd. She visited a Mobile, Alabama, home in which she found a room crowded with furniture. The walls were plastered with Sunday supplements of the *Mobile Register*, and bore seven calendars and three wall pockets, one with a lace doily. Over the door was a large lithograph illustrating the Treaty of Versailles being signed with a Waterman pen. Behind the display, Hurston thought, was the assumption that "there can never be enough beauty, let alone too much." [19] Much the same might have been said of Negro dress. Among those who tried, it went beyond simple elegance into delightfully extravagant elegance. Overdressing, overacting, and overprancing were the very essence of that most popular Negro dance of the 1890s, the Cakewalk.

At the bottom of the Negro's expression, Hurston thought, lay drama, "something that permeates his entire self." In a sense, the Negro was still the primitive who thought in terms of pictures rather than words. Thus he was led to act out his thought, to illustrate it in some drama using his body. "There is an impromptu ceremony always ready for every hour of life," she concluded. "No little moment passes unadorned." She felt, apparently, that the Negro had not adopted the English language so much as he had adapted it. Because he used one thing to explain another, Negro expression was abundant in similes and metaphors. Because he saw pictures in motion, he would add an an action word to the noun to make a "close fitting word." Thus Negroes used such terms as "cook-pot," "chop-axe," and "sitting-chair." Because he acted out his thoughts, he would engage in the most extravagant language in describing how he would absolutely demolish his enemy. "I'll beat you till you smell like onions," he might say. Or, again, witness a verse by Langston Hughes in which a man speaks about his unfaithful lover:

> I brought her from the South and she's going on back,
> Else I'll use her head for a carpet tack.

Besides making up similes and metaphors, such as "syndicating" for gossiping, Negro language made verbs of nouns, as in "funeralize" and "jooking" for playing the jook (the guitar). Also very expressive (close-fitting) were double descriptives, such as "high-tall," "little-teeny" ("teeny" standing for tiny), and "kill 'em dead." [20]

Zora Hurston also saw a distinctive lack of privacy among Negroes. This she ascribed to their traditionally outdoor and communal style of life, and to their sense of drama. Thus good fighting and suggestions of good loving were as much to be performed publicly as a wedding or a funeral. Emotions were to be displaced and acted out in a dramatic fashion. Sexuality, she thought, was more explicit among Negroes. The songs, the dances, the folk tales were explicitly sexual, and lovemaking was raised to an art. "He swaggers. She struts hippily about," observed Hurston. "Songs are built on the power to charm beneath the bed-clothes." [21]

Hurston picked up the great truth that Negro life was not static, but rather highly fluid. She caught many of the blues songs and "new" dances in the flight of creation in the "jook" joints of the Negro world. A jook, sometimes spelled "juke," was a pleasure house, a place where men and women could drink, dance, gamble, and find sex. Jooks were usually located in the least attractive places in the Negro community—the "black bottoms," "Catfish Rows," and "blue heavens" of America. Beginning about 1890 the music in such resorts was provided by "boxes," which was another word for guitar, or jook. In time the guitar was supplanted by the piano; then came the foot-pumped player piano operated mechanically off a paper scroll, later the hand-cranked victrola, and finally the electric "Juke Box." Songs and dances would begin somewhere in the jooks and travel from one to another for years, up and down the Mississippi or along the "Seaboard" or anywhere, developing infinite variations. Finally, one version would burst into the white world and become the rage. For instance, the dance that was called the "Black Bottom" probably started in the jook section of Nashville, a rough and ready neighborhood around Fourth Avenue close to the Cumberland River. "Bottom" refers, not to a dancer's anatomy, but to the "bottom land" that is the river's flood plain, dark with silt but not the most valuable real estate in town. Often when the whites absorbed the new performance, they so altered it that Negroes did not recognize their own creation and referred to a dance as, for instance, the "new Black Bottom" and hastened to learn it.[22]

Hurston was a social scientist, and she attempted to separate out and examine the parts of Negro culture. She knew, as do we, that it was all of a piece and ultimately inseparable. It was impossible to describe in mere words each of the parts, mesh them together, and set them in motion. One place, however, where all came together in living motion was in the Negro church. Mary Cunard, an English aristocrat belonging to that distinguished family which, among other things, ran a steamship line, visited the United States in the 1930s. She was advised to attend a Negro church service. She chose Cullen's Seventh Avenue Methodist Church in Harlem. The preacher for the occasion was the famous "dancing evangelist" Elder Becton. Becton was said to have a faithful following of 200,000 souls from New York to Florida to Kansas. In the church Mary Cunard saw on the stage the special band of sisters clad in white, and the twelve disciples. She heard the superb band of musicians, the foot-patting, double-clapping, swinging and shouting joy of the singing. She saw Becton slip quietly onto the stage and was impressed with his "exquisite smartness (pearl-grey suit, top hat, cane, ivory gloves, his youthful look and lovely figure)." He preached, dancing about the stage, improvising, catching the audience up again and again with one rich image after another, elaborating, spinning out the theme. Sin was a "cat-foot" and a "double-dare devil" out to get you. The congregation joined in, punctuating his performance with shouts of "yeah man" and "tell it, tell it." Then, at the peak of excitement, Becton would turn suddenly, fall to a quiet mood, and whisper a phrase, such as "that inexpressible something by which I raise my hand," with an appropriate and graceful movement. Becton was supported in high style by his followers and their repeated gifts of what he called the "consecrated dime." "I told you, Lord, before I started out that I was a high-priced man, but you wanted me," he shouted. "God ain't broke!" [23]

In picking up the black heritage, Zora Hurston was doing what scores of other artists and intellectuals in the Renaissance were doing. Arthur Schomberg, for instance, began to gather what has become one of the great collections of materials relating to Negroes in America, today housed in the Schomberg Library in Harlem. Arthur Huff Fauset began the systematic collection of black folklore. Scores and scores of musicians picked up ragtime, blues, and jazz and elaborated

endlessly upon them. Langston Hughes celebrated Negro music in
poetry in *Weary Blues;* James Weldon Johnson eulogized black sermons by writing up seven sermons in poetic form and publishing
them under the title *God's Trombones.*[24] In song, in dance, in painting and sculpture, and in the theater, Renaissance people lauded black
as beautiful. Claude McKay loved to see Broadway productions performed in Harlem after their run on the great white way. "To me the
greatest charm is that the erotic movements are different," he explained. "And besides, 'The Negroes make their eyes talk.' Such eyes!
So luminously alive!"[25]

All of this was new, and it was, in terms of culture and race relations, revolutionary. Charles Chesnutt, for instance, in his pre-1900
stories took great pains to illustrate that there was really nothing mysterious or even very different about Negro culture in America. Indeed, for Chesnutt in those years, such difference as existed was tragic
because it was little more than the fruit of denial.[26] Even James Weldon Johnson, so ardent a convert later, early in the century could
only assume that ragtime was a low form of music that would make
its contribution ultimately, not by being appreciated in its own character, but by being absorbed into the classical forms of western music.
In his 1912 novel *Autobiography of an Ex-Colored Man,* he illustrated
that idea by having his protagonist, a ragtime pianist, play a piece for
an assembly of white musical sophisticates. Then he has one of these,
"a big bespectacled, bushy-headed man," rush over to the piano and
play the same piece beautifully enfolded in a sequence of western
forms—to the amazement and admiration of the protagonist.[27] After
the Renaissance, it was fully possible to think that black music could
stand by itself and was not dependent for its salvation upon inclusion
in the white world.

In picking up the culture of the Negro mass, artists and intellectuals in the Renaissance necessarily involved themselves in recognizing
the beauty of all colors and features among Negroes, from the darkest
to the lightest. Sometimes they did so in art, sometimes in literature,
folklore, and music. It meant, of course, the ultimate end of the mulatto elite and the full acceptance of the one-drop rule.

Unlike social scientists who confidently predicted her demise, Renaissance people did not intend to let the black girl vanish. Wallace

Thurman, who possessed one of the quickest and most critical minds of his time and who was himself black, wrote a novel in which he illustrated her very real problems and pointed to a solution—the acceptance of blackness. His protagonist is a black girl of intelligence and talent who suffers exploitation, material and sexual, precisely because she is black rather than brown. Ultimately, she finds her answer is to "accept her black skin as being real and unchangeable, to realize that certain things were, had been, and would be, and with this in mind to begin life anew, always fighting, not so much for acceptance by other people, but for acceptance of herself by herself." [28]

The black woman had her ready defenders and admirers in almost every genre, including the folklore from which Thurman derived the title of his novel, *The Blacker the Berry*. In the folklore the old saying ran, "the blacker the berry, the sweeter the juice." Equally popular, and suggestive of the machine age, was this often chanted verse:

> Oh de white gal rides in a Cadillac
> De yaller gal rides de same,
> Black gal rides in a rusty Ford
> But she gits dere just de same.[29]

There were blacks—and Negroes who were mostly black—who were not willing to forget their strong color and their African features. Nor did they despise themselves and want only to melt into the middle ground of the New Negro American. Blacks had pride, and their pride too had its exclusiveness. Always someone held up the sable banner. Martin Delany, for example, was a Virginia-born black abolitionist whose affinities led him to visit Africa before the Civil War and steadily to preach pride in blackness. In Renaissance Harlem itself, however, came the first great evocation of pure blackness in America.

The apostle of pure blackness in the 1920s was Marcus Garvey, a Jamaican of solely African ancestry. Paradoxically, Garvey was both in the Renaissance and out of it. He was in the movement in the sense that he shared and was a leader in the conscious promotion of black as beautiful. He was out of it in that he tended to equate pure blackness with pure morality and sought to excise black people from the corruption of mixture in America, primarily by transporting those of pure blood back to Africa.

Like Claude McKay, another black Jamaican, Garvey first came to America attracted by the Booker T. Washington style of bootstrap self-lift. Soon, however, he moved on to catch a vision of fundamental kinship between black people in Africa and the Americas. His plan was to colonize Afro-Americans in Liberia and build a strong base there to push the white imperialists off the continent. Once the pioneers had established a stronghold in the African homeland, their very success would attract waves of migrants from America, thus relieving the plight of the Afro-American while developing Africa. "Africa for the Africans" was his rallying cry. In Harlem in 1917 Garvey founded the Universal Negro Improvement Association and soon established his newspaper *Negro World* to promote his program. With flashing rhetoric, an imperious manner, and Napoleonic uniforms, Garvey gathered about 200,000 paying members into his organization. The association purchased ships that it formed into the "Black Star Line" to effect the return to Africa.

Garvey's affinity for an exclusive blackness might not have seemed so impossible in his native Jamaica, where 80 percent of the people were black and faced a distinct discrimination from the 18 percent who were mulatto. But in America, where Negroes were only about 10 percent of the total population and probably more than 75 percent of the Negroes were mulattoes, such an appeal was inherently limited. Garvey built a highly effective organization and mustered a very strong and very dark following, but his own emphasis upon racial purism was bound to render his followers a minority within a minority in the United States. Moreover, Garvey was soon to come into direct conflict with mulattoes in the Negro elite, and he came to hate them bitterly. Directly in his path stood W. E. B. Du Bois, and Garvey showed no hesitation in attempting to cut him down, and with him all the light-skinned leaders in the New World. "It will be useless," he warned, "for bombastic Negroes to leave America and the West Indies to go to Africa, thinking that they will have privileged positions to inflict upon the race that bastard aristocracy that they had tried to maintain in this Western world at the expense of the masses." [30] The mulatto elite retaliated, and, like the wolf going for the jugular, it went for Garvey's black racism. He made a good fight, but he was outnumbered, outgunned, and, within the American racial context, fundamentally wrong. A purely black racism could not long survive in the land. Even though Garvey could never have won, in the end he was defeated, not on the issue of his ideas, but rather on a technical matter. The Black Star Line was grossly mismanaged (shipping being a highly technical and complicated business), the Liberian government proved less than faithful to its commitments, and Garvey was forced out of the United States by the federal government under threat of imprisonment for fraud. [31]

Marcus Garvey failed in his purpose, but he had an important and lasting effect upon Negro America, as even his rivals conceded. First, he carried the idea of Africa as a homeland to the mass of American Negroes, who had theretofore been less touched by the idea than the intellectuals. Second, he demonstrated that Negroes in large numbers in America could organize themselves for racial ends outside of such white-allied institutions as the Republican party and the NAACP and beyond such limited Negro institutions as the churches and the fraternal orders. Finally, because he was a "purist" in race, he exalted the unmixed black as a superior type and tended to scorn people of mixed blood as mongrels. This was of course an impossible position, but it did serve effectively as a corrective to the premium that had long been given gratis to whiteness in the Negro community. In brief, Garvey offered black people a clear and pure heritage, an ideal of destiny and power, and a sense of self. When Garvey was done, the black berry was sweeter indeed.

The Renaissance also moved to save the very light Negro from slander. Ironically, by the 1920s the wheel had turned, and popular opinion supported the idea that a very light child born to a darker woman was the offspring of "white trash." Unfortunately, origins of that sort came to be associated, as we have seen, with certain complexions—e.g., "high yellow." In men, that color was often tied to the high-living, superdressed, sexually seductive trickster. He was represented by Du Bose Heyward in *Porgy* in a character beautifully named "Sportin' Life." [32] In real life, the singer Eartha Kitt knew all too well what it was to suffer abuse for having a skin too light and no visible father. She was born Eartha Mae Kitt on a South Carolina plantation where her mother was a farm worker. Her mother was dark, she was light. The next child was dark, and somehow Eartha Mae felt that it was her light skin that caused them to be driven away from the plantation. One of her first memories is of that awful flight. She was perhaps three, walking down "the long, dark, dusty road" at sundown, her mother carrying her baby sister, Pearl, she "holding tightly to my mother's hand," struggling to keep up. They slept in the woods that night, the next morning her mother foraged food from someone's garden. They arrived at her uncle's house; he refused them. "I don't want that yella gal in my house, I told you that before!", Eartha Mae heard as she was trying to distract herself by playing with the dog on the front porch. Her mother sobbed, pleaded; Eartha ran crying into the woods. A few days later the little family came to rest, employed to take care of an elderly woman and her farm. Eartha Mae was terrified that the woman would notice her light skin and send them away. She tried desperately to stay out of her sight. Finally, she realized with great relief that the woman was blind.[33]

Lena Horne knew the experience too. After she starred as an actress, singer, and dancer in the film *Stormy Weather* in 1942, she became the archetypal image in the white mind of the supersexy and probably sinful "high-yellow" woman. Actually she was purely a descendant of the mulatto elite and, on the white side, of the Carolina Calhouns. Her great-aunt, Lena Calhoun, had attended Fisk University. When W. E. B. Du Bois arrived at Fisk in 1885 to begin his freshman year, the very first night at supper he sat opposite "two of the most beautiful beings God ever revealed to the eyes of 17." One of them was Lena Calhoun. He always remembered that "far-off September night of 1885" when he first saw her.[34] Because her parents were separated, for a time in the 1920s Lena Horne lived with her uncle, a college professor, in Fort Valley, Georgia. In the local school she suffered all kinds of slander from other Negro children because of her "too light" skin. "I was often called a little yellow bastard because I had no visible, immediate family," she later recalled.[35]

Zora Neale Hurston, who knew so much about the life of the common folk, wrote a novel, *Jonah's Gourd Vine* (1934), in which the hero, John Buddy, is very light, the firstborn of a dark mother on a lower South plantation, and whose father is never identified. His mother marries, and bears a sequence of darker children by her husband. In an early scene Hurston has the mother defend, not John Buddy's origins, but his character in spite of his color before the onslaughts of the boy's dark stepfather. Finally the man, Ned, an ex-slave, invokes the white authority. "Dese white folks orta know and dey say dese half-white niggers got de worst part uf bofe de white and de black folks," he declares.

"Dey ain't got no call tuh say dat," John Buddy's mother replies. "Is mo' yaller folks on de chain-gang den black? Naw! Is dey harder tuh learn? Naw! Do dey work and have things lak other folks? Yas."[36]

Ironically, Renaissance leaders had to combat both extremes simultaneously. Even as they fought to save the black woman, they had to fight black purists like Garvey; and while they defended the "high yellow," they had to oppose a persisting exclusiveness among scattered elements of the mulatto elite. The "blue vein societies" had become very weak by the 1920s, but they did still exist. In Harlem itself there was "Striver's Row," a three-street section in which lived the more successful professional and business people of light color. Striver's Row actually was not very pernicious in exclusiveness, but nevertheless it took its full share of punishment for any pretensions it might make on grounds of color. The bon ton mulatto society in Washington in the 1920s was still the hard core of mulatto exclusiveness, and Renaissance leaders heaped coals of fire upon its head.

Artists and intellectuals in the Renaissance exalted all colors within the Negro community as beautiful. Claude McKay reviewed the most famous of the Harlem musicals, *Shuffle Along,* and loved it. But he did think the producers had missed a great opportunity to show the richness of variety in Negro beauty when they chose to display a very light line of chorus girls. "Instead of making up to achieve a uniform near-white complexion the chorus might have made up to accentuate the diversity of shades among 'Afro Americans' and let the white audience in on the secret of the color nomenclature of the Negro world. For, as the whites have their blonde and brunette, so do the blacks have their chocolate, chocolate-to-the-bone, brown, low-brown, teasing-brown, high-brown, yellow, high-yellow and so on. The difference on our side is so much more interesting. . . ."[37]

It is a paradox that in crushing color exclusiveness, the mulatto elite in the 1920s dissolved itself. Hughes, Johnson, Du Bois, Walter White, and Zora Hurston simply refused to see themselves as separated from their people by their light skin and Caucasian features. By the end of the 1920s it was no longer relevant to talk of a mulatto elite in other than personal terms. The mulatto elite had, in fact, dissolved itself willingly into the Negro elite, and the Negro elite would lead in "the fire next time."

The Harlem Renaissance exalted blackness, but it was also a conscious attempt to marry smoothly together the blackness and the whiteness inherent in Negro life in America. It was an attempt to melt together within the Negro community the African and the European heritage, each transformed and unconsciously mixed in this New World in slavery and in freedom. The Renaissance was a continuation and a new high plateau in the process, now conscious, of amalgamation that had begun significantly in the lower South during Reconstruction and received its first signal recognition in 1897 when W. E. B. Du Bois eloquently described "twoness" as the central experience of Negro life in America.[38] The Harlem Renaissance was an effort, the first great effort, to make a fusion, to melt the two into one. In a way it was an attempt to answer the question—not of whether to be or not to be, for that had already been answered—but of how to be. In part, the Renaissance was a meeting of the challenge raised by Du Bois to begin to merge those disparate and seemingly conflicting parts of white and black into a viable life. How to play black music on white instruments, how to say dark things in white words, how, figuratively, to offer black bodies in white suits—that was the initial task.

The special capacity that mulatto artists and intellectuals brought to the Harlem Renaissance was precisely a great facility with white instruments, white words, and white suits. Du Bois, James Weldon Johnson, Walter White, Langston Hughes, and Jean Toomer were not only very light of skin, they were very light in culture. They and other mulattoes in the movement were generations deep into whiteness—not just into its words and schemes of words, but into its ideas, the very essentials of whiteness as evolved over centuries. They had learned—almost intuited—the structure from their white fathers and mothers, they had taught it to their black students, and they knew it very well. What they brought to the marriage was valuable, as bones are valuable to a body. But for them it was valueless without the flesh of blackness. The black part was deep, and yet it was not well defined; it was more felt than explicated. Nevertheless, in the Negro world blackness was the difference that would give life to whiteness. And that exactly was the task: somehow to encompass whiteness with blackness, to give Negro life its most viable shape, really to make one world of two in the dark body.

First of all, it is necessary to say that artists and intellectuals in the Renaissance only effected the engagement and the marriage. They did not perfect the union, nor did they produce a progeny of perfect combination. What they did, essentially, was to make a beginning and to point the way. Jean Toomer was then and is today recognized by eminent scholars as the writer who made the first signal breakthrough in his book *Cane* in 1923. What he did in that volume was eagerly to embrace his black ancestry—not only the black peasant who followed emancipation but even the slave who had come before. For two generations the Negro elite had sternly, earnestly beat its way away from the slave experience. Now Toomer signaled the beginning of a revolution in Negro life by turning to accept a slave ancestry. It was but a beginning, but it was a commencement that would achieve great force in the 1960s and 1970s as scholars, black and white, turned to study black culture in slavery and to find there great strength and beauty. Admittedly, Toomer's marriage to deep blackness was ephemeral, but other artists and intellectuals in the Renaissance were more persistent and, in many ways, more successful.

One of these was Countee Cullen, probably the premier poet of the Harlem Renaissance. In his art he lived willingly in the thrall of the Romantic poets. His forms, his rhymes, his meters, and often even his passions were those of Byron, Keats, and Shelley. But yet the messages that he laid upon those vehicles were deeply black. The pair of poems that follow illustrate his superb talent for work in this vein. The form of the poems is classically western. They are lyrics consisting of three open quatrains with a rhyme scheme ABAB. They have the formal completeness of sonnets—that is, each raises a problem and offers a solution. The meter is jauntily western, resembling that used in "The Boy Stood on the Burning Deck":

### TO A BROWN GIRL

What if his glance is bold and free,
  His mouth the lash of whips?
So should the eyes of lovers be,
  And so a lover's lips.

What if no puritanic strain
  Confines him to the nice?
He will not pass this way again
  Nor hunger for you twice.

Since in the end consort together
  Magdalen and Mary,
Youth is the time for careless weather;
  Later, lass, be wary.
                                —Countee Cullen.


### TO A BROWN BOY

That brown girl's swagger gives a twitch
  To beauty like a queen;
Lad, never dam your body's itch
  When loveliness is seen.

For there is ample room for bliss
  In pride in clean, brown limbs,
And lips know better how to kiss
  Than how to raise white hymns.

And when your body's death gives birth
  To soil for spring to crown,
Men will not ask if that rare earth
  Was white flesh once, or brown.
                                —Countee Cullen.

The message seems to be that sexuality in youth is not only permissible but natural and highly desirable. Such lusty sentiments seem to reject outrightly the Calvinistic coolness and Victorian conventions of the white world. The poetry borders on blasphemy in suggesting that Magdalen, the whore, and Mary, the virgin, go hand in hand and are contained in the brown girl herself. Still, the girl is warned later to be wary, and, presumably, to settle down for the long pull, and the boy is reminded of the universality of death that dissolves color and gives life. Ultimately, one's own color is dissolved and so nourishes the life that follows.

The interpretation of poems in a literary way always seems a precarious endeavor; but a student of Negro life and history has little difficulty in interpreting the substance of these twin poems in his own terms. One thinks immediately of Charles S. Johnson's study of Negro youth in the black-belt South where the testimony of the lower-class children—the darker girls and boys—clearly demonstrated the high value placed on sexuality before marriage. Their words also indicated the general willingness of parties to marry if the girl became pregnant. After marriage, one was to be faithful—"later . . . be wary." [39]

One thinks too of the deeper history that Herbert G. Gutman affords in his close study of the Negro family. Looking at the census of 1900, he found that among Negro mothers "a significant number everywhere but especially in the rural places reported the birth of a child either prior to marriage or during the first year of marriage." Looking further back into plantation records duing slavery, he found a pattern in which slave girls ordinarily had sexual relations before marriage. Sometimes the single girl bore a child, but whether she did or not, she almost invariably married and remained faithful to a single husband until either he or she died and by him had a sequence of children. Gutman concluded that what he found in the South "closely resembled practices found in many other premodern cultures." [40]

John Blassingame, looking to Africa, observed that some peoples, though not all, institutionalized premarital sex in the interest of preparation for continuing family lines. "Because Africans viewed sex as a natural act and so highly valued children, they could neither conceive of the European concept of celibacy nor, like the European, regard sexual intercourse as dirty, evil, or sinful," he asserted. Nevertheless, strict fidelity was required after marriage. "While providing socially sanctioned forms for engaging in premarital sex, African societies generally forbade extramarital sex, punishing adulterers with heavy fines, divorce, slavery and sometimes death," Blassingame concluded. [41] It seems that Countee Cullen in that beautifully matched set of poems was, after all, neatly encapsulating an American fruit of African seed.

Cullen mixed black and white well in his art; he also mixed them well in his life. As a youth in New York he opted to attend De Witt Clinton High School. Almost totally white, Clinton was the public school for the gifted and college-bound. Countee meshed easily with his fellow students, was a leader among them, and finished twenty-fifth in a class of 600. Next he entered New York University, where he meshed well again and stood with the top eleven in his class to take his Phi Beta Kappa key. While he was a senior at the university, he published his first book, *Color* (1925)—with Harper's, an eminent white press. He had published some of the poems contained therein in *The Bookman, Harper's Magazine, The American Mercury, The Nation,* and *Poetry*—the most sophisticated popular journals of that time. *Color* won Cullen high praise. The appropriate professor at Harvard was widely noted to have judged one of his pieces the best lyrical ballad yet produced in America. In 1926 and 1927 he went on to Harvard to earn a master's degree with distinction. In 1928 he won a Guggenheim fellowship and had two years abroad, mostly in Paris in intimate association with other American writers. From De Witt Clinton on, Cullen moved often in the white world, and he moved well.

Culturally, Countee Cullen could be white, he could be black—he was both. To offer him as one who made the marriage well is not to argue that he made it perfectly. No one did, and probably no one could. It was Cullen himself, after all, who wrote the poetic echo to Du Bois's superb prose on the "twoness" of Afro-American life:

> Yet do I marvel at this curious thing:
> To make a poet black, and bid him sing!

And still Countee Cullen was black and he strove to sing. In his assessment of Cullen's work Houston A. Baker, Jr., concluded that "there is much continuity between the career of the Harlem Renaissance poet and the generations that have followed. As one glances from Cullen to present works and back, it is sometimes hard to tell the difference." [42] It seems very likely that the similarity springs from the fact that Harlem began what is not yet finished—the smooth union of white and black within the Negro world. That was, after all, a massive labor, and one could not expect it to be accomplished in one short decade, or even in a generation or two. It seems fully appropriate here to repeat Nathan Huggins's recent conclusion, in speaking of the Renaissance, that "we have worked from that moment ever since." [43]

The Harlem Renaissance was an internal integration of black and white within the Negro world, but it was also a reengagement of the white world, as such, and the Negro world. It could be said that the years from about 1830 to 1877 were years of relatively intense engagement between white and Negro cultures. Up until 1865 Southern whites were trying hard to convert black people into childlike replicas of white people, and the result was the infusion of a significant amount of white culture into the slave community and, of course, of black culture into the white community. During Reconstruction Northern whites came south to continue the effort as missionaries of all kinds—political, religious, economic, familial, and educational. After Reconstruction Northern missionaries retired, and Southerners failed to resume their prewar mission. Resulting was the disengagement and alienation of the two worlds. Black life went its own way, generating its own power and forging ahead in its own directions. Growing alienation reached its extreme during the turn-of-the-century years, an era that one historian has called the "nadir of the Negro." Apart and rigidly segregated from the white world, the Negro world was left to mature a culture very much its own. Negro culture did indeed mature, and in the Renaissance came to a rich bloom. Simultaneously reengagement was also growing, and alienation was on the decline. The reintegration of black and white that marks the twentieth century had its real beginning in the Harlem Renaissance in the 1920s.

The reengagement of white and Negro culture that evolved in Harlem differed from any that went before. For one thing, it proceeded from a very different array of human geography. In that earlier, mid-nineteenth-century integrative phase, more than 90 percent of the Negro people in the United States were scattered across fifteen slaveholding and ex-slaveholding Southern states, and they were vastly rural. In this twentieth-century phase, Negroes were concentrating in sections of the great cities, especially in the North, and most strikingly in Harlem. The reengagement of white and black, then, proceeded from relatively solid, discrete Negro bases. It was almost as if Negroes had fortresses from which they could sally forth into the white world and to which they could retire when they chose to do so. There was a new and rare sense of security, for instance, among Harlem Negroes. In the Harlem enclave, as Langston Hughes represents well through his character Jesse B. Simple, Negroes often felt that they had protection "from white folks."

Negroes in the Renaissance also came to reengagement and the new integration with an altered sense of self. They were learning to appreciate their blackness, and that very awareness gave them a new kind of strength. Now they came to white culture looking across, so to speak, rather than looking up or down. Whereas previously they had been largely unconscious of their blackness, or saw it on balance as a detriment to their progress, they now saw it as a positive value. The positiveness of the Renaissance exuded tremendous energy, it was attractive, and it had goods to trade at parity with the white world.

During the Renaissance Negro people for the first time in America broke into "high culture" in a way that white people recognized. The depth itself was often very impressive—as in music—but the breadth of the Renaissance was no less than astounding. From Walter White, W. E. B. Du Bois, Charles S. Johnson, and A. Philip Randolph in social and political action, to the writers, scholars, composers, musicians, dancers, and actors, and across to the painter Aaron Douglas, the sculptor Richmond Barthé, and the collectors of Afro-American cultural materials Arthur Schomburg and Arthur H. Fauset, Negro artists and intellectuals were spilling across the frontiers of high culture on a broad front. The breadth and the depth of the thrust reflected the essential maturity of the people whence it sprang. The Renaissance was compelling, in a large way, both to those who were in it and to those who touched it because it was, like that of Italy in the fourteenth century, the effort of a people in full if early bloom. It was a growth at the level of Petrarch rather than Dante. Again like that earlier movement, it was a profound revolution, a major change in cultural direction. The Harlem Renaissance was a pulling of the focus of life and living and of creative energy more fully into this world—to where Negro Americans had been and actually were. It said, in brief, that this life is worth living. One need not simply pray and wait. Rather relish this life as it is, and see its beauty. It was as if Negro Americans had come at last into the possession of their own bodies and the conscious exercise by themselves of their arms, legs, and minds. Like the child discovering control of his hands, the power of manouver was fascinating. Renaissance people seemed to shout, "Look what we can do!"

White America clearly felt the energy and the attraction of the

Renaissance, and it came consciously, deliberately to drink of the pleasant waters. Whites saw Negro shows, did Negro dances, sang and played Negro songs, read Negro books, and looked at Negro art. In addition to the ever ongoing unconscious contact, there was now appreciative contact. And the contacts went both ways—there would be conscious interpenetration in this integration.

The Renaissance contained the real beginning of the modern, twentieth-century phase of integration, the phase in which America is still involved. It was not an integration in politics or economics, but rather in the all-important cultural realm. Cultural integration in the Renaissance operated at various levels and in various ways. There were white intellectuals coming to Harlem, and Negro artists, intellectuals, and performers reached out of Harlem, not only into New York City, but into all America through poems, novels, plays, songs, humor, and performances of a wide variety.

White people shared in the Renaissance as white people in America had never shared in Negro culture before. At its most superficial level, contact consisted of white people simply coming to Harlem to enjoy the night life. Harlem in the time of prohibition became a place where one went after the theater to visit the cabarets, listen to the music, watch the dancing, and talk and drink the bootleg booze. At its worst it was slumming, at its best it grew into appreciation. Carl Van Vechten, born in 1880 in Cedar Rapids, Iowa, an English major at the University of Chicago, a music critic, novelist, and scintillating member of Manhattan's "smart set," was one of those who came to Harlem to play. Soon he brought with him a host of others. There seemed to be something in his desire for sharp contrasts and vivid experiences that drew him compulsively to Harlem virtually every evening in the first half of 1925.[44] Possibly Van Vechten came at first simply to exploit, but he remained to praise and finally to serve as cultural liaison between the Harlem elite and that of Manhattan. One level of that communication was revealed by a note which James Weldon Johnson, then executive secretary of the NAACP, wrote to Van Vechten after a night on Harlem. "I enjoyed myself inordinately on the cabaret jaunt," he confessed. "I guess it does a fellow good once in a while." [45]

Van Vechten served the Renaissance in a multitude of ways. He encouraged Negro writers and introduced them to eminent white publishers. Specifically, he took Langston Hughes as his protégé and solidly promoted his first important book in 1925. He brought Alfred A. Knopf and his wife to Harlem, with the result that Knopf's interest was increasingly stimulated, and a series of works came out of his presses by Negro authors, including a reprint of Johnson's own *Autobiography of an Ex-Colored Man* (1912). Before the Renaissance Negro writers were published typically either as curiosities or in disguise. As was the case with Charles Chesnutt, most people did not know that they were Negroes. During the Renaissance, and in part through the help of intermediaries like Van Vechten, Knopf, and others, Negro writers suddenly found themselves supported in their work and able not only to publish books in presses heretofore lily white but also to penetrate the most expensive and intellectual of the popular white magazines.[46]

Another facet of the coming of the white writers and intellectuals to Harlem was that they did indeed begin to take up Negro characters and themes in their own work in a new and praising way, and with compelling intensity. White writers had written about Negroes before, of course. Herman Melville and Harriet Beecher Stowe had published very powerful novels in the previous century. In 1892 William Dean Howells had published a novel about the tragedy of the light mulatto, *An Imperative Duty*, and Gertrude Stein did *Melanctha* in 1909. But during the Renaissance the volume of production by white writers on Negro themes swelled impressively. Van Vechten himself wrote *Nigger Heaven* (1925), in which the protagonist was a Harlemite named Byron Kasson who failed ultimately because he was not true to his blackness. Du Bose Heyward, a low-country South Carolina aristocrat and friend of James Weldon Johnson, wrote the book *Porgy*. That story became the basis for the great musical *Porgy and Bess*, featuring music by George Gershwin and including the song "Bess You Is My Woman Now." In the same rush Paul Green, a young North Carolinian, did *Abraham's Bosom*, Eugene O'Neill did *Emperor Jones*, and Marc Connelly did *Green Pastures*. Waldo Frank, the critic and writer who had befriended Jean Toomer, published his novel *Holliday*. What writers were doing in literature Paul Whiteman was doing in music. He translated Negro music into white forms and discovered that his work had instant and widespread appeal—with the result that his own style was widely copied and Negro styles were broadcast across the western world.[47]

White people came into Harlem and carried Negro culture away; Negro artists and intellectuals also carried their work directly out into the white world. Literature offers an obvious example, but music probably reached more people than any other form. Noble Sissle, one of the producers of *Shuffle Along*, organized a large band that traveled in much the same style as did Whiteman's, moving from one city to another playing to very large audiences. On one occasion the band was in Cincinnati when Sissle was hospitalized by an automobile accident. In the crisis he summoned his seventeen-year-old singer to his bedside and passed the baton to her less than willing fingers. She would have to conduct, he insisted. That night a thoroughly frightened young woman stood before the band. To her surprise she found that no matter what she did, the band played as smoothly and superbly as usual. She soon learned that the band followed the first saxophone regardless of the vagaries of the baton. Moreover, the audience loved her performance, whatever it was. Lena Horne would always insist that she was a better actress than conductor.[48] Very often, Negro artists created specifically for the white world things that the white world came to relish—even though it did not always remember their sources. Noble Sissle and Eubie Blake, for example, wrote the song "You Were Meant for Me," with which Noel Coward and Gertrude Lawrence debuted as a team.[49]

Negro actors also began to penetrate the white world. As late as 1917 a play written by Ridgely Torrence about Negro people was done by white actors in blackface. It was an extreme irony that even when Negro actors played the parts of Negroes in stage plays, they were often required to make up in blackface. The stereotype of wide mouth and big eyes had gained such strength that a Negro actor could not simply portray a Negro; he had to be the Negro that the whites in their minds had made. In the Renaissance that all began to change rapidly. First Charles Gilpin in 1921 and then Paul Robeson after 1925 did much to shatter the tradition when they so brilliantly played the lead role in Eugene O'Neill's *Emperor Jones* (1921). Of course white entertainers in blackface continued, Al Jolson doing "Mammy" in vaudeville and Eric Von Stroheim portraying a Negro soldier in the film *The Birth of a Nation*. Amos and Andy in effect did blackface by voice on radio. But from *Emperor Jones* on, Negroes somewhere were always seriously portraying Negroes on the American stage.[50]

As whites came to Harlem and Harlem went out into the white world, each was giving to each—and taking. The exchange was always in motion and symbiotic. Of course, the filters of each culture were always at work. When white people heard a Negro song or saw a Negro dance, they heard it with white ears and saw it with white eyes. The result was that something always changed in translation. When Negro people saw white culture, their filter also functioned. A good example of such symbiosis with filters is the history of the "Black Bottom," as described above. Whites learned it from Negroes, but when Negroes saw it performed by whites, they did not recognize their own creation. They rushed to learn the "new Black Bottom," and without doubt created still another mutation in that translation.

The interchange between Negro and white was strikingly evident in music and dancing. These two came brilliantly together in the Harlem "reviews" of the 1920s. The reviews included very simple stories and fantastically rich singing and dancing. The all-Negro musical went back to the minstrel shows of the mid-nineteenth century. In that time many of the minstrels who played Negroes were white, but in the 1890s Negro artists began to come into their own, not only as performers but also as composers, writers, and producers. One of the pioneers was Ernest Hogan. In a Chicago brothel in the 1880s Hogan discovered a ragtime tune that he refined into one of the hit songs of the 1890s, "All Coons Look Alike to Me." Thus was born the genre of the "Coon song," which was simply a ragtime piece with words about Negroes. Later he used the same ragtime form to write two other hits, "Rufus Rastus Johnson" and "Won't You Come Home Bill Bailey." Essentially Hogan had merely discovered an aspect of the basic creative vigor of Negro culture and exploited it. He had plugged into a strong and growing current of Negro music that sparked across America from brothel to brothel, from brothel to juke joint and back again. It was carried by precisely such people as Scott Joplin, who was to become famous for his own "Maple Leaf Rag," and the fictional protagonist of Johnson's *Autobiography of an Ex-Colored Man*, and it possessed a variety and richness that was almost incredible. In the early years of the twentieth century, for instance, Negro piano players in brothels and juke joints were actually primary contributors to the rash of "Indian" songs that appeared about that time. In the year 1912 the sporting houses rang with ragtime tunes carrying Indian themes, including such lasting favorites as "Red Wing," "Pony Boy," and "Come with Me to My Big Teepee." It is debatable whether or not such interest was inspired by the fact that several million Negroes were in part Indian, but it is clear that Negro musicians did much to shape the musical imagery of Indians in the white American mind.[51]

In the 1890s two pioneer Negro musical performers, George Walker and Bert Williams, conceived of the idea of having Negro Americans actually play Negro Americans for white audiences by the device of putting them into a foreign and hence neutral setting. At first, the setting used was Africa. The inspiration came from their participation in the Dahomeyan exhibit in the San Francisco Winter Fair in 1893. The native Dahomeyans employed did not arrive in time to open the exhibit. American Negroes substituted, including Walker and Williams, with no sign of disapproval from whites who were aware of the fact. It seemed that American Negroes could portray real people without offending white racial sensibilities . . . if the setting were foreign. Walker's and Williams's first production in this style, *In Dahomey* (1902), was a great success. It consisted of a thin story about two American Negroes in that African country, their adventures, funny and hazardous, and intriguing songs and dances. The show allowed the authors to offer Negroes in royal settings and regal attitudes. In short, it allowed them to break the stereotype and be themselves. This production and those that followed—*Abyssinia* (1906) and *Bandana Land* (1908)—carried low-key messages about race relations in the United States. George Walker died in 1909, just as relations between whites and blacks in America reached a new low level of intolerance. From 1910 to 1917 Bert Williams was the sole Negro permitted to appear in the otherwise lily-white mainstream American theater. He survived only as a singer and dancer doing a blackface single act in the Ziegfield Follies. Being too light, he was required, ironically, to use burnt cork to darken his face and thus to fulfill the stereotypical white image of the Negro.[52]

In 1921, after a slow reentry by Negroes into show business, Noble Sissle and Eubie Blake produced an all-Negro musical review that they called *Shuffle Along*. *Shuffle Along* was all-Negro in cast, and it first played in what was generally regarded as a Negro theater, but it combined what had been going on in the white musical reviews with elements that were uniquely Negro. It started a style that gained great strength in the mid-twentieth century—on stage, in films, and, finally, in television.

Before 1921 and *Shuffle Along* there was really no such thing as a chorus line that both sang and danced. There were dancing acts, and there were beautiful girls on stage who sang in chorus, but the two were not joined effectively. There were, for example, "the Floradora Girls," an English import in the early 1900s. They were a sextet of lovely girls in the style of that age, very round of limb, figure and face, with rosebud lips, peaches-and-cream complexions, and volumes of hair. They were gorgeously attired, with frills, flounces, and low necklines. They sang sweetly as they moved slowly and regally about the stage. Most appealingly, each girl picked out some gentleman in the audience at whom she smiled and winked. Needless to say, the original set of Floradora Girls did not last long, as one after another made an advantageous American marriage. They were replaced by American girls, who, in turn, soon passed on to their marital rewards. Though the "team" was only six in number, the players eventually

numbered about seventy.[53] The Floradora Girls were more ornamental than active. *Shuffle Along* not only had beautiful girls, beautifully and briefly dressed, but they danced and sang. They danced
and sang, not in the structured way of the white world, but in a way
that would delight America.

Eubie Blake, who composed much of the music for *Shuffle Along*,
told Nathan Huggins in an interview in 1973 just how that show
differed from what had gone before:

> E. B. But I'll tell you how we changed shows. Ziegfeld, George
> White, the Shuberts. . . . They all had reviews with girls—beauti-
> ful girls. They walked around in beautiful clothes. The people
> who danced in these shows were specialties. These shows didn't
> have a real chorus. These girls in beautiful costumes would just
> walk and kick a little. So, we came in with our show. Our girls
> were beautiful, and they *danced!!!* They *danced!!!* And they
> *sang!!!* Those others didn't do nothing but [sing] "A Pretty Girl is
> Like a Melody . . ." and all were beautiful. But after you had
> seen them once, well, that's it. But our girls were—white people
> have a name they call dancers—hoofers—these girls DANCED!!!
> There had never been anything like it. You could see a little danc-
> ing in burlesque, but better people didn't go to burlesque, espe-
> cially ladies.
>
> N. H. So, *Shuffle Along* brought the dancing chorus to the shows.
>
> E. B. They danced. You see, I wrote rhythmic tunes so that they
> could dance. You know rhythm is the most—rhythm and laughing
> is the most contagious thing in the whole world. . . .[54]

In *Shuffle Along* Negro people were doing what they felt came
naturally. It was beautiful, it was dynamic, and white people were
attracted. They saw in it a kind of "letting go" from the straight,
pressurized Victorian life that they usually pursued. It was an emotional and a physical liberation. *Shuffle Along* was free, loose, as unrestrained as its most popular song, "I'm Just Wild about Harry."
And it was as satisfying as the second line that added that "Harry's
wild about me." All of this was celebrated appropriately by enthusi-
astic, ecstatic steps, gestures, and faces. White people came, and they
were lifted out of themselves. The reviewer for the New York
*Herald* thought that when "the chorus and the principals" danced,
"the world seems a brighter place to live in." In his eyes, "they fling
their limbs about without stopping to make sure that they are securely

fastened on." Puritan America, Victorian and sedate America, could hardly imagine being so careless with one's limbs, and flapper America was barely beginning to allow itself to be insecure. In the Negro musical white "strivers" found a looseness, an abandon not afforded in their tight worlds, little or large, and they let themselves go vicariously. The reviewer in the *American* caught it just so as he described the cast on stage. "They revelled in their work; they simply pulsed with it, and there was no let-up at all. And gradually any tired feeling that you might have been nursing vanished in the sun of their good humor and you didn't mind how long they 'shuffled along.' You even felt like shuffling a bit with them," he confessed. "How they enjoyed themselves! How they jigged and pranced and cavorted and wriggled and laughed. . . ." [55]

*Shuffle Along* was indeed a signal beginning. It launched such stars as Josephine Baker, who was a young girl in the chorus line, and Florence Mills, who had a brief but spectacular show-business career in that decade, including starring roles in hit musicals in Paris and London. In the 1920s every year saw its Negro review, sometimes two of them, and they moved downtown to Broadway. Following *Shuffle Along*, came *Seven-Eleven, Strut Miss Lizzie, Liza,* and *Dixie to Broadway. Runnin' Wild* in 1924 introduced a dance called the Charleston. The Charleston was another of those "juke joint" dances that probably began in Carolina and moved up and down the east coast for a dozen years before emerging into the white world. Ethel Waters did *Africana* in 1927, and Bill "Bojangles" Robinson opened in *Blackbirds* in 1928, a show that ran for 518 performances. The era closed in 1929 with *Hot Chocolates*, featuring Thomas "Fats" Waller's song "Ain't Misbehavin'." [56]

In its highest essence the Renaissance never died, and it lived and grew in the white world as well as the black. During portions of the 1940s, one could not turn on the radio for half a day without hearing Phil Harris sing one of Bert Williams's most famous songs, "Darktown Poker Club." During the 1950s and on into the 1960s, every Saturday night millions of Americans sat down in front of their television sets to watch "The Jackie Gleason Show." First they saw a series of ravishingly beautiful girls, gorgeously dressed, who moved about a bit and smiled and said a line just as the Floradora Girls used to do. Then they saw the June Taylor Dancers performing like a chorus line out of a Eubie Blake show. None of the dancers seemed Negro, and the dances were a bit too structured to be Negro, but lord, did they dance—arms and legs flying at such a rate that one feared for their continuing bodily unity. And did they ever have pep

and vitality! There were angular, sharp turns and thrusts and kicks—
their movements did almost defy belief. When they had finished, even
the viewers wiped their brows and breathed hard. *Shuffle Along*
seemed alive and well, and so too were the Floradora Girls. They
were not yet totally merged, but they did exist in a happy contigu-
ity. And few viewers, probably, had an idea how "Negro" was this
most popular dance performance of its kind in that era.

All of this might seem a bit far from the subject of the mulatto,
but the point is that during the Harlem Renaissance and after, black
and mulatto people in America were generating a mulatto culture.
American Negroes were themselves by this time vastly fused, and the
color line within the Negro world was rapidly becoming little more
than a matter of personal preference. In the vastly more important
cultural sphere what was happening was that all Negroes were involved in the marrying of their white heritage to their black heritage,
and evolving a culture that would afford a new and higher satisfaction
to Negro life.

The tradition is that the Harlem Renaissance died in the 1930s, the
victim of the great depression. In one sense, the tradition is accurate.
The money was important, and it did evaporate. More vitally, the
positiveness, the joyousness, the celebration that often marked the productions of the Renaissance gave way to bitter feelings about the injustices done to Negro people in America. In bitterness, in frustration,
some Negro artists and intellectuals such as Du Bois and the actor Paul
Robeson turned to Marxism, communism, and Russia for relief. However, many of those who turned away soon discovered that a white
man's ideology, for instance, Marxism, was hardly less ruthless than a
white man's personal ego in its readiness to use and abuse people of
other races for its own ends. In the 1940s many of these thoughtful
people, disillusioned, were adrift, and a few even lost their grip on
their blackness and melted into the white world. In that decade Ralph
Ellison's "invisible man," a man in search of his identity, beautifully
bespoke the incertitude of the future of Negroes in America—even
as he also symbolized the determination of Negroes never to say die.

The 1950s brought both great unity and clear directions to the
evolution of Negro life. The change came during an era in which
European civilization was engaged in a great civil war between fas-

cism and liberalism, when the imperialist world order of the previous three centuries was in the final stages of dissolution, and when communism had become a serious contender for international dominance. The United States from 1941 to the present has been reluctantly but vitally involved in each of these great events, and each has impacted upon race relations in America to improve the bargaining potential of Negro leadership. During World War II America needed the help of its Negro tenth in a massive effort to win that struggle, and Negro leaders exacted a price for that aid, primarily in the economic realm. During the Cold War that followed, communist leadership made much of its commitment to the freedom of the imperialized peoples of the world, most of whom were nonwhite and who, just then, were emerging into independence amid the ruins of crumbling empires. Color distinctions, communist leaders insisted, were but another device of the imperialists to divide and rule the working masses everywhere. In identifying imperialist exploitation with whiteness, communists developed a very powerful tool for expanding their influence among the colored peoples of Africa, Asia, and elsewhere. The United States, casting itself as the leading defender of freedom against the communist champion Russia, could hardly seem to oppress colored people at home if it would vie with the Russians for alliances with colored peoples abroad. Equal-opportunity employment in defense industries during the war, the desegregation of the armed services by presidential order after the war, the series of Supreme Court rulings that led to the Brown decision in 1954, the subsequent desegregation of public accommodations generally, and the official honoring of the civil rights of Negroes were all, among many things, white necessities in the power play of great nations.

White leadership was forced to make concessions, but Negro leadership defined what would be conceded, and that, in turn, was broadly decided by what Negro people wanted. What Negro people wanted in the civil rights movement (often termed "the second Reconstruction") as it occurred between 1941 and 1965 was very much what they had wanted and not achieved in the first Reconstruction. In a word, they wanted "in." They wanted equal access with whites to economic opportunity, to public accommodations, to participation in politics, government, and the courts. More broadly, they wanted the dignity of unabridged citizenship. In the first Reconstruction the pursuit of these goals had been highly optimistic, perhaps naively so in the face of the realities. In the dozen years after general emancipation in 1865 Negroes were still too much split by divisions between the old free and the newly freed, and by profound differences in wealth, education, sophistication, and color to confront successfully the myriad manifestations of white racism. A century of hard striving since the 1850s had not reduced white racism, but it had, as we have seen, increasingly melded the Negro people together, not only in the genetic sense but also in the all-important cultural sense. By the end of World War II Afro-Americans were preset for union, and they were poised to move with power. When they began a mass movement in 1955, it possessed terrific force, and it had a concerted leadership.

In the first Reconstruction Negro leadership had been much diffused; in the second it was to be distinctly concentrated. Probably Frederick Douglass, who had made his reputation initially as the foremost Negro abolitionist, was the Negro leader most widely known in the years after the Civil War. Real power, however, was spread broadly and thinly among hundreds of less famous folk, mostly in the South, beginning with two United States senators and twenty-two congressmen and working on down through numerous local politicians and across to hundreds of ministers and educators. In 1895 Booker T. Washington was catapulted to the fore and thereafter he presumed to speak for all Negroes. But he had hardly arrived at the head before he was vigorously challenged by W. E. B. Du Bois and others. In 1955 Martin Luther King, Jr., the twenty-six-year-old minister of the Dexter Avenue Baptist Church in Montgomery, was tapped to lead a bus boycott in Alabama's capital city. King was not so much the ambitious volunteer as he was the conscientious draftee. Nevertheless, he emerged from the year-long struggle not only victorious but nationally known and powerful as the head of the Southern Christian Leadership Conference. The SCLC, which was very much a grand coalition of Southern Negro churches as institutions and ministers and members as individuals, was the civil rights organization that grew out of the boycott.[57] Negro America had generated a preeminent leader, and the leader evinced a style distinctly different from any that had gone before. Moreover, the leader and his lieutenants perfected a method, nonviolent demonstrations, that would work to promote great unity among Negroes and prove to be highly effective in securing their rights.

One should not overemphasize the dominance in the civil rights movement of the SCLC or of Martin Luther King. There were other organizations, and there were other leaders. But for a time the style in which the SCLC operated set the style of the civil rights movement generally, and the Conference stood first among organizations formed to achieve the civil rights of Negroes, eclipsing even the venerable, prestigious, and secular NAACP. And Martin Luther King did speak for Negro Americans with a consent that was overt, willing, and effective in a degree that no other person had ever achieved. King at first had not offered himself boldly or with the seeming self-confidence of Washington or Douglass or Du Bois. Indeed, like that other prime-moving protestant for whom he was named, he stood where he stood because, in conscience, he could do no other. In a sense Washington was appointed by whites to speak for Negroes; in every sense King was appointed by Negroes. Washington had stirred great loyalties among Negroes, but he had also roused great and serious animosities. Comparatively, before 1965 King generated only loyalty. Even though both men were mulattoes, Washington was an educator, the primal profession of the mulatto elite, and King was a minister, the primal profession of the black elite. Washington was consciously, even assiduously secular, as were Du Bois and Douglass. King was profoundly religious—in style, in tone, and in his essence. So too were such close lieutenants as Ralph Abernathy, Jesse Jackson, and Andrew Young—and the movement they all represented.

King's power was, ultimately, the rising power of the Negro people. If there had been conflict within the Negro world before, if there had been rivalry between mulatto and black perspectives, King inherited the rising synthesis of a Negro perspective a century in the making and the power that went with the emergence of that great conjunction. It is almost inconceivable that one person could have stood out as the leader of the Negro people in the first Reconstruction, so disparate were the personal histories of Negroes, their values, and goals. In 1895 when Booker T. Washington stepped onto the stage in Atlanta, it is inconceivable that Negroes could have chosen a leader who could announce goals that were not highly acceptable to the white world. By 1955, however, color was gaining power in the world, and Negro Americans had progressed far in the building of a cultural synthesis out of the rich and many-parted materials of their past. They were ready and able to claim a larger and fairer share of American life for themselves, and King appeared to lead them to that goal.

When King brought Negroes to confront whites, the effect was to cause whites to confront themselves. In some degree the confrontation was generated by what Gunnar Myrdal had called "an American dilemma," the fact that America claimed to be democratic yet excluded its Negro tenth from the democracy. But there was involved another, often much more disturbing confrontation of white ideals with white practice. Christianity did not license racial discrimination, America in its own eyes was religious, and perhaps nowhere more so than in the South. Rightly or wrongly the South had gained a reputation as the "Bible belt," and undeniably it had given rise to a stream of crusading evangelists whose ministry was enthusiastically welcomed outside of the region. But the South was also a stronghold of racism, and it would be the prime target in the civil rights movement. Frederick Douglass had been forced to wage his campaign for the recognition of the humanity of Negroes from the North. Booker T. Washington based his campaign in the South, but made it soft. W. E. B. Du Bois and the NAACP revived the hard line, but, like Douglass, they cast it forth from Northern bases.[58] King brought the flag of command south again. He led a campaign that was nonviolent, but it was not soft and it was effective.

It was the genius of Martin Luther King that he used Southern religion to attack Southern racism. He was himself a proper son of the South, and the heir of all that I have talked about heretofore in the mixing of black and white. He carried within his own body white blood as well as black, and he carried too in himself the peculiar mixture of black and white that was Southern Christianity. In his very bones he knew the whole South, and he spoke the language. He spoke most of all as a man of God. The round voice, the rich imagery, the rhythm and repetition were classic to the black ministry. His message from the Negro people to Southern whites was unmistakably Christian. It was that we are all God's children, that we Negro people are walking as Christ walked, that we love—as Christ loved—even those who oppress us, and that we offer our bodies to the fire hoses, the police dogs, and the beating sticks of Birmingham for the salvation of all our souls. It would be a happy thing if one could say that white Southerners recognized the rightness of the cause and revolutionized their lives to deal humanely with black people. But they did not. Most often in the crisis of confrontation, they became violent. But in the process they fell into confusion and disorientation, with the result that old lines were loosened, ranks were broken, and Negroes were able, with outside assistance, to move through the breech. The nonviolent method of the movement hacked the Christian sensibilities of the white South. It also excited the active sympathy of the nation and, indeed, the world. It was totally fitting that in 1964 Martin Luther King was awarded the Nobel Peace Prize. In leading Negroes in America as he did, he had indeed served the cause of world peace.

By the time the second Reconstruction got underway, the mulatto elite had given way to a Negro elite, and the strategy was to achieve equal rights through integration. In effect the Negro elite between 1941 and 1965 carried through the last phase of the mission that the mulatto elite had undertaken in the first Reconstruction. The civil rights movement was a last hard push to get into the white world. The Harlem Renaissance gave great power to that movement—and to the "Soul movement" that followed. By the end of the Renaissance the integration of black and mulatto had already proceeded so far as to establish, genetically, the "brown" American as the norm. But as I have said, the greatly important mixing was cultural. The marrying of black with white that had begun in the 1850s proceeded rapidly during Reconstruction and was pursued assiduously during the Renaissance. It was perfectly symbolic that, at the end of the Renaissance decade, Horace Mann Bond heard a seemingly "blue-eyed Anglo-Saxon" speaker declare to an assembly of Negroes "the necessity that all of us black men in America and the world stand together." The speaker was probably Walter White, field secretary of the NAACP. White exemplified Bond's assertion that those who chose to pass had passed quietly over the line, and those who remained could then devote themselves unequivocally and wholeheartedly—as did White—to "the immediate task of survival." By the 1930s the Gibsons and mulattoes of lighter hue who had chosen the white side were indeed lost to the Negro world. Their black past was increasingly dissolved in the rushing white waters, and the thought of their blackness was perhaps often more a lingering suspicion than a certain memory. On the other side, the Metoyers, the Walter Whites, and the Bonds themselves had picked up the cross of their blackness and cast their lives with Negro America.

The civil rights movement was, relative to all that went before, a new high success for the Negro in America. That success was in some measure made possible by the state of the world, but it was greatly the product of a unity of Negro leadership and Negro followership, and that conjunction had much to do with what came out of the 1920s generally and the Harlem Renaissance in particular. Renaissance writers, artists, and intellectuals had given the mass of Negro Americans elements through which they could establish a communion. For instance, in the 1930s and 1940s Negro children, taught by teachers who had themselves been taught in Negro institutions, did learn black history, black music, and black literature. They knew who Langston Hughes and W. E. B. Du Bois were when white children did not. The commonality of their knowledge was not always conscious even as it grew stronger in the 1930s and 1940s, but it was made very evident in the quick and ready union of Afro-Americans in the 1950s and early 1960s.

Civil rights leadership too had direct connections with the Renaissance. A. Philip Randolph organized a march on Washington in 1941 from his long-time Harlem office, the headquarters of the Brother-hood of Sleeping Car Porters. In the 1930s and 1940s the NAACP under Harlemites James Weldon Johnson and Walter White, with W. E. B. Du Bois in close support, pushed with deliberate speed down the judicial road to compel America to honor its promise of civil equality to all its people. The Brown case in 1954 was an NAACP effort, and if it had not been the Brown case that broke the back of legal segregation, it would have been another of the several cases the Association was bringing to the fore.

It might mean nothing at all that Martin Luther King, Jr., and his wife named their firstborn daughter Yolanda and Du Bois had named his child Yolande, but it is a striking continuity that the Montgomery bus boycott King came to lead had actually been planned by the local chapter of the NAACP and its associates for months before it occurred. Rosa Parks, who began the action by refusing to yield her seat to a white person, was no simple seamstress, tired of body by a long day of labor and tired of spirit by years of denial, who all by her single self declared that she had had enough. She was, in fact, lately the secretary of the Montgomery chapter of the NAACP and had attended the Association's leadership school in Monteagle in east Tennessee. She and her colleagues had already achieved a number of minor victories against discrimination in the city, and they had orig-inally planned the protest and boycott to begin several months before. A postponement was thought wise when the young woman who was supposed to "sit in" had become pregnant. Rosa Parks did act upon impulse, but the chain of action in the Negro community that fol-lowed had long been pondered by local Negro leadership. The local NAACP itself eagerly inaugurated the active response in the Negro community, and it was the head of the Montgomery chapter (E. D. Nixon, a vigorous member of Randolph's Brotherhood of Sleeping Car Porters) who recruited an initially careful Reverend King to join the effort. King soon rose both to lead and to personify the civil rights movement, and it would seem at first glance that he and the movement sprang fully matured and without visible parentage from a Montgomery bus boycott spontaneously begun. In reality he in-herited a movement already underway and a leadership cadre pre-formed and well prepared for its role.[59]

Thus the debt of King's power to the organized leadership that had gone before was direct and great, but no more so than its debt to a risingly self-conscious Negro culture. For all their great diversity and internal rivalries, Negro Americans had come to value the same essential things, and they spoke the same language. Through the schools and the churches, through a common culture and a common religion, King, the SCLC, and the other organizations in the civil rights movement united Negro leaders and followers throughout the South and the nation as they had never been united before, and this time when Negroes moved they moved with great concert. The power of the fusion was evident when they met in the schools and the churches to move together in great numbers out into and through the streets. The goal remained the achievement of a fair share of the good things in American life, but the tactics were the tactics of a new generation, the next generation of the Negro elite. Previously, Negro leaders had come into courts as plaintiffs under the laws; now they came in as defendants protesting the laws. And in the new generation, there was no mulatto elite. In that vanguard were such young people as Horace Mann Bond's son, Julian. His career, like that of others among his contemporaries, rapidly took him from the streets and student activism into politics. He went first into the Georgia House of Representatives and then into the Democratic National Convention in 1968, where he stood for the vice presidential nomination of the party. Julian Bond was more than half white, but no one ever accused him of not being black.

The civil rights movement was a vast effort at integration. Ultimately, however, Negro Americans decided, quite prudently, that they did not want simply to be "in," to be merely white Americans with dark skins. In 1965 and for roughly a decade thereafter, "black separatism" gained strength and with it rose ideas of "black power" and "black nationalism." Violence displaced nonviolence as riots came to Watts, Washington, and dozens of other major cities in the North and West. Raised black fists displaced the interlocking of black and white arms and the singing of "We Shall Overcome." Malcolm X and the young radicals Stokely Carmichael, Rap Brown, and Huey Newton took stage center, and the South lost its nearly exclusive reputation as the heartland of racism in America.

As the ideal of getting into the white world declined in attractiveness after 1965, the ideal of getting out gained, and Negroes at large began to turn back again toward their blackness. This aspect of the Negro Revolution has often been called the "Soul movement." Inevitably in that movement, the Harlem of the 1920s would be re-discovered and revived in close detail, and the legacy of the Renais-sance would be brought forward and utilized to fulfill modern needs. Just as the civil rights phase of the Negro Revolution had pushed for-ward the work signally advanced by the mulatto elite in the first Reconstruction to integrate Negroes into the good things of American life, so would the Soul movement push forward the work promoted by the mulatto elite in the Harlem Renaissance to keep Negro Ameri-cans significantly black.

In the broadest sense the Renaissance had never died. Like its Euro-pean model, it was a part of all that followed. Many Renaissance people lived through the 1930s and some on into the 1960s. Some of them changed, others did not. Those who continued to sing loudly the beauties of blackness were, in a measure, divorced from the neces-sities of Negro life and lost much of their audience. In the last half of the 1960s and in the 1970s, however, black and white in the Negro world came together again. The full Renaissance was revived and elaborated and fared smoothly into the Soul movement. "Black is beautiful" was the explicit slogan of the Soul movement, and modern Americans naturally remembered that precisely such had been the essential message of the Renaissance. The Soul movement was in every major way an extension of the Renaissance. White people shared in both in a highly similar fashion. But most centrally, in the Soul movement as in the Renaissance, Negro people evoked their black-ness, studied it, and worked at building it into their lives. Africa, for instance, was roused again as a part of the Negro past—this time with such strength as to be institutionalized into courses, library col-lections, and professorships at leading universities and colleges all over America. Further, the special history of Negro people in the Americas, in the United States, and in the slave South received the same treat-ment. These are institutions that are likely to persist.

The Soul movement was the direct heir to the Renaissance, but it was at once more broad and more intense than the earlier movement. In its more thoughtful aspects the Renaissance had always been a rela-tively elite affair. In the 1960s everyone, white and Negro, who as-pired to a reasonable awareness of the world about him began to buy, read, and think about works from the Renaissance. Printings that had run into the hundreds in the 1920s ran into the tens of thousands in the revival, and authors known previously only to a few professors of literature became semifamous. Jean Toomer, for example, became a popular literary hero such as he had never been in the 1920s, when his book sold barely 500 copies. Where the original authors had survived looking level-eyed at poverty, publishers of reprints and writers of introductions prospered in the revival. The loss of income notwithstanding, it seems likely that those hard-driving, dedicated souls of Harlem, nearly all of whom had died by 1965, would have relished the belated currency of their labors.

The Soul movement was a mass affair that also mustered to its cause vast numbers of young people. The wearing of African dress and hair styles, the taking of Moslem names to signify non-European, non-white-American roots, and the rise and popularity of Afro-American studies in the public schools were things that intimately involved millions of Negro youth. Black was definitely "in," and it has indelibly marked the generation that came to maturity in and after the 1960s. It was neatly symbolic of the transition that the heavyweight champion of the world from 1937 to 1949 had been "the Brown Bomber," Joe Louis, while the champion from 1964 to 1967 began his career as Cassius Marcellus Clay and ended it as Muhammad Ali.

The Soul movement, then, represented a turning back to blackness—to Africa and the slave and peasant past—begun in a signal way in the Renaissance. In the movement the idea of blackness was raised to a new, more popular, pervasive, and powerful fruition. The results of that movement, like the effects of the Renaissance, now seem firmly woven into the fabric of American life.

# Today and
# Tomorrow

NUMBERING more than 22 million people, Afro-Americans constitute one of the largest communities of Negroes in the world outside of Africa. They are also the richest, probably the most powerful, and they are here to stay. The only question is, in what manner shall they stay?

It seems abundantly clear that the assimilation of blacks and whites predicted by the social scientists in the first two-thirds of the twentieth century is not taking place and probably will not take place in the near future. The black girls did not vanish, and tens of thousands of very light men did not pass yearly over the color bar into whiteness. More importantly, Negro people have not proved willing to dissolve that part of themselves that is black into a melting pot dominantly white. On the contrary, Negroes as a people are finding strength in their blackness, and in that strength lies the power to stand apart from the white world. Separatism is becoming institutionalized and, consequently, more probably perpetual. The Negro world is becoming an enclave that the whites are too disorganized to penetrate and manage, even if they should chose to make the attempt.

The great fact about miscegenation today is that it is minimal, and further has been minimal since 1865. There has been relatively little mating between the races, and the transfer of genes across the race line has been so small as to be practically inconsequential. Thus today, even though the great majority of Negroes have some white heritage, the quantity of that heritage is not great and is not growing significantly. Geneticists estimate that the "gene pool" among Negroes is about 20 percent white, while the gene pool among whites is about 1 percent black.[1] What has changed, and what has continued to change over the centuries, is who is mating with whom. Shortly after the turn of the century, it appears that most of the mixing was done by the lower orders of society on both sides. Up into the 1950s, probably most of the mixing was of that kind. Malcolm X caught the reality beautifully in the person of a white prostitute of his acquaintance in Harlem. She was born and bred in Alabama, yet she never went with white men. As she expressed it, "Ah jes lu-uv ni-uh-guhs." [2] Miscegenation after 1865 was minimal, and Negro offspring of white parents were few. Social scientists theorized that the number of offspring diminished in the 1920s and 1930s because of the introduction of contraceptives. No doubt contraceptives had an effect, but the real diminution probably came from the fact that there was simply much less mixing going on.

Interracial marriage, as distinguished from interracial mating outside of marriage, clearly declined drastically in the early years of the twentieth century. Boston was probably the most tolerant large city in America in regard to interracial unions. There, in the time period from 1900 to 1904 about 14 out of every 100 Negro grooms married white wives. Between 1914 and 1918 only 5 out of every 100 did so. On the other hand, only 1 out of every 100 Negro brides married white men, a ratio that held fairly constant in Boston over the early decades of the century. There was not much intermarriage, and such as there was often involved immigrant whites who apparently had not absorbed the racial mores of the native whites or else were native whites of the lower economic orders who had no great stake in social conformity. In a study of marriages between Negroes and whites in Boston and New York State from 1914 to 1938, researchers found that foreign white males and native white females were "over-represented." Further, they found that Negro grooms occupied high social status within their communities, Negro brides were average, and white grooms and brides were low.

The author of a study of mixed marriages in Philadelphia from 1922 to 1947 reached findings that varied somewhat from those earlier studies. He agreed that the rate of intermarriage was low (about 7 each year in the city of Brotherly Love), but he found that white women crossed the race line for marriage much more frequently than white men. In one sample of 50 mixed marriages, 44 of the whites involved were women and only 6 were men. Whites of both sexes ranked higher in social status than in the earlier studies of Boston and New York State, and both races tended to marry across race lines within their occupational class. All studies agreed that interracial marriage often involved immigrants or persons somehow alien to the native white society. In one sample of 41 mixed marriages in Philadelphia, 16 of the whites were foreign born, most of them war brides. In another sample of 50 mixed marriages, 19 of the 44 white brides were Jewish. The researcher thought that this phenomenon might arise from a shared sense of oppression. Inexplicably, however, none of the 6 white grooms were Jewish. In any event, it is clear that in the twentieth century before the civil rights movement the pressures against interracial marriage ran very high, they were effective, and the few white people who married across the race line tended to have some immunity from the full effects of the sanctions of white society.[3]

The civil rights movement saw an upsurge in interracial dating, mating, and marriage, though the proportions were far from overwhelming. Interracial marriage has been easiest to chart. The census of 1960 counted 51,409 black-white couples, or 12 out of every 1,000 in the United States. In the decade of the 1960s the rate of new interracial marriages accelerated by 63 percent, totally because of an increase in the number of white women taking Negro grooms. The number of Negro women taking white grooms actually declined. Very significantly, along with the increase in numbers went a change in the status of both brides and grooms. Many of those who intermarried in this decade were in the middle and upper middle class in terms of income and education.[4]

In spite of the relative increase in miscegenation, the total quantity of interracial unions in the whole population remained very small during the civil rights movement. Available evidence suggests that up through 1965 fewer than 2 out of every 1,000 new marriages in the United States were between whites and Negroes. Pressures upon youth from white parents and society against dating, mating, and marrying across the race line continued. The same animus worked in the Negro community. As Negro men dated across the race line, Negro women in racially mixed schools, colleges, and universities felt the impact and reacted distinctly negatively. Seemingly, Negro women either did not have that option or, more likely, chose not to take it. Many Negroes, especially women, were critical of Negroes who dated and married white and levied charges of opportunism, particularly of a material kind, against those who did so. Thus students of interracial mating conclude that the rate is presently up from its very low level of a generation ago, but they do not anticipate that the rate will exceed 1.0 percent in the coming generation. In genetic terms, the rate of miscegenation is not such as to excite any anticipation of a near-term assimilation.[5]

The Soul movement, carrying such slogans as "black power," "black nationalism," and "Black is beautiful," has pressed further the trend within Negro society to value darkness in color that began in the Harlem Renaissance. Darker people have gained in status and prestige, and lighter people have come to be regarded with less favor, and sometimes even with disfavor. Looking at graduates from Howard University between 1963 and 1973, Laurence Glasco found that while the number of lighter graduates remained small, the number of darker graduates increased from 17 percent to 31 percent for males and from 7 percent to 26 percent for females.[6] In the last decade mulattoes of lighter hues have suffered a serious decline in prestige because of their color, even though their wealth, education, and experience have enabled them to maintain positions well up in the status hierarchy. Whereas the problem for mulattoes used to be "not white enough" to be accepted in the white world, now the problem, sometimes, is "too white" to be accepted in the "black" world. Very light mulattoes, mulattoes who could pass for white, frequently suffer from an extreme discrimination within the Negro world, one that borders on a rejection of the one-drop rule. The tragic plight of the lightest mulattoes these days is that they have been reared to a Negro world, and too often that world would deny them. The alternatives are to fight the discrimination within the world to which they were born or to move into a white culture that is alien and uncomfortable.

During the early 1970s I had a vivid personal encounter with the effects of the Soul movement upon light mulattoes. I was visited in my office by a Negro student then enrolled in my class in "Race Relations in America." She was very light, very attractive, intelligent, and well educated. The daughter of modestly affluent and caring parents, she was obviously nurtured to move with ease and grace in the white world as well as the Negro. Her language and manner, however, soon evidenced that she was an ardent, even a stringent black militant. On the surface, it seemed incongruous to hear such extravagant blackness from one whose color and culture were so light. She, after all, had been spared so much. Finally, I concluded that I had encountered a new paradox: "white guilt" among black people. She and her forebears for generations past had benefited from the simple accident of skin color, much as had white people. Now it was as if she, like some young Southern whites, was attempting to erase her sense of guilt by taking up the black revolution with terrific intensity. Such is the plight of the light mulatto, the double jeopardy of being both very light and "black" in the biracial universe in which we now find ourselves.

The Soul movement is altering color preferences within the Negro world, with the result that self-images and mating patterns are shifting. As late as 1966 it appeared to some observers that successful darker men were still marrying lighter women.[7] Seemingly, the "ornamental effect" was still operative. Surveys of high school and college students about the same time also indicated that black was still not generally preferred. But what was new and striking was that the lightest colors were even less attractive than black. Moreover, the great preference for brown that Charles S. Johnson had noted among boys and girls in the black belts in the late 1930s was still present and growing.[8] The emphasis on darkness has had an adverse psychological effect on mulattoes of lighter colors, especially men. Recent study suggests that light males have suffered in their sense of self-esteem and are not winning the mates they desire. Tests indicate that they experience a less positive self-image, are less certain of their goals in life, and lose out to darker men in attracting high-status women.[9] Light men are having difficulty marrying as they chose; light women seem to be calculating the advantages to their future children of marrying darker. "I have had light-skinned female students describe their insecurities over their color and features," reports Laurence Glasco. "One assured me that her marriage plans definitely included a dark man, because she did not want her children to go through the peer rejection that she had experienced." [10]

The resultant of these forces is a line that points toward brown as the color most admired among Negroes. Given the facts that only about 20 percent of the genes in the gene pool of the Negro world are white, that new infusions proceed at a very low level, and that lighter women are purposefully thinking of marrying darker, it appears that "brownness" is not only desired, it is inevitable. The brown person seems destined to become the ideal—the "somatic norm"—in Negro culture. As we have seen, this is no new development. By the 1920s a hundred years of intensive mixing between blacks and mulattoes was producing, physically, the "brown American" that Herskovits and others were busily describing. At the same time, Negro artists and intellectuals in the Renaissance were generating a mixture of black and white culture that was equally "brown." In retrospect it seems, again, that very much of what is Negro America today commenced during the era of the Harlem Renaissance.

Apparently there is a rule in society just as in physics that what is in motion will continue in motion unless operated upon by some compelling outside force. Negroes are not going to choose to marry whites in any great numbers, and the internal mixture within the Negro world is going to continue to refine the "brownness" of Negro people. More important, American Negroes are in the process of synthesizing a new culture that is neither African nor European, neither white nor black, but rather both. The people are brown and so too is the culture. Even so, "black" does not seem a misnomer as applied to Negro culture in America. Negro culture is indeed precisely black in that it is not white. For there to be a Negro America, Negroes ultimately have to reject white America—in some degree and in some style. It is not unlike the American Revolution, which was accomplished not solely by military action. The American Revolution was, after all, fundamentally cultural and was achieved only over several generations both before and after the war. The real Revolution was a process in which America passed through a long and painful cultural self-separation, almost a cutting away from the parent, created distance in a sufficiently distinct American life style, and completed its independence in thought and art. Once the separateness was clearly established, America could grow much more tolerant and even fond, as it did, of the parent. Among Negro Americans a certain posture of aggressive independence is necessary to integrity. Adver-

tisements to whites, even redundant and irritating advertisements, are
also necessary to achieve that end. Thus demurrers and rejections that
are perpetually unexpected and often shocking to whites, clothing
and hairdos that are absolutely unmatchable, and a language that
simply gallops along faster than whites can run are all declarations of
black independence. They say, "Give us room in which to be."

In 1965 the Soul movement ushered in a new era in Negro life in
America. It is, in a sense, a re-Renaissance. Like the original Harlem
Renaissance, it is ultimately much more broadly cultural than it is
political or economic. It is more shapeless than structured and institutional. And its ends are not amenable to sharp definition. Contrasted
with the unity of the civil rights movement, there was a splintering in
leadership, a diffusion in goals, and a fragmentation of followers. Yet
the unitary and hard thrust of the civil rights movement had made it
all possible. It had opened up a free space in which Negro people
could afford a broad variety of possibilities. The very formlessness of
the Soul movement in an era of reduced pressures, without a great
depression and with "the law of the land" in a supportive mood, is a
source of strength. Out of the lack of imposed focus comes a spontaneous and healthy diversity. That diversity has operated and will
continue to operate within the broad range of Afro-American tradition to generate an array of resources out of which the next stage of
Negro culture will be built.

And so, what of tomorrow? There does seem to be much that is
generational in race relations in America, and it often appears that
major plateaus come in trigenerational cycles. It is almost as if all the
people of a past age have to die away at three score and ten and be
lost from sight before a new age can emerge. Thus the people of the
Harlem Renaissance, so many of whom were in their twenties, had to
wait for the generation born before 1850 to fade away before they
could be what they would be. We might date the high point of the
Renaissance at 1925, by which time most of the freedmen had gone
on to their rewards and mulatto exclusiveness was passing into its
grave.

Today's middle generation, born in the Renaissance and its aftermath, is transitional. Its members were born and reared to embrace
their blackness with rising surety, and somehow to marry the black
and the white, to bridge over the gap first within the Negro world
and then within the world at large. It is a massive task, and theirs will
be a life of unending double struggle. There is confusion, there is
frustration, and often despair at the seeming lack of progress. But
what that middle generation is truly doing—with the support of the

next older generation—is maintaining an open field for the potentiali-
ties in Negro life. The people of that generation are spending their
lives to hold free that space, that *lebensraum* in which the vital thing
is going to happen.

The legacy of the labors of today's middle generation will be
passed in full strength to the next generation, to the Negro child who
was born, say, in 1975 and toddles about today. That child was born
to a world where the law of the land declared equality of opportunity
in all things public and civic. Obviously racial equality is an ideal that
has not yet been realized, yet the principle has never before been so
deeply, so broadly, and so firmly integrated into the fundamental
legal and social constitutions of America as it now is. That child has
been born into an age in which black men do have rights that white
men are bound to respect. Regardless of the fact that prejudice in
white minds is still rampant and discrimination, visible and invisible,
exists on every hand, there has been a revolution in the posture of
government and law and national image vis-à-vis Negro people.

Even more important than the fact that this child, unlike his parents,
was born into an America officially committed to equality is the fact
that he is a part of a Negro world risingly aware of itself as separate,
powerful, and attractive. That rise is not without difficulties. Almost
certainly, the integrity of Negro life is going to be assaulted in diverse
and disorganized ways by the white world in the years to come—a
phenomenon already clearly evident in debates over job and educational quotas and the movement in international relations by some
prominent Negro leaders and organizations toward favoring Arabs as
opposed to Israelis. Furthermore, the next generation of young whites
will carry only a very light burden of guilt compared with that of
their parents. It will seem evident to these young whites, having
passed through the schools and into jobs alongside young Negroes,
that their darker contemporaries have had every chance that they
have had. Indeed, they are liable to conclude that their Negro cohorts,
having benefited by quotas and preferential treatment, have had more
chances than they, and they will probably not be receptive to the
suggestion that simply being born white in America is, in reality,
"headstart." Finally, the integrity of Negro life is also going to be
damaged by large numbers of talented Negroes being recruited into
the great white way, where they will strive, consciously and unconsciously, to leave their blackness behind and to gain full membership
in the sterile, materialistic club of middle-class Americana. Still, Negro
leadership seems steadfast and well enough concerted in its determination to hold its people together and to defend that enclave of freedom

they both fought so hard to win—even as it divides on the issue of what method will best achieve those ends and searches for the new direction in which to move.

In the year 2000 A.D. our imagined child will have reached the age of twenty-five, the age that seems somehow a miracle in maturation not only to automobile insurance companies. No one can say what the Negro children of 1975 will be as men and women. Nevertheless, it seems probable that they will be much more at ease with both their whiteness and their blackness than their parents have been with theirs. Indeed, the next generation, the third generation after the Renaissance, might well be a cultural mutation, a new stage in a long and significant line that has struggled to join black and white comfortably together in America. He and she might well be, in fact, the first fully evolved, smoothly functioning model of a people who have transcended both an exclusive whiteness and an exclusive blackness and moved into a world in which they accept and value themselves for themselves alone—as new and unique, as, indeed, a new people in the human universe.

# Notes

### Preface

1. Edward Byron Reuter, *The Mulatto in the United States: Including a Study of the Role of Mixed-Blood Races throughout the World* (Boston: Richard G. Badger, 1918).
2. Charles W. Chesnutt, *The House behind the Cedars*, (New York: Page, Doubleday, 1899), p. 83.

### Introduction

1. Edna Ferber, *Showboat* (New York: Doubleday, 1926), pp. 90–92, 134–245.
2. Horace Mann Bond, "Two Racial Islands in Alabama," *American Journal of Sociology* 36 (1930–31): 554.

### Chapter I: Genesis

1. Economic historians Fogel and Engerman, in their provocative and highly controversial book *Time on the Cross,* constructed a model through which they examined race mixing in the South during slavery. Their model posited a "straight line" mixing of pure black women and pure white men over eight generations. Using the statistics in the censuses of 1850 and 1860, supported by other data, they concluded that the mulatto populations in those counts were consistent with a very low rate of miscegenation, perhaps one out of every hundred Negro children born in each generation having a white father. I would not take issue with the basic finding that the quantity of race mixing in slavery was fairly low. But I would caution that the relatively late arrival of black people in large numbers suggests that eight generations might be too many, one cannot really assume that

substantially all of the mixing by whites was done by men, and we certainly know that after the first issue the mixing was not always between pure whites and pure blacks. It seems probable that the amount of "white blood" among Negroes in 1850 and 1860 was indeed not great, but Fogel's and Engerman's model does not well explain how this came to be. Robert William Fogel and Stanley L. Engerman, *Time on the Cross: The Economics of American Negro Slavery* (Boston-Toronto: Little, Brown, 1974), 1:130–36; see also *Evidence and Methods: A Supplement*, pp. 106–13.

2. Evarts Boutell Greene and Virginia D. Harrington, *American Population before the Federal Census of 1790* (New York: Columbia University Press, 1932), p. 136. The first count of slaves in Maryland occurred in the eighteenth century only after importations had probably accelerated significantly. However, in 1707 there were 4,657 slaves and 3,003 servants in a total population of 34,000. Ibid., p. 124.

3. In describing contact between slaves and servants in early Virginia, colonialist Edmund S. Morgan wrote, "It was common, for example, for servants and slaves to run away together, steal hogs together, get drunk together. It was not uncommon for them to make love together." Edmund S. Morgan, *American Slavery, American Freedom: The Ordeal of Colonial Virginia* (New York: Norton, 1975), p. 327.

4. Helen T. Caterall, ed., *Judicial Cases Concerning American Slavery*, 5 vols. (Washington, D.C.: Carnegie Institute of Washington, 1926–37), 1:77–78.

5. Ibid., 1:58.

6. William Waller Hening, ed., *The Statutes at Large: Being a Collection of All the Laws of Virginia, from the First Session of the Legislature in the Year 1619*, 13 vols. (New York: R. & W. & G. Bartow, 1823), 2:170.

7. Ibid., 3:86–87.

8. Ibid., 3:453–54.

9. James Hugo Johnston, *Race Relations in Virginia and Miscegenation in the South. 1776–1860*, with a foreword by Winthrop Jordan (Amherst: University of Massachusetts Press, 1970), pp. 175–76, citing County Records, Elizabeth City County, Virginia, vol. 1684–1699.

10. Morgan, *American Slavery, American Freedom*, p. 336.

11. Johnston, *Race Relations*, pp. 177–78, citing Charles G. Chamberlyne, *The Vestry Book and Register of Bristol Parish, Virginia* (Richmond, 1898), pp. 2–63.

12. Hening, ed., *Statutes*, 3:86–88.

13. Ibid., 3:250–52, 298.

14. Ibid., 4:131, 133–34; John Henderson Russell, *The Free Negro in Virginia, 1619–1865* (Baltimore: Johns Hopkins Press, 1913), p. 52.

15. William Hand Browne, ed., *Archives of Maryland: Proceedings and Acts of the General Assembly of Maryland, January, 1637/8–September, 1664* (Baltimore: Maryland Historical Society, 1883), pp. 533–34.

16. Jeffrey Richardson Brackett, *The Negro in Maryland, 1634–1860, a Study of the Institution of Slavery* (Baltimore: Johns Hopkins University, 1889), pp. 32–34, 34fn. See also James Martin Wright, *The Free Negro in Maryland, 1634–1860*, Columbia Studies in History, Economics and Public Law, 97 (New York: Columbia University Press, 1921), pp. 27–28.

17. Brackett, *Negro in Maryland*, pp. 33–34.

18. Edward Raymond Turner, *The Negro in Pennsylvania: Slavery—Servi-*

*tude–Freedom, 1639–1861* (Washington: American Historical Association, 1911), pp. 29–31, 91–92.

19. Bureau of the Census, *A Century of Population Growth, from the First Census of the United States to the Twelfth, 1790–1900* (Washington, D.C.: Document Printing Office, 1909), pp. 6, 185.

20. Ira Berlin, *Slaves without Masters: The Free Negro in the Antebellum South* (New York: Pantheon Books, 1975), pp. 49, 97–99. This was a significant retreat by the legislature from the law of 1705. It meant that one had to be only slightly more than three-fourths white to qualify as legally white, whereas previously one had to be more than seven-eighths white to do so. In Virginia after 1785, if only one grandparent was a Negro and that grandparent had the slightest trace of non-African ancestry, then one was white. Thus many people generally judged as quadroons would be deemed legally white.

21. Ibid., pp. 365–66.

22. Ibid., pp. 48–49.

23. Richard S. Dunn, *Sugar and Slaves: The Rise of the Planter Class in the English West Indies, 1624–1713* (Chapel Hill: University of North Carolina Press, 1972), pp. 111–14.

24. Peter H. Wood, *Black Majority: Negroes in Colonial South Carolina from 1670 through the Stono Rebellion* (New York: Knopf, 1974), p. 36.

25. Ibid., pp. 234–35; Winthrop D. Jordan, *White over Black: American Attitudes toward the Negro, 1550–1812* (Chapel Hill: University of North Carolina Press, 1968), pp. 146–47.

26. Wood, *Black Majority*, pp. 235–36.

27. Ibid., p. 99.

28. Ibid., pp. 102–103.

29. Marina Wikramanayake, *A World in Shadow: The Free Black in Antebellum South Carolina* (Columbia: University of South Carolina Press, 1973), pp. 150–51.

30. Johnston, *Race Relations*, pp. 300–301, citing *A South Carolinian, a Refutation of the Calumnies Circulated against the Southern and Western States, Respecting the Existence of Slavery among Them, to Which Is Added a Minute and Particular Account of the Actual Condition of the Negro Population* (Charleston: 1822), pp. 84–85.

31. Catterall, ed., *Judicial Cases Concerning American Slavery*, 2:269.

32. Johnston, *Race Relations*, pp. 199–200, citing *State v. Cantey*, 2 Hill, *South Carolina Reports*, p. 278 (1857).

33. Wikramanayake, *World in Shadow*, pp. 76–77, 82, 167–70.

34. O. Vernon Burton, "The Antebellum Free Black Community: Edgefield's Rehearsal for Reconstruction," *Furman Review* 5:24; idem, "The Slave Community in Edgefield, South Carolina, 1850–1880," Ph.D. dissertation, Princeton University, 1975, *passim*.

35. Research Department, Association for the Study of Negro Life and History, "Free Negro Owners of Slaves in the U.S. in 1830," *Journal of Negro History* 9 (January 1924):41–85. Two of the others were low-country South Carolinians, and the third was a Virginian.

36. Henry E. Sterkx, *The Free Negro in Ante-Bellum Louisiana* (Rutherford, N.J.: Fairleigh Dickinson University Press, 1972), pp. 202–212.

37. Gary B. Mills, *The Forgotten People: Cane River's Creoles of Color*

(Baton Rouge: Louisiana State University Press, 1977), pp. 1–3, 10, 20–49, 79, 144, and *passim.*

38. Ibid., pp. 49, 108–110, 139.

39. Ibid., pp. xiii, 77–79, 96–100, 156–58.

40. Ibid., pp. 139, 145, 153, 164, 216, 217.

41. John Blassingame, *Black New Orleans, 1860–1880* (Chicago: University of Chicago Press, 1973), pp. 17–21.

42. Berlin, *Slaves without Masters,* p. 198.

43. Edward Byron Reuter, *The Mulatto in the United States: Including a Study of the Role of Mixed-Blood Races throughout the World* (Boston: Richard G. Badger, 1918), pp. 12–13.

44. James Hugo Johnston, in his 1937 study of miscegenation in the South before 1860, remarked upon the difference between the upper South and the lower, asserting that "in the lower South, because of its liberal attitudes and traditions handed down from the Spanish and French colonists, there appears to have been more sympathy for the mulatto. . . ." Johnston, *Race Relations,* p. 226,

45. *Negro Population in the United States, 1790–1918* (Washington, D.C.: Government Printing Office, 1918), pp. 207–208, 210, 221. For the total national population, see *The Seventh Census of the United States: 1850* (Washington, D.C.: Robert Armstrong, Public Printer, 1853), p. ix.

46. *Seventh Census,* p. ix.

47. *Negro Population,* p. 221.

48. *Negro Population,* p. 221; Berlin, *Slaves without Masters,* pp. 179–80, 221–22. The subject of Berlin's study is the free Negro, not the free mulatto. One grand theme in his book is that during the Revolutionary era private emancipations in the upper South rapidly darkened the free Negro population, while in the lower South the absence of such a wave of emancipations left its complexion about three-quarters mulatto, a ratio that prevailed up to the time of the Civil War. Thus when Berlin writes about free Negroes in the lower South as a group, he is referring to a people about 75 percent mulatto. The situation of free mulattoes in Louisiana is described in Sterkx, *Free Negro,* pp. 200–239.

49. *Century of Population Growth,* p. 185; *Negro Population,* p. 221.

50. *Negro Population,* p. 221.

51. Ibid.

52. Ibid.

53. E. Merton Coulter, *A Short History of Georgia* (Chapel Hill: University of North Carolina Press, 1933), pp. 64–65, 88–90, 121.

54. Allen Daniel Candler, comp., *The Colonial Records of the State of Georgia* (Atlanta: Charles P. Byrd, State Printer, 1910), 18:659. In passing this law, the assembly indicated that it wanted to correct a situation in which it had made no distinction in status between slaves and free people of color.

55. Bureau of the Census, *Compendium of the United States Census, 1850* (Washington: A. O. P. Nicholson, Public Printer, 1854), p. 68; *Negro Population,* p. 221.

56. Morgan, *American Slavery, American Freedom.*

57. A student of emancipation in colonial South Carolina found that three-fourths of the recorded adult manumissions were of females and one-third of all manumissions were of mulatto children. John D. Duncan, "Slave

Emancipation in Colonial South Carolina," *American Chronicle, a Magazine of History* 1 (1972): 66.

58. For a general description of the high degree of tolerance of Carolinians for free mulattoes up to the eve of the Civil War, see Wikramanayake, *World in Shadow, passim.*

59. An excellent account of the Gibson family in the early years is in Jordan, *White over Black,* pp. 171–73. See also Wood, *Black Majority,* pp. 100–101. The local history in which the color of the Gibsons went unnoted was published first in 1867 by the Episcopal Bishop of Texas, a descendant of an old Carolina family: Alexander Gregg, *History of the Old Cheraws* (Columbia: The State Company, 1925); reprint ed. (Baltimore: Genealogical Publishing Company, 1967), pp. 72*fn,* 73–74, 139–61, 354. For Edgefield see the discussion above, and for the state at large see Wikramanayake, *World in Shadow,* pp. 76–77.

60. Good indicators of time of settlement are dates of admission to the Union as states. These are Kentucky 1792, Tennessee 1796, Louisiana 1812, Mississippi 1817, Alabama 1819, Missouri 1821, Arkansas 1836, Florida 1846, and Texas 1846.

61. For an excellent display of the details in this matter state by state, see Berlin, *Slaves without Masters,* pp. 138–39, *fn* 2.

62. Greene and Harrington, *American Population,* pp. 172–76.

63. Ibid., pp. 135–40, 125.

64. Dunn, *Sugar and Slaves,* p. 326.

65. Winthrop D. Jordan, "American Chiaroscuro: The Status and Definition of Mulattoes in the British Colonies," *William and Mary Quarterly* 19 (1962): 197.

66. Dunn, *Sugar and Slaves,* pp. 314–17.

67. *Century of Population Growth,* p. 185.

68. Greene and Harrington, *American Population,* pp. 172–73.

69. For Maryland see Arthur E. Karinen, "Maryland Population: 1631–1730: Numerical and Distributional Aspects" (part II of a two-part article), *Maryland Historical Magazine* 60 (1965): 141.

70. Greene and Harrington, *American Population,* pp. 136–37. Abbott Emerson Smith, *Colonists in Bondage: White Servitude and Convict Labor in America, 1607–1776* (Chapel Hill, University of North Carolina Press, 1947), pp. 330, 336.

71. Wesley Frank Craven, *The Southern Colonies in the Seventeenth Century, 1607–1689* (Baton Rouge: Louisiana State University Press, 1949), p. 400. Smith, *Colonists in Bondage,* p. 335. One writer observed in Virginia in 1724 that "these servants are but an insignificant number, who compared with *shoals* of Negroes. . . ." Quoted in ibid., p. 330.

72. Wood, *Black Majority,* pp. 25–26. The account that follows draws heavily upon Professor Wood's study.

73. Ibid., p. 132.

74. *Negro Population,* p. 221.

75. Peter Fontaine to Moses Fontaine, Mar. 30, 1757, cited in Robert Eldon Brown and B. Katherine Brown, *Virginia, 1705–1786: Democracy or Aristocracy?* (East Lansing: Michigan State University Press, 1964), pp. 68, 78.

76. The following account relies upon factual information supplied in a study by Fawn Brodie, *Thomas Jefferson: An Intimate History* (New York:

Norton, 1974), *passim.* See also Jordan, *White over Black,* pp. 464–69, and Merrill D. Peterson, *The Jeffersonian Image in the American Mind* (New York: Oxford University Press, 1960), pp. 181–87.

77. Gerda Lerner, *The Grimké Sisters from South Carolina, Rebels against Slavery* (Boston: Houghton Mifflin, 1967), pp. 358–66.

78. John Mercer Langston, *From the Virginia Plantation to the National Capitol, or The First and Only Negro Representative in Congress from the Old Dominion* (Hartford, Conn.: American Publishing Co., 1894) pp. 11–36 *et seq.*

79. Johnston, *Race Relations,* pp. 246–47, citing Petition 16315, Henry, Dec. 20, 1848.

80. Estimation of the rate of such mixing is made difficult, however, by the fact that some of these women were simply taken by the census taker to be white when in reality they were of mixed blood. In Virginia the situation was further obscured by the rule that if a person was less than one-fourth black, he or she was defined legally as white; census takers often responded according to the legal classification. Thus Eston Hemings was listed in the census of 1830 as white, while his wife was classed as black, as were their four children. Brodie, *Thomas Jefferson,* pp. 469; 475; 554, *fn* 51.

81. Johnston, *Race Relations,* p. 254, citing Petition 5370, Amherst, Dec. 6, 1809.

82. Ibid., pp. 254–55, citing Petitions 8218, Louisa, Dec. 16, 1824, and 8305, Louisa, Jan. 20, 1825.

83. Kenneth M. Stampp, *The Peculiar Institution: Slavery in the Ante-Bellum South* (New York: Knopf, 1956), pp. 353–55. See pp. 350–61 for a succinct summary of the author's findings on miscegenation after completing the most exhaustive study of manuscript sources relating to slavery in the American South done in the last sixty years.

84. Frederic May Holland, *Frederick Douglass: The Colored Orator* (New York: Funk & Wagnalls, 1891), pp. 7–9.

85. Louis R. Harlan, *Booker T. Washington: The Making of a Black Leader, 1856–1901* (New York: Oxford University Press, 1972), pp. 3–4; 326, *fn* 11. Harlan gave his chapter on Washington's origins a title that Washington, Douglass, and other sons of the unknown father would have appreciated. Like Moses, they had been found "In the Bulrushes."

86. Johnston, *Race Relations,* pp. 306–307, citing *Alfred, a slave* v. *State of Mississippi,* 37 Mississippi Reports, p. 296 (1859).

87. Ibid., pp. 307–308, citing Executive Papers, Sept. 10, 1830.

88. A copy of this letter is in my possession. This material was supplied to me through the courtesy of an archive in which papers of this family are deposited.

89. *Negro Population,* p. 221.

90. Ibid.

### Chapter II: Changeover, 1850–1915

1. Bureau of the Census, *Negro Population in the United States, 1790–1918* (Washington, D.C.: Government Printing Office, 1918), p. 208.

2. Ibid., pp. 220–21.

3. Virginians sometimes used the term "mustee" to mean octoroon. Cited in Ira Berlin, *Slaves without Masters: The Free Negro in the Antebellum South* (New York: Pantheon Books, 1975), pp. 365–66.

4. Marina Wikramanayake, *A World in Shadow: The Free Black in Antebellum South Carolina* (Columbia: University of South Carolina Press, 1973), pp. 169–70.

5. O. Vernon Burton, "The Slave Community in Edgefield, South Carolina, 1850–1880," Ph.D. dissertation, Princeton University, 1975, *passim*.

6. Henry E. Sterkx, *The Free Negro in Antebellum Louisiana* (Rutherford, N.J.: Fairleigh Dickenson University, 1972), pp. 285, 297.

7. David C. Rankin, "The Origins of Black Leadership in New Orleans during Reconstruction," *Journal of Southern History* 40 (November 1974): 422, citing *Picayune*, Mar. 8, 1856.

8. Sterkx, *Free Negro* pp. 196–98, 292–315.

9. Diary of Ella Gertrude (Clanton) Thomas, Jan. 2, 1858, Manuscripts Division, Duke University Library, Durham, North Carolina.

10. Frederic Bancroft, *Slave-Trading in the Old South* (Baltimore: J. J. H. Furst, 1931), pp. 131, 315, 321.

11. Fredricka Bremer, *The Homes of the New World: Impressions of America*, trans. Mary Howitt, 3 vols. (London: A. Hall, Virtue, & Co., 1853), 1:492–93; 2:534–35; Bancroft, *Slave-Trading*, pp. 130–31.

12. Bremer, *Homes of the New World*, 3:7–11; Bancroft, *Slave-Trading*, pp. 333–36.

13. Mary Boykin Chesnut, *A Diary from Dixie*, ed. Ben Ames Williams (Boston: Houghton Mifflin, 1949), pp. 121–22.

14. Ibid., pp. 21–22.

15. *Report and Treatise on Slavery and the Slavery Agitation*, printed by order of the House of Representatives of Texas (Austin: John Marshall and Company, 1857), pp. 38–40. For a compact description of the abolitionists' attack on miscegenation in the slave South, see Robert Brent Toplin, "Between Black and White: Attitudes toward Southern Mulattoes 1830–1961," *Journal of Southern History* 45 (May 1979): 185–200.

16. Harvey Wish, *George Fitzhugh: Propagandist of the Old South* (Baton Rouge: Louisiana State University Press, 1943), p. 54; George Fitzhugh, *Sociology for the South: Or the Failure of Free Society* (Richmond, Va.: A. Morris, 1854), p. 93.

17. George M. Fredrickson, *The Black Image in the White Mind: The Debate on Afro-American Character and Destiny, 1817–1914* (New York: Harper & Row, 1971), *passim*, especially pp. 223–35. See also Toplin, "Between Black and White," pp. 197–200.

18. Charles W. Chesnutt Diary, entry for Mar. 30, 1880, Charles W. Chesnutt Collection, Fisk University Library, Nashville, Tennessee.

19. Sterkx, *Free Negro*, pp. 301–304.

20. Joseph Karl Menn, *The Large Slaveholders of Louisiana—1860* (New Orleans: Pelican Publishing Company, 1964), p. 92.

21. C. Peter Ripley, *Slaves and Freedmen in Civil War Louisiana* (Baton Rouge: Louisiana State University Press, 1976), pp. 102–105, 116–17; John Blassingame, *Black New Orleans, 1860–1880* (Chicago: University of Chicago

Press, 1973), pp. 25–47; Mary F. Berry, "Negro Troops in Blue and Gray: The Louisiana Native Guards, 1861–1863," *Louisiana History* 8 (Spring 1967): 165–90. One might well question the depth of the support offered by members of the mulatto elite to the Southern cause. They had property to defend. They were in an armed camp alert to—and ready to punish—dissent. They had just passed through several years of severe abuse. Nevertheless, tokens of support were given—and taken. Gary B. Mills noted that even though the sympathies of a small portion of the Cane River population were later questioned, "the colony publicly favored the Confederacy throughout the conflict." These people had always been known for their loyalty to Louisiana, he observed, and only a handful enlisted in the Union army. Gary B. Mills, *The Forgotten People: Cane River's Creoles of Color* (Baton Rouge: Louisiana State University Press, 1977), pp. 229–36. It seems probable that such indecisiveness reflected the fact that the mulatto elite was in transition from a more or less effective pre-1850s alliance with the white elite to a new level of independence.

22. Geraldine McTigue, "The Free People of Color in New Orleans: Contributions toward a Group Portrait," paper given at the Convention of the Organization of American Historians, April 17–20, 1974, *passim.*

23. Rankin, "Black Leadership in New Orleans," pp. 433–34, citing *Tribune,* Feb. 1, 1865.

24. Charles Vincent, *Black Legislators in Louisiana during Reconstruction* (Baton Rouge: Louisiana State University Press, 1976), p. xiv *et seq.*

25. In an exhaustive study of the end of slavery Leon Litwack noted the move toward unity among Negroes in the first months of freedom. Persistent divisiveness would occasionally appear, but, he concluded, "the common hostility they confronted usually forced the various groups that made up the black community to minimize and surmount their differences." Leon Litwack, *Been in the Storm So Long: The Aftermath of Slavery* (New York: Knopf, 1979), p. 514.

26. Jack Pendleton Maddex, Jr., *The Virginia Conservatives, 1867–1879: A Study in Reconstruction Politics* (Chapel Hill: University of North Carolina Press, 1979).

27. In fact, their assaults upon the white bastions were usually so ineffective that their efforts have largely escaped the attention of historians. However, two excellent studies recently published bring these efforts to light: Joseph H. Cartwright, *The Triumph of Jim Crow: Tennessee Race Relations in the 1880s* (Knoxville: University of Tennessee Press, 1976), and J. Morgan Kousser, *The Shaping of Southern Politics: Suffrage Restriction and the Establishment of the One-Party South, 1880–1910* (New Haven, Conn.: Yale University Press, 1974).

28. Carter G. Woodson, *A Century of Negro Migration* (Washington, D.C.: Association for the Study of Negro Life and History, 1918), pp. 123–24.

29. The early division in goals between mulatto and black political leaders is well demonstrated for Alabama in an excellent study by Peter Kolchin, *First Freedom: The Response of Alabama's Blacks to Emancipation and Reconstruction* (Westport, Conn.: Greenwood Press, 1972), p. 170. For the same phenomenon in Louisiana, see Roger A. Fischer, *The Segregation Struggle in Louisiana, 1862–77* (Urbana: University of Illinois Press, 1974), pp. x–xi, 86–87. In an admirably close and careful study of Negro political

leadership in South Carolina during Reconstruction, Thomas Holt found that the division was persistent and ultimately so destructive as to constitute a primary cause of the downfall of the Republican regime in that state in 1877. The key leaders, he concluded, were out of the free mulatto elite, they were "basically bourgeois in their origins and orientation," and, while some were affected by their constituents, they "oftener than not failed to act in the interests of black peasants." Thomas Holt, *Black over White: Negro Political Leadership in South Carolina during Reconstruction* (Urbana: University of Illinois Press, 1977), pp. 3, 43, 58–59, 69–71.

30. Howard N. Rabinowitz, *Race Relations in the Urban South, 1865–1890* (New York: Oxford University Press, 1978), pp. 248–49.

31. Holt, *Black over White*, p. 49, table 5.

32. Ibid., pp. 53–54, 70, 71, 86; Joel Williamson, *After Slavery: The Negro in South Carolina during Reconstruction, 1861–1877* (Chapel Hill: University of North Carolina Press, 1965), pp. 210–11.

33. Ten Negro soldiers were commissioned officers in the Union army in South Carolina. All ten were Northerners who had come south during the war. Williamson, *After Slavery*, pp. 28–29; Holt, *Black over White*, table 5.

34. Williamson, *After Slavery*, pp. 365–66; Holt, *Black over White*, table 5.

35. Williamson, *After Slavery*, p. 211.

36. Holt, *Black over White*, pp. 81–82.

37. Ibid., pp. 79, 115, table 5.

38. Ibid., pp. 76*fn*, table 5.

39. Ibid., table 5; Williamson, *After Slavery*, p. 357.

40. Williamson, *After Slavery*, p. 211.

41. Holt, *Black over White*, p. 83.

42. Ibid., pp. 85–86.

43. Ibid., pp. 38, 39*fn*, 59.

44. Ibid., pp. 150–51.

45. David C. Rankin identified 240 Negro politicians of significance in New Orleans. Of the 102 whose color is known 93 were mulatto and 9 were black. Rankin, "Black Leadership in New Orleans," pp. 419, 426–27.

46. Holt, *Black over White*, table 5.

47. Ibid., p. 68.

48. *The Nation* 1 (Sept. 14, 1865): 332.

49. Caroline Bond Day, *A Study of Some Negro-White Families in the United States*, with a foreword and notes on the anthropometric data by Ernest A. Hooton, Harvard African Studies, no. 10 (Cambridge, Mass.: Peabody Museum of Harvard University, 1932). For a detailed and fascinating exhibition of the Negro family in this transition, see Herbert G. Gutman, *The Black Family in Slavery and Freedom, 1750–1925* (New York: Pantheon Books, 1976).

50. James H. Croushore and David A. Potter, eds., *John William De Forest: A Union Officer in the Reconstruction* (New Haven, Conn.: Yale University Press, 1948), p. 138.

51. Edward Lipscomb to Smith Lipscomb, June 19, 1874, Lipscomb Family Papers, Southern Historical Collection, University of North Carolina, Chapel Hill.

52. Blassingame, *Black New Orleans*, pp. 203, 207, 210.

53. For South Carolina, see Williamson, *After Slavery*, p. 297.

54. Emma E. Holmes ms Diary, entry for "End of May" 1865, Southern Historical Collection, University of North Carolina, Chapel Hill.

55. Williamson, *After Slavery*, pp. 295–96.

56. William Heyward to James Gregorie, Jan. 12, 1868, Gregorie-Elliott Papers, Southern Historical Collection, University of North Carolina, Chapel Hill.

57. U.S. Congress, Senate, *South Carolina in 1876: Testimony as to the Denial of the Elective Franchise in South Carolina at the Election of 1875 and 1876*, 3 vols., Senate Miscellaneous Document no. 48, 44th Congress, 2d session (Washington: Government Printing Office, 1877), 1:234.

58. Blassingame, *Black New Orleans*, pp. 206–207. For an excellent discussion of miscegenation in New Orleans in the postwar years, see pp. 202–210.

59. George Brown Tindall, *South Carolina Negroes, 1877–1900* (Columbia: University of South Carolina Press, 1949), pp. 147–48.

60. Mills, *Forgotten People*, p. 247.

61. Blassingame, *Black New Orleans*, p. 204.

62. Lawrence D. Rice, *The Negro in Texas, 1877–1900* (Baton Rouge; Louisiana State University Press, 1971), pp. 148–50.

63. Ray Stannard Baker, *Following the Color Line* (New York: Doubleday, Page, 1908), pp. 167–68.

64. That the situation was that of the temptation and the fall was precisely the message of Thomas Dixon's highly popular novel, *The Sins of the Father* (New York: Doubleday, Page, 1911).

65. For an excellent discussion of both popular and scientific thought concerning mulattoes in the turn-of-the-century decades, see John German Mencke, "Mulattoes and Race Mixture: American Attitudes and Images from Reconstruction to World War I," Ph.D. dissertation, University of North Carolina, Chapel Hill, 1976, pp. 68–237.

66. Edgar Gardner Murphy, *The Problems of the Present South* (New York: Macmillan, 1904), pp. 272–73.

67. Quoted in Joseph Blotner, *Faulkner, a Biography*, 2 vols. (New York: Random House, 1974), 1:498.

68. Charles Staples Mangum, Jr., *The Legal Status of the Negro in the United States* (Chapel Hill: University of North Carolina Press, 1940), p. 246.

69. Ibid., pp. 238–48.

70. Blassingame, *Black New Orleans*, p. 201.

71. Rankin, "Black Leadership in New Orleans," pp. 427–28.

72. William Faulkner, *Light in August* (New York: Random House, 1936).

73. Various letters, especially T. L. Grant to Whitefield McKinlay, Nov. 29, 1909 (with note added about Grant's passing in another hand), Whitefield McKinlay Papers, Carter G. Woodson Collection, Manuscripts Division, Library of Congress, Washington, D.C.

74. Baker, *Following the Color Line*, p. 164.

75. Ibid., pp. 160–61.

76. Gunnar Myrdal, *An American Dilemma: The Negro Problem and Modern Democracy* (New York: Harper & Brothers, 1944), p. 687; Baker, *Following the Color Line*, p. 161.

77. Baker, *Following the Color Line*, p. 156.

78. Blassingame, *Black New Orleans*, p. 201.
79. Baker, *Following the Color Line*, pp. 158, 160–61.
80. Myrdal, *An American Dilemma*, pp. 1207–1208; Walter Francis White, *A Man Called White: The Autobiography of Walter White* (New York: Viking Press, 1948), p. 3.
81. John H. Burma, "The Measurement of Negro 'Passing,' " *American Journal of Sociology* 52 (July 1946): 1822.
82. Horace Mann Bond, "Two Racial Islands in Alabama," *American Journal of Sociology* 36 (January 1931): 554.
83. Baker, *Following the Color Line*, p. 52, citing the Atlanta *Georgian*, Mar. 6, 1907, for the expulsion and the Albany *Herald* for the return.
84. Lillian Smith, *Killers of the Dream* (New York: Norton, 1949), pp. 34–39.
85. White, *A Man Called White*, pp. 135–36.
86. William Watts Ball, *The State That Forgot: South Carolina's Surrender to Democracy* (Indianapolis: Bobbs-Merrill, 1932), p. 265.
87. William Faulkner, *Absalom, Absalom* (New York: Random House, 1936), pp. 192–216.
88. Baker, *Following the Color Line*, p. 172.
89. William Edward Burghardt Du Bois, *The Philadelphia Negro* (Philadelphia: Published for the University [of Pennsylvania], 1899), pp. 361–66.
90. Joseph Golden, "Characteristics of Negro-White Marriages in Philadelphia," *American Sociological Review* 18 (April 1953): 177–83.
91. Randolph Chandler Downes, *The Rise of Warren Gamaliel Harding, 1865–1920* (Columbus: Ohio State University Press, 1970), pp. 553–59.
92. The great fear of Negro rebelliousness that swept through the white South during the war and the winds of rumor that blew with it have been catalogued by sociologist Howard W. Odum in his book *Race and Rumors of Race* (Chapel Hill: University of North Carolina Press, 1944). Pages 54–56 related especially to race and sex.
93. Ernest Sevier Cox to Charles R. Henderson, May 1, 1913, Ernest Sevier Cox Papers, Manuscripts Division, Duke University, Durham, North Carolina.
94. The Hancock story can be pieced together from materials in the Marion Butler Papers, Southern Historical Collection, University of North Carolina.
95. William Faulkner, *Intruder in the Dust* (New York: Random House, 1948).
96. Bond, "Two Racial Islands in Alabama," p. 554.
97. Edwin R. Embree, *Brown America: The Story of a New Race* (New York: Viking Press, 1931), pp. 272–79.

**Chapter III: Brown America**

1. Langston Hughes, *Not without Laughter* (New York: Alfred A. Knopf, Inc., 1930), p. 121. Copyright © 1930 by Alfred A. Knopf, Inc. Reprinted by permission.
2. *Negro Population in the United States, 1790–1918* (Washington, D.C.: Government Printing Office, 1918), pp. 207–208.
3. Ibid., pp. 1, 209.

4. Bureau of the Census, *Abstract of the Census of 1920* (Washington, D.C.: Government Printing Office, 1923), p. 97.

5. Bureau of the Census, *Fourteenth Census of the United States, 1920: Population*, 2:35; *Abstract of the Census of 1920*, p. 102; *Negro Population*, p. 208.

6. Bureau of the Census, *Negroes in the United States, 1920–32* (Washington, D.C.: Government Printing Office, 1935), *passim.*

7. Edward Byron Reuter, *The Mulatto in the United States: Including a Study of the Role of Mixed-Blood Races throughout the World* (Boston: Richard G. Badger, 1918).

8. Melville J. Herskovits, *The American Negro: A Study in Racial Crossing* (New York: Knopf, 1928).

9. Gunnar Myrdal, *An American Dilemma: The Negro Problem and Modern Democracy* (New York: Harper & Brothers, 1944).

10. Kelly Miller, *Out of the House of Bondage* (New York: Neal Publishing Co., 1914), p. 55.

11. Melville J. Herskovits, *The Anthropometry of the American Negro*, Columbia University Contributions to Anthropology, vol. 11 (New York: Columbia University Press, 1930), pp. 240–41.

12. For such feelings in the North, see David Fowler, "Northern Attitudes toward Interracial Marriage: A Study of Legislation and Public Opinion in the Middle Atlantic States and the States of the Old Northwest," Ph.D. dissertation, Yale University, 1963.

13. Caroline Bond Day, *A Study of Some Negro-White Families in the United States*, with a foreword and notes on the anthropometric data by Ernest A. Hooton, Harvard African Studies, no. 10 (Cambridge, Mass.: Peabody Museum of Harvard University, 1932), pp. 109–110.

14. Carter G. Woodson, "The Beginnings of the Miscegenation of the Whites and Blacks," *Journal of Negro History* 3 (October 1918): 339.

15. Charles S. Johnson, *Growing Up in the Black Belt: Negro Youth in the Rural South* (Washington; D.C.: American Council on Education, 1941), p. 262.

16. Edward Franklin Frazier, *The Negro Family in Chicago* (Chicago: University of Chicago Press, 1932), p. 103.

17. Lena Horne, *Lena*, with Richard Schickel (Garden City, N.Y.: Doubleday, 1965), pp. 51, 56–57.

18. Malcolm X, *The Autobiography of Malcolm X*, with the assistance of Alex Haley (New York: Grove Press, 1964), pp. 97, 119.

19. Ralph Linton, "The Vanishing American Negro," *The American Mercury* 6 (February 1947): 135.

20. Herskovits, *American Negro*, pp. 62–66.

21. Myrdal, *American Dilemma*, p. 131.

22. Reuter, *Mulatto in the United States*, p. 396.

23. Herskovits, *American Negro*, pp. 65–66; Linton, "Vanishing American Negro," 136.

24. Gustavas Adolphus Steward, "The Black Girl Passes," *Social Forces* 6 (September 1927): 99–103.

25. Herskovits, *American Negro*, p. 65; Edwin R. Embree, *Brown America: The Story of a New Race* (New York: Viking Press, 1931), p. 46; Myrdal,

*American Dilemma*, pp. 130, 687, 1207–1208; Charles S. Johnson, "The Vanishing Mulatto," *Opportunity* 3 (October 1925): 291; Everett V. Stonequist, *The Marginal Man: A Study in Personality and Culture Conflict* (New York: Scribner, 1937), pp. 190–191.

26. William M. Kephardt, "Is the American Negro becoming Lighter? An Analysis of the Sociological and Biological Trends," *American Sociological Review* 13 (August 1948): 437–43, citing Edward W. Edwards and Lane Duntley, "The Pigments and Color of Living Human Skin," *American Journal of Anatomy* 65 (July 1935): 1–35.

27. Stanford M. Lyman, *The Black American in Sociological Thought* (New York: Putnam, 1972), pp. 27–28.

28. Myrdal, *American Dilemma*, pp. 131, 1207–1208.

29. Linton, "Vanishing American Negro," 133, 135.

30. W. G. Weatherby, "Race and Marriage," *American Journal of Sociology* 15 (January 1910): 433.

31. E. Franklin Frazier, "Children in Black and Mulatto Families," *American Journal of Sociology* 39 (July 1933): 12–29.

32. Franz Boas, *The Mind of Primitive Man* (New York: Macmillan, 1911), pp. 53–65, 262, 275, 277. The flow of Boas's thinking was concisely rendered by Gunnar Myrdal in his 1944 study; see Myrdal, *American Dilemma*, pp. 90–91, 122, 146, 150, 1202–1203.

33. Herskovits, *American Negro*, pp. 8–9, 22.

34. Ibid., pp. 20, 32; Embree, *Brown America*, p. 10.

35. Herskovits, *American Negro*, pp. 8–10; Embree, *Brown America*, p. 10.

36. Day, *Some Negro-White Families*, pp. 9–11.

37. Ibid.

38. Ibid., pp. 106–127.

39. Steward, "The Black Girl Passes," p. 99.

40. Laurence Glasco, "The Mulatto: A Neglected Dimension of Afro-American Social Structure," paper given at the Convention of the Organization of American Historians, Apr. 17–20, 1974, pp. 23–26, 38.

41. Gilbert F. Edwards, *The Negro Professional Class* (New York: Free Press, 1958), pp. 112–15.

42. Johnson, *Growing Up in the Black Belt*, pp. 258–66.

43. Hans Hoetink, *The Two Variants in Caribbean Race Relations*, trans. Eva. M. Hooykaas (London: Oxford University Press, 1967), p. 120.

44. Myrdal, *American Dilemma*, p. 1211.

45. Embree, *Brown America*.

46. Reuter, *Mulatto in the United States*, pp. 309–312.

47. Day, *Some Negro-White Families*, pp. 120, 122.

48. Ibid., pp. 108–126. The quote is from p. 109.

49. Ibid., pp. 113–15, 117–19.

50. A full story of this movement is contained in the files of the Board of Domestic and Foreign Missions held by the Church History Archives in Austin, Texas.

51. Day, *Some White-Negro Families*, p. 116.

52. Ibid., pp. 109–111.

53. Ibid., pp. 111–13, 119.

54. Ibid., p. 126.

55. Ibid., pp. 119–21.
56. Ibid., p. 121.
57. Ibid., pp. 121–22.
58. Ibid., pp. 123–26.
59. Madison Grant, *The Passing of the Great Race: Or the Racial Basis of European History* (New York: Scribner, 1916), pp. 15–16. Grant's book went through four editions before 1923.
60. Myrdal, *American Dilemma*, p. 114.
61. Ralph Ellison, *Invisible Man* (New York: Random House, 1952).
62. Margaret Mitchell, *Gone with the Wind* (New York: Macmillan, 1936), p. 253.
63. Lillian Smith, *Killers of the Dream* (New York: Norton, 1949); *Strange Fruit: A Novel* (New York: Reynal & Hitchcock, 1944).
64. Morton Sosna, *In Search of the Silent South: Southern Liberals and the Race Issue* (New York: Columbia University Press, 1977), pp. 188–93.
65. Theodore Gilmore Bilbo, *Take Your Choice: Separation or Mongrelization* (Poplarville, Miss.: Dream House Publishing Company, 1947), pp. 57–58.

**Chapter IV: Harlem and After**

1. Langston Hughes, *Simple Speaks His Mind* (New York: Simon & Schuster, 1974), p. 31.
2. Gilbert Osofsky, *Harlem, the Making of a Ghetto: New York, 1890–1930* (New York: Harper & Row, 1966), pp. 81–135; Seth Scheiner, *Negro Mecca: A History of the Negro in New York City, 1865–1920* (New York: New York University Press, 1965), pp. 18–20, 34–38; Bureau of the Census, *Negroes in the United States, 1920–32* (Washington, D.C.: Government Printing Office, 1935), p. 17. Ironically, the National Origins Act of 1924 did not apply to the New World, with the result that a large percentage of the 100,000 foreign-born Negroes in the United States in 1930 had come into the country during the 1920s, primarily from the islands of the Caribbean.
3. Eugene Levy, *James Weldon Johnson, Black Leader, Black Voice*, Negro American Biographies and Autobiographies, ed. John Hope Franklin (Chicago: University of Chicago Press, 1973), pp. 178–87.
4. Nathan I. Huggins, *Harlem Renaissance* (New York: Oxford University Press, 1971), pp. 27–28.
5. Langston Hughes, *The Big Sea* (New York: Knopf, 1940), p. 81.
6. Loften Mitchell, *Voices of the Black Theatre* (Clifton, N. J.: James T. White & Co., 1975), pp. 121–22, 67–68.
7. Levy, *Johnson*, pp. 303–304, 309.
8. James S. Haskins, *Always Movin' On: The Life of Langston Hughes* (New York: Franklin Watts, 1976), pp. 1–22; Milton Meltzer, *Langston Hughes: A Biography* (New York: Crowell, 1968), pp. 2–17, 29–80.
9. James S. Haskins, *Pinckney Benton Stewart Pinchback* (New York: Macmillan, 1973), pp. 1–23, 252, 256; Constance McLaughlin Green, *Secret City: A History of Race Relations in the Nation's Capital* (Princeton, N.J.: Princeton University Press, 1967), pp. 121–42.

10. Haskins, *Pinchback*, p. 258; Jean Toomer, *Cane* (New York: Boni & Liveright, 1923).

11. Darwin Turner, *In a Minor Chord: Three Afro-American Writers and Their Search for Identity* (Carbondale and Edwardsville: Southern Illinois University Press, 1971), pp. 5–14, 30–38, 56–59.

12. Blanche E. Ferguson, *Countee Cullen and the Harlem Renaissance* (New York: Dodd, Mead, 1966), *passim.*

13. Nathan Irvin Huggins, ed., *Voices from the Harlem Renaissance* (New York: Oxford University Press, 1976), p. 10.

14. Ibid.. pp. 72–73.

15. Ibid., p. 231.

16. Alain Locke, ed., *The New Negro: An Interpretation* (New York: Albert and Charles Boni, 1925), p. 44.

17. Turner, *In a Minor Chord*, pp. 89–90; Melville J. Herskovits, *The Anthropometry of the American Negro*, Columbia University Contributions to Anthropology, vol. 11 (New York: Columbia University Press, 1930), p. xiv.

18. Huggins, ed., *Voices from the Harlem Renaissance*, p. 228. Zora Neale Hurston's theory of asymmetry appeared in 1935 in her essay "Characteristics of Negro Expression: Conversions and Visions" in *Negro: An Anthology*, collected and edited by Nancy Cunard; edited and abridged, with an introduction, by Hugh Ford (New York: Frederick Ungar, 1935). The verse by Langston Hughes is from his poem "Evil Woman" in *Fine Clothes to the Jew*, published in 1927 by Alfred A. Knopf, Inc., reprinted by permission of Harold Ober Associates, Inc.

19. Higgins, ed., *Voices from the Harlem Renaissance*, p. 227.

20. Ibid., pp. 224–26. The verse by Langston Hughes is from his poem "Evil Woman" in *Fine Clothes to the Jew*, published in 1927 by Alfred A. Knopf, Inc. Copyright © 1927 by Langston Hughes. All rights reserved. Reprinted by permission of Harold Ober Associates.

21. Ibid., pp. 231–32. One wonders if Hurston deliberately built an adverb out of "hip."

22. Ibid., pp. 232–34. The authenticity of these early labors by Zora Neal Hurston and other Negro folklorists in the Renaissance has recently been validated in a study beautifully matured by Lawrence Levine. Lawrence W. Levine, *Black Culture and Black Consciousness: Afro-American Folk Thought from Slavery to Freedom* (New York: Oxford University Press, 1977).

23. Mary Cunard, "Harlem Reviewed," in Huggins, ed., *Voices from the Harlem Renaissance*, 126–28.

24. Huggins, *Harlem Renaissance*, pp. 72–83.

25. Ibid., p. 133.

26. See, for example, *The Conjure Woman*, where Chesnutt's stories turn precisely upon the point that white characters at first interpret Negro behavior as strange, exotic, and mysterious, only to discover in the end that the Negroes had been tricking them to achieve goals that were, in terms of values, very white. Charles W. Chesnutt, *The Conjure Woman* (Boston: Houghton Mifflin, 1899).

27. James Weldon Johnson, *Autobiography of an Ex-Colored Man* (Boston: Sherman, French and Co., 1912), pp. 141–42.

28. Wallace Thurman, *The Blacker the Berry: A Novel of Negro Life* (New York: Macaulay Co., 1929), p. 237.

29. Huggins, ed., *Voices from the Harlem Renaissance*, p. 234. The verse is taken from Zora Neale Hurston, "Characteristics of Negro Expression: Conversions and Visions" in *Negro: An Anthology*, collected and edited by Nancy Cunard; edited and abridged, with an introduction, by Hugh Ford. Copyright © 1970 by Frederick Ungar Publishing Co., Inc.; reprinted by permission of the publisher.

30. Huggins, *Harlem Renaissance*, pp. 41–47; Huggins, ed., *Voices from the Harlem Renaissance*, p. 37.

31. E. David Cronin, *Black Moses: The Story of Marcus Garvey and the Universal Negro Improvement Association* (Madison: University of Wisconsin Press, 1962).

32. Du Bose Heyward, *Porgy* (New York: G. H. Doran, 1925), p. 55.

33. Eartha Kitt, *Alone with Me* (Chicago: Regnery, 1976), pp. 7–14.

34. W. E. B. Du Bois *The Autobiography of W. E. B. Du Bois* (New York: International Press, 1968), pp. 107–108.

35. Lena Horne, *Lena*, with Richard Schickel (London: Andre Deutsch, 1966), p. 31.

36. Zora Neal Hurston, *Jonah's Gourd Vine*, reprint ed. (Philadelphia: Lippincott, 1971), p. 24.

37. Huggins, ed., *Voices from the Harlem Renaissance*, pp. 133–34.

38. W. E. B. Du Bois, "Strivings of the Negro People," *Atlantic Monthly* 80 (July 1897): 94–98.

39. Charles S. Johnson, *Growing Up in the Black Belt: Negro Youth in the Rural South* (Washington, D.C.: American Council on Education, 1941), pp. 224–29. Countee Cullen's poems "To a Brown Girl" and "To a Brown Boy" are taken from his book *Color*, copyright © 1925 by Harper & Row, Publishers, Inc., and renewed 1953 by Ida M. Cullen; reprinted by permission of the publisher.

40. Herbert G. Gutman, *The Black Family in Slavery and Freedom, 1750–1925* (New York: Pantheon Books, 1976), pp. 60–67, 449.

41. John Blassingame, "Southern White Churches and the Evolution of the Slave Family," paper given at the University of Missouri–St. Louis Conference on the First and Second Reconstructions, Feb. 15–17, 1978.

42. Houston A. Baker, Jr., *A Many-colored Coat of Dreams: The Poetry of Countee Cullen* (Detroit: Broadside Press, 1974), pp. 15, 33, 52. The two lines of verse by Countee Cullen are from his poem "Yet Do I Marvel" in *On These I Stand*, copyright 1925 by Harper & Row, Publishers, Inc., and renewed 1953 by Ida M. Cullen; reprinted by permission of the publisher.

43. Huggins, ed., *Voices from the Harlem Renaissance*, p. 10.

44. Edward Lueders, *Carl Van Vechten* (New York: Twayne, 1965), pp. 21–37, 97.

45. Levy, *James Weldon Johnson*, p. 318.

46. Huggins, *Harlem Renaissance*, pp. 93–116, 127–36.

47. Ibid.. pp. 116, 295–301.

48. Horne, *Lena*, pp. 73–75.

49. Eileen Southern, *The Music of Black Americans: A History* (New York: Norton, 1971), pp. 439–40.

50. For a summary discussion of Negroes in the theater during the era of the Renaissance, see Huggins, *Harlem Renaissance*, pp. 292–300. See also Mitchell, *Voices of the Black Theatre.*

51. Huggins, *Harlem Renaissance*, pp. 274–77; Huggins, ed., *Voices from the Harlem Renaissance*, pp. 326–27. The latter reprints a 1920s interview with one of the great ragtime pianists, James P. Johnson, who described the pattern.

52. Mitchell, *Voice of the Black Theatre*, pp. 23–26; Huggins, *Harlem Renaissance*, pp. 279–86.

53. Abe Laufe, *Broadway's Greatest Musicals* (New York: Funk & Wagnalls, 1970), pp. 6–9.

54. Huggins, ed., *Voices from the Harlem Renaissance*, pp. 337–38.

55. Huggins, *Harlem Renaissance*, pp. 288–90.

56. Ibid., pp. 288–91.

57. The emergence of King was admirably captured by Eugene P. Walker in "Montgomery Revisited," a paper presented at the First Anniversary Meeting of the State Committee on the Life and History of Black Georgians, Feb. 9–11, 1978.

58. The continuity between the abolitionists and the early NAACP has been closely traced by James M. McPherson in his study *The Abolitionist Legacy: From Reconstruction to the NAACP* (Princeton, N.J.: Princeton University Press, 1975.

59. Walker, "Montgomery Revisited." See also David L. Lewis, *King: A Critical Biography* (New York and Washington, D.C.: Praeger, 1970), pp. 47–53, and Coretta Scott King, *My Life With Martin Luther King, Jr.* (New York: Holt, Rinehart and Winston, 1969), pp. 108–115.

## Epilogue: Today and Tomorrow

1. Laura Newell Morris, *Human Populations, Genetic Variation and Evolution* (San Francisco: Chandler Publishing Company, 1971), pp. 419–21, 448. All agree that these figures are very rough estimates. The variation in "whiteness" among Negroes in different parts of the United States is great. In Charleston, South Carolina, current evidence suggests that Negroes are about 4 percent white, in two counties in Georgia 11 percent, New York City 19 percent, Oakland, California, 22 percent, and Detroit 25 percent.

2. Malcolm X, *The Autobiography of Malcom X*, with Alex Haley (New York: Grove Press, 1964), pp. 89–90.

3. Louis Wirth and Herbert Goldhamer, "The Hybrid and the Problem of Miscegenation," in Otto Klineberg, ed., *Characteristics of the American Negro* (New York: Harper & Brothers, 1944), pp. 249–369, especially pp. 276–300; Joseph Golden, "Characteristics of Negro-White Marriages in Philadelphia," *American Sociological Review* 18 (April 1953): 177–83.

4. James E. Blackwell, "Social and Legal Dimensions of Interracial Liaisons," in *The Black Male in America: Perspectives on His Status in Contemporary Society*, comps. Doris Y. Wilkinson and Ronald L. Taylor (Chicago: Nelson-Hall, 1977), pp. 232–33. In 1967 the Supreme Court disallowed the last

of the bans against interracial marriage. In striking down Virginia's anti-miscegenation law, the Supreme Court ruled out such legislation in the sixteen states in which it was still in effect. Benjamin Muse, *The American Negro Revolution* (Bloomington: Indiana University Press, 1968), p. 280.

5. Daniel M. Heer, "Negro-White Marriage," *Journal of Marriage and the Family* 28 (August 1966): 262–73; Joan Downs, "Black/White Dating," in *The Black Male in America*, p. 208.

6. Laurence Glasco, "The Mulatto: A Neglected Dimension of Afro-American Social Structure," paper given at the Convention of the Organization of American Historians, 17–20, 1974, pp. 23–26.

7. K. Richard Udry et al., "Skin Color, Status, and Mate Selection," *American Journal of Sociology* 76 (January 1971): 722–23.

8. John M. Goering, "Changing Perceptions and Evaluations of Physical Characteristics among Blacks, 1950–1970," *Phylon* 33 (September 1972): 231–41; Jo Holzman, "Color, Caste Changes among Black College Students," *Journal of Black Studies* 4 (September 1973): 92–101.

9. Udry, "Skin Color, Status, and Mate Selection," pp. 722–33.

10. Glasco, "The Mulatto," p. 33.

# Index